BORN AND RAISED IN THE STREETS OF

Compton

BORN AND RAISED IN THE STREETS OF

Compton

KEVIN "SALT ROCC" LEWIS

Rowe Publishing

REVISED EDITION

ISBN 13: 978-1-939054-26-5

ISBN 10: 1-939054-26-5

3 5 7 9 8 6 4 2

Printed in the United States of America

Published by

Rowe Publishing

www.rowepub.com

DEDICATION

To my dear parents, without your patience, love, guidance, and forgiveness, I could have never grown into the man I am today. To have parents like you is truly a work of God.

PREFACE

This is a book that is not to be taken lightly; it is a rich history of betrayal, hate, intraracial violence, love, and deception backed by concrete facts. Not one incident or thought is that of fiction. Many of the negative events that occur within this story have been changed in regards to time and place. This is done in order to protect those who were living in their time of ignorance. The violence within this work is to be examined, challenged, and cured. This can only be achieved by us, the true soldiers of the struggle ~ a struggle that will prove to culminate in the battle of all battles.

INTRODUCTION

Born and Raised in the Streets of Compton is a true story based upon many events among the urban black youth growing up amidst poverty in the notorious city of Compton, California, a place where the navigation of daily life for young black men is, literally, a never ending tightrope between life and death.

This story follows the path of a second generation Crip member, who weaves his journey into the context of the United States sociological history and governmental action that propagated the birth and escalation of gangs and gang violence, now careening out of control. This work represents the personal history of a young black man's struggle in the context of racism, poverty, and violence.

This book also serves as a valuable historical resource. Included in this work is a report that was released by the United States Senate Select Committee on COINTELPRO's activities against the Black Panther Party and Martin Luther King, Jr. in 1975, along with another report that outlined a plot to dismantle stability in the black community. Finally added, is a historical break-down of the evolution of street gangs from the 1930's to the present, which includes a complete compilation of gangs and gang territories in the United States as well as statistical material and an extensive reference listing.

CONTENTS

1

The Rites of Passage

In these bloody days and frightful nights when an urban warrior can find no face more despicable than his own, no ammunition more deadly than self-hate, and no target more deserving of his true aim than his brother, we must wonder how we came so late and lonely to this place...

— Maya Angelou, August 1965

"Boy, get yo' ass outta' that window!" screamed Michael's mother, as the sounds of gunfire rang in a rising crescendo just outside of his bedroom window.

"Aw Mom, you never let me have any fun."

"Yo stupid butt won't think it's any fun when one of those bullets slams into your little black ass!"

As Michael stepped away from the window, reality began to take a firm hold of him. It was August 11, the summer of 1965, in Watts, Los Angeles, California, where he experienced the sight of death firsthand. This deadly cycle of death was much different from what he had viewed upon their old raggedy black and white television in those episodes of *The Fugitive* (1963-1967, see Appendix) and *The F.B.I.* The faces he now viewed were somewhat familiar. They were like the faces of people to whom his parents had considered friends, people he often saw, hanging around alleyways, sitting upon wooden crates playing dominoes, and drinking cheap Silver Satin wine, while others stood around in front of the stores begging for some pocket change ~ pimps and hustlers, all of whom he considered his peers were now either dead or dying. For what reason, he didn't know.

Michael suddenly ran through his living room and into the kitchen where his mother was and asked, "Why is everyone shootin,' and why are they burning the stores and other buildings on Central Avenue?" (See Appendix).

"It's just another one of those riots boy, so keep yo' little ass in here."

But to Michael's eight–year-old mind, what was happening outside of his home was more than a riot. The prophecy of God destroying the world by fire was coming true, and black people were out in the streets trying to stop God from prevailing by shooting up everything that represented the devil. After all, every time Michael heard black folks speak about white people they referred to them as being devils and things, so to his young mind that's what they were. Black people were out there in the streets fighting in the battle of Armageddon ~ and losing.

"But why are they rioting?" he asked his mother.

"Because things have been bad lately for us black people, and we're tired of it, so we're fighting back."

"Why ain't you out there fighting?"

"I'm not fighting because men do the fighting."

"Daddy ain't out there."

"Boy, you know your daddy is a working man, plus if he was out there fighting and got himself killed, who's gonna take care of us?"

Trying to sound grown, he replied, "Me."

"How?" his mother asked.

"Pimping, or I'll be a gangsta' just like Ms. Johnson's son."

Turning to face him, his mother grabbed him by the shoulders and asked, "Boy, who put that shit in yo' head?"

"No...nobody, I mean everybody who don't have any money is either hustling or pimping, I see em' do it every day, so if I had no father and we needed some money, I'd hustle for it."

Letting go of him, Michael's mother stood straight up, and from where she stood, she appeared to be about ten feet tall. From the look that was present in her eyes it seemed as if she was about to give him one of those good backhands to his forehead.

Stepping back a safe distance from her reach, he quickly said, "I ain't done nuthin'!"

Taking a step toward him, his mother said, "Listen to me you little black-ass nigga. I ain't raising you to be somebody's damn ghetto thug, understand me?"

Confused, he replied, "But Mom, I haven't done anything."

"I know that boy, but I'm letting you know before you do, plus I don't want your ass hangin' wit' those bad-ass little niggas at Will Rogers Park."

"Ah, Mom, they are my friends, and they got my back at all times; plus they jumped on those boys who used to pick on me."

"What boys?"

"You know…the boys who live in the Nickerson's Garden projects."

"I never knew about that."

"Only a sissy runs to his momma with problems."

"Who told you that, boy?"

"It's the law of the streets," he answered.

His mother suddenly stared at him as if he was a stranger. She couldn't believe, that at eight years old, his mind was rapidly advancing faster than his body. And what she didn't know was that by the time he would reach ten, he would have experienced everything from sex to murder.

Placing her index finger within inches of his nose, his mother said, "The only law that you're gonna be following is mine, and if you think you're too big to obey the laws of this house, then I'm gonna introduce yo' ass to the laws of gravity, understand me?"

"Yes, Momma."

"Now go clean up that funky-ass room of yours!"

Complying with her demand he quickly stepped out of the kitchen and within four steps, he was in his bedroom. The place they lived in was very small and cheap, and from what they later learned, the whole apartment building and the surrounding housing projects were built by the Southern Pacific Railroad Corporation. It was in an effort to keep its minority work force near the work site and out of the white community; a clever plan that is still in practice to this very day.

Doing what his mother asked, he began cleaning his room until he was startled by a loud crash that occurred just outside of his bedroom window. Cautiously, he moved toward the window until he was within inches of the curtains. Slowly, he pulled them back and saw a scene that would be a part of his memory for the rest of his life.

Three white policemen were chasing three black youths in which one had fallen while the other two had escaped their pursuers by jumping over a nearby fence. The lone black youth that had fallen was immediately surrounded by the policemen who began beating him as he pleaded for his life. They were kicking, punching, and hitting him with everything they had. Hoping to put an end to this vicious assault, Michael cried out, "Hey, Momma! Hurry up! Come quick!"

"Fool, who do you think you are screaming at me like some raving lunatic!" responded his mother, as she appeared at the doorway of his room.

"Look," he screamed, gesturing toward the window.

Walking up to the window, Michael and his mother watched the next series of events in terror. She was awestruck as one of the policemen placed his foot on the back of the young child; the other policeman removed a large nightstick from his belt and quickly smashed it into the head of the youngster. Finally, the third policeman spat a wad of saliva upon the boy's fallen body while the other one said, "One less nigger to deal with and one less monkey to fry."

"Ain't that the title of a song?" asked one of the officers.

"I dunno, but it sho' sound good," answered one of the policeman, laughing as they left the bloody scene.

Michael and his mother were at a loss for words as the policemen exited their backyard. It seemed at that very moment they were replaying through their minds the chain of events that occurred before them ~ an event that had left a lasting impression upon Michael's psyche for years to come. In fact, many years later, as he reflected upon this episode, anger and hate would often build up inside of him. He remembered that day as his first encounter with racism. At that point in his young life, he wanted to kill anyone that was white, and wore a uniform that represented the power structure which white people were sworn to protect, along with those who were known to be corrupt, and hiding behind badges, which gave them the authority to rape, maim, and kill at will.

Michael was also puzzled by the atrocities that black people suffered at the hands of others. During that time he couldn't understand why so many black people had allowed the white man to get away with what they had done to many of them, especially when cultural encounters were virtually unavoidable.

Every day, black people encountered white faces in stores, doctor offices, and on television ~ all smiling and saying nice things about them during the day, but calling them niggers at night. The ones who were bold enough to call them a nigger in their face did so because the black person in question was either out-of-bounds, wandering within the white man's neighborhood, or because they were packing a big gun, which some of them called their "niggerlizer."

Breaking the silence that had overwhelmed them, Michael turned to his mother and said, "Momma, we got to let people know what just happened."

Silently, his mother moved away from the window and pulled him out of his room and into the hallway where she said, in a quiet manner, "No one, absolutely no one can ever know about this."

"But, Mom!"

"No one!" she suddenly shouted.

Afraid, he slid away from her reach and said, "I'm telling daddy, he'll know what to do."

"Yo' daddy won't do nuthin' but git' us all killed, now is that what you want?"

"But Momma, we ain't done nuthin' wrong."

"That's just it boy, those police are racist. They hate us black people, so bad that they'll put the crime on us, so keep yo' mouth shut!"

Nodding his head as if he understood, he slowly sat down upon their cold hardwood floor. Everything was happening much too fast for his young mind to comprehend. It did seem to him that when a black person got killed, nobody did anything about it, but let it be someone white, and you'd see the police kicking black people's butts until they break weak.

As he grew older, he discovered that, in fear, black people would sell-out their own brothers and sisters to the police in an attempt to save the neighborhood from further unprovoked attacks. But the unfair practice against black people wouldn't end there, because the police believed that when they were brutally beating black people, it was justified because they were protecting the American citizenry from the systematic violence of its niggers.

In other words, in the unseeing eyes of whites, black people didn't rank as being a part of the human race. Like circus animals and toys, they were to be sold and distributed, used and totally abused. They had no political voice, and in some white people's minds they had no souls. Blacks were regarded as nothing but a bunch of wild niggers ~ a piece of discarded garbage, hated and despised until death.

Suddenly looking up at his mother, Michael said, "I'm gonna keep my mouth shut for now; but later, I'm gonna git' my weight up with my hate and pay em' back when I'm bigger."

Smiling, she said, "When you get bigger you can do all of that; but for right now, let me fix cha' some of that fried chicken that you love so much."

Reluctantly, he got up and followed her into the kitchen. Like always, in every black household, community function, or event when a problem occurs, it was quickly resolved with a plate of fried chicken, black-eyed peas, and a piece of sweet potato pie. For most black people in general would call this action the great black copout. Everyone did it, and therefore it was an easy practice.

2

The Coming of Age

*In the search of freedom, the urban warrior finds
many roads, a road to understanding, a road to
knowledge, a road to guidance, and a road to destruction, but it's often the road to destruction that
cuts his life short, a life that was once endowed with
the precious gift of higher intelligence and brotherly
love...*

—Kevin "Salt Rocc" Lewis

April 1968

Michael's father was a hardworking and caring individual. He always displayed a smile and was
quick to greet his neighbors with something positive.
His love and sole purpose was for his family as well
as his friends. He never cursed or raised his voice in
anger, even if there was a conflict in his home. He
showed his wife the uppermost respect; but still, in all
the good that he displayed, his lifestyle wasn't what
Michael had in mind for himself. Michael wanted to

be hard, gifted, and feared; but most of all, he wanted to be a hardcore gangster, like the ones in the movies, and he couldn't learn that from his father.

When Michael and his friends came together and conversed about their fathers, Michael had to lie because his dad was employed at a hospital in Los Angeles as a cook, and he also worked part time as a janitor. Michael friends' fathers were said to be gangsters, hustlers, street players, pimps, and much more. In his neighborhood it was often said that whatever your father was would reflect in what you would become. Don't let your father be viewed as some sucker, or you'd be treated like a punk until you proved otherwise, so Michael made his father out to be the hardest of the hard, a ghetto assassin, straight-up hideous, plain ruthless, a thug of thugs, and the shot caller of the black mafia. And he was lying. Little did he know, the rest of his friends were lying too, but he didn't realize that until later, years later.

One morning Michael awakened with his mind hard set against going to school. He was tired of the constant regime of waking up; getting dressed, just in order to sit in class among other children who, too, didn't want to be in school. So he ditched his class and his after-school baseball practice along with several other youngsters who were his closest comrades in street crime, and they ventured out to complete one of the many tasks they had set for themselves ~ the scoring of some good ole' malt liquor.

After two hours of bottle hustling and collecting cans, they finally had enough money to score some beer. They then headed for their secret hide out, an old well-kept cemetery, located in the city of Inglewood, California. There, they sat among the tombstones of their older comrades, role models who passed away in gun battles with the police. Those fallen brothers were their martyrs and they were said to have belonged to the legendary Slausons, one of the largest and most respected street organizations in the neighborhood.

They had heard many stories about the Black Panthers, the Businessmen, the United Slaves, and other street organizations from around the city, and they vowed to be just like them. The more alcohol that was consumed, the bolder they had become, and they would have continued their facade if it wasn't for one of their comrades who realized the sun had begun to set and it would soon be dark. They all needed to get home before they got caught, and they sure didn't want that to happen, especially Michael. So with that thought in mind, each of them shook hands with their special grasp and headed on their separate ways.

During his journey back home, Michael was confronted by something very strange. He couldn't see it, but yet it was there, lying just below the surface of his thoughts, waiting ~ a deadly omen ready to consume or be consumed.

Quickening his pace, he noticed that something was missing during his route back home: the children. Usually on days like this there would be a lot of bad-acting neighborhood kids running up and down the block like little escaped convicts, but today there wasn't a child in sight. There was no screaming, nor was there any laughter. There were no birds singing and playing in the trees like they usually do just before sunset, and there were no sounds of traffic racing up and down Central Avenue. Stranger still, there wasn't a black soul to be found on any of the blocks he passed. It was like all the black people in the city of Los Angeles had been kidnapped and taken to some unknown destination ~ everyone gone, except Michael.

Becoming afraid, he took off running until he reached his block. There he stopped, regained his composure, and stepped into his front yard, only to be badgered by one of his older, smart-mouthed sisters, Marie, whom he argued and fought with on a daily basis. "Boy, where have you been?" She asked.

Surprised and caught off guard, he answered, "It ain't none of yo' business where I been, plus I was playin' baseball with my friends."

"Boy, your baseball practice was cancelled early today because King was shot and killed."

"What King?"

"Dr. Martin Luther King."

Damn! Was his first thought and his second thought was...*why did this nigga pick this day, Thursday, April 4, to go and get himself killed ~ shit, it was always someone else who got me busted and in trouble when I was doing something wrong.*

Gathering himself, he lied and said, "I was at the park playin' a game of pickle with my homies."

"Boy, you need to stop lying because every black soul in this city is either in front of their television sets or out in the streets preparing for another riot, and anyone who is stupid enough to be to be caught in those streets right now is either a damn fool or a white policeman with no fear in his heart because he's supported by ten others who have the same objective in mind ~ to kill themselves a nigga, and yo' little-ass sho' ain't no super nigga, so where have yo' ass been?"

"I ain't gotta tell you nuthin'."

"But you gotta tell **me**," said his mother, suddenly appearing from out of nowhere. "Now, tell where yo' ass..."

"Don't do that here," interrupted his father, seemingly coming to his rescue.

Frowning, his mother turned toward his father and said, "You let this boy git' away with everything. He has no respect for you, himself, or the people around him...and I'll be damn if I let him drive me to an early grave, so you better do something 'bout his attitude right here and now, or else you're gonna have to call the police on me because I'm gonna kill his little-ass."

"Ha-ha-aha-ha!" his little sister chimed in.

"You betta' shut yo' mouth, girl, before I tap yo' little yellow-ass as well."

As his mother focused her attention upon his little sister, Michael tried to take advantage of the situation; he stepped around his mother and headed for the front door of their home.

"Where in the hell do you think you're going?" asked his father, halting his progress.

Shocked by his father's sudden outburst and choice of words, he answered, "I'm going to my room."

"You can forget about going to your room. Instead, I want you to get yourself a rake and go to the backyard and rake-up those leaves until I tell you to stop."

"But it's gettin' dark."

"You heard me, boy, now do what I told you to do!"

Angry, Michael ran into his backyard, picked up a rake, and began raking leaves like crazy. He was mad as hell. At that moment he hated everyone, even that damn Martin Luther King. Why was everyone so upset? What did his death mean? What made him different from other black people? In Michael's eyes he was just another black man; and like all black people, they were hated and despised by everyone who wasn't like them. There wasn't anything they could do to change that fact, at least that's what he thought at the time.

Michael's thoughts were suddenly interrupted by some movement he caught out of the corner of his eyes. He quickly turned only to see that it was his father sitting upon an old orange crate, curiously staring at him.

After watching him for a few moments, the silence between them was broken when his father said, "Come here, boy."

Tossing the rake into the pile of leaves, he walked over to where his father sat and he attempted to say something, but was stopped short when his father raised his hand to silence him. "Don't say anything, boy, just listen."

Looking somewhat dumbfounded, he just stood there looking at his father as he began to speak. "Every day, I go to work and I work hard without complaining, just so you children can have the things in life I didn't have when I was growing up ~ things that other children can only wish for. And I'll be damned if I let you destroy all that I've achieved for this family and myself. I've sacrificed way too much for you, boy, plus I gave you money so you can look good in school and play baseball as well. Son, you're very lucky to have me as a father, and I say this because when I was growing up my father didn't give a damn about me having nice things. Most often, he would take me out of school and force me to work in the fields as a laborer so I could make money for him to buy something to drink. He took every penny I made, and he wouldn't buy no food, no clothes, nothing ~ just alcohol and whores. That was his priority in life. His behavior made my life almost unbearable. Many times I lived in shame because the children I came in contact with often teased me by calling my dad a drunken hobo and other awful things, but all in all, I loved him regardless."

Breaking the silence, Michael asked, "How can you love someone who treated you like that?"

Placing his hand on Michael's shoulder and smiling for the first time, his father answered, "Son, I know my dad loved me. I was his first born, his pride and bundle of black joy. Everything that I know today I can thank my father for because he taught me things that most children would never learn. He always listened to what I had to say, but all that began to change when he started drinking."

"Why did he start drinking?"

"He had problems," he answered while looking at something far off in the distance.

"Does alcohol help people with their problems?" Michael asked.

"Naw son, alcohol doesn't help people with their problems. It does just the opposite. It makes things worse."

"Then, why do people choose to drink?"

"Maybe for the same reason why you choose not to go to school and ditch baseball practice as well."

The subject of Michael not going to school came as a surprise. He thought he had an airtight alibi because his homeboy's older brother forged some absentee letters for him and his comrades, so they could ditch school, commit burglaries, and do other illegal activities.

Dropping his head, he said, "I go to school sometimes."

"And what do you do when you don't go to school?"

He hunched his shoulders and answered, "Nothing really," and then added, "Sometimes we go downtown to catch a movie, and sometimes we just ride around."

"And who is we?"

"Me and my homeboys."

"Are you talking about those bad-ass niggas that live over on Compton Avenue?"

Michael didn't answer immediately because this was the first time in his life that he heard his father refer to a black person as being a nigga. Just hearing the word come from his dad's mouth made him place both feet on instant escape-prepared-to-run mode.

Turning his body slightly away from his father's reach, he answered, "Yes," while at the same time he allowed his eyes to scan the backyard for a possible avenue of escape if needed.

Frowning slightly, his father said, "I already knew that, and there's a whole lot more that I know about yo' little ass that you think I don't know."

"Like what?" He asked defensively.

"Like how you got that money to go to the movies."

Shocked by his father's sudden knowledge and information, Michael dropped his head for a moment, then quickly recovered and said, "I got that money from bottle hustling."

"And purse creeping!" his father added.

"What?"

"Don't stand here and act dumb with me, boy. Don't you know that everything you have done so far in your life has been done by me as well as others...don't you know that?"

"Yeah," He answered weakly.

His father then cleared his throat and said, "Did you think we all were fools? Or did you think we're so absentminded that we wouldn't notice the things you were up to? Don't you know we knew all along you had been skipping school, drinking beer, and stealing money out your mother's purse? At first we felt like we hadn't given you enough, but we did, didn't we?"

He didn't answer.

"We did give you enough, didn't we?"

He still didn't answer.

"I guess your mother was right ~ should have whipped yo' ass a long time ago."

Michael wanted to say something in his defense, but at the moment he couldn't find the right words to express himself. The anger in which he felt, was too hard for him to dissipate, despite the fact that his father was right in what he had said. He did have more than the other children in his neighborhood, but that didn't stop his personal suffering. He felt the same pain other children in his neighborhood endured. He still lived the life of a black child growing up in a white world. He was still hated and despised by everyone who wasn't in the same social class as himself. Those facts alone played a big role in how Michael reacted to certain people in certain situations, but he wasn't aware of those facts at the time.

Looking toward his father, he started to say something, but tears began to flow uncontrollably down his cheeks and that made him even angrier. Michael believed that the sight of tears was a definite sign of weakness, a sign that most people in his neighborhood preyed upon. That alone could get you killed in the notorious ghetto streets of Los Angeles.

Upon seeing his tears, Michael's father reached out to pull him toward him, but Michael backed away. He didn't want his father's sympathy; instead, he wanted him to understand what he was going through so he tried to express what he was feeling through questions.

Establishing eye contact with his father, he asked, "Do you know why I stole that money?"

"Why?" asked his father, looking somewhat confused.

"Because every time my homeboys and I would go somewhere outside of the neighborhood people treat us like dogs."

"What people?"

"Those white people."

"Where in the hell do ya'll be going to be confronted by white people?"

"We go to the city of Carson, sometimes Long Beach."

"But how does stolen money change the fact of how you and your friends are treated?"

"Because when we have money, white people treat us as equals. They smile and help us find the things we need, and they don't follow us all over the entire store."

"That don't mean they like you, they just want you to get your stuff and then get the hell out of their store."

"But having money does change things," he insisted.

Michael father paused for a moment and then asked, "Do you really think by you having money in your pocket changes the way white people feel about you?"

"Yes, I do," he answered.

"Okay, if you believe that, then let me ask you a question?"

"Okay, go on."

"A few minutes ago you said that when you and your friends have money, ya'll catch a bus to the city of Carson."

"Yes, we do, and sometimes we catch the bus to Inglewood as well as other places."

"When you went to these places, did ya'll ever leave the bus just to walk around and check out the sights?"

"Yes, because we like to go through their neighborhoods to look at their big 'ole houses and cars, pretending that one day we'll have the same things like them."

"Okay, now when ya'll are walking around in their neighborhoods, and you come in contact with white people who may be sitting in their cars as you cross the street at the traffic signal, have you noticed the strange way they react to ya'll once ya'll invade their world?"

Michael searched his mind for a moment, but he couldn't figure out the point his father was making, nor did he notice anything in reference to the behavior of white people when he personally came in contact with them, so he looked his father in his eyes and answered, "No."

Michael's father smiled, and then asked, "You didn't notice all those white people locking their doors and rolling up their windows as ya'll pass by?"

Damn, he thought as reality hit him like a hard left jab, right between the eyes. White people did react strangely to us when we invaded their environment.

Suddenly, he turned to his father and in a sudden rush of words, said, "I know whatcha' be talkin' 'bout now cause every time when webe' walkin' down the street and we cross over in front of their cars, those white people be ah closin' their doors, rollin' up their windows and we can hear the sounds of those electric locks when webe' walkin' in front of their cars."

"How did you feel when that happens?"

"Mad."

"And what did you do?"

"We didn't do anything."

"Why?"

"You know we can't do anything to those white people."

"Then money won't change that fact as well, right?"

Michael was now dumbfounded. He couldn't answer that question, so he replied, "I guess having money makes us feel good about ourselves, and it makes us feel like we're really important."

"But once the money is gone, again you'll be treated as some dumb-ass ghetto Negroes. Now do you understand what I'm trying to say?"

"I guess so," he answered, weakly.

"Listen, Son, all I'm trying to show you is what's real. The true fact is if I made big money at my job and moved our family into a white neighborhood, it wouldn't make any difference. Because as long as we're black, we'll still be hated, money or no money, and you children would be attacked with so many negative insults that we would be forced to move out of the community. But don't worry about it, because we're better than those who are ignorant. As people of color we can overcome just about anything."

"How is that?"

"We can do that just by using our minds, Son."

"How does using our minds make us better?"

"The way we use our minds to create," his father answered.

Michael stared at his father for a moment because he was confused. He couldn't understand what his father meant by using their minds to create. In school they were taught that white people were the ones who were responsible for inventing something great. This was taught to them by teachers who were black, so in a way, black children were being conditioned to feel inferior from the very beginning.

"Daddy," he said after a long moment of pondering, "The mind of black people will never be accepted by anyone because we're hated by the police, by the people who placed them in power, and it seems that we're even hated and rejected by God."

Surprised by his son's intellect, Michael's father asked, "Boy, where did you learn that information from?"

Smiling, he answered, "When we ditched school we didn't always go to the movies or to the white neighborhoods. A lot of times we would go and listen to the Black Muslim brothers speak, or to the old black church front in downtown Los Angeles and listen to these brothers known as the United Slaves."

"And what do they be talking about?"

"They be talking 'bout Blackness, Control, Courage, and Black Pride."

"And what do you think Black Pride is?"

"I don't know really," he answered honestly.

"Have you ever heard of the Black Panthers?"

"Hell yes! I mean heck yeah," he corrected.

Laughing slightly, Michael's father asked, "How much do you know about them?"

"A whole lot," he quickly answered. "Those brothers are really bad. They're not scared of the police or the government. Nobody scares them."

"That's good that you know about them, but do you know they couldn't achieve their strength or intellect without first finishing school."

"C'mon Dad, school?"

"Yes Son, school."

"But all our school does is teaches us things about white people."

"Learn it anyway, Son, because the more you learn about other people who you see as a threat, the better chances you'll have of overcoming the threat that they pose."

Michael didn't understand what his father meant; but it sounded like what he was saying was true, so he asked, "Daddy, if I go to school and learn, can I be a Black Panther?"

"You can do that and much more, Son."

After hearing that, he really wanted to be somebody important. He wanted people to fear him; especially those people in power who were corrupt, and those who were racist. He wanted them to know that he was armed and dangerous; mentally, physically, and spiritually. The only way he could do that was by being a Black Panther.

Suddenly he looked up at his father, and said, "Don't worry yourself about me anymore. I won't be stealing and I'll go to school, too."

"Now that's what I wanted to hear," said his father as he began to pull his son close but stopped short to ask, "Now you're not too big for me to give you a hug, are you?"

Michael displayed a big smile and said, "No, I'm not that big yet."

3

From Watts to Compton

For the urban warrior religion holds no purpose,
his faith lies in the products he uses for survival, his
strength comes from deception, his pride is his honor,
his love is for no one, and his God is his blue steel
enforcer dealing death on a daily basis to those of the
same pigmentation, thus destroying a nation, possess-
ing no remorse ~ a fucking rebel without a cause...

—For Dawn Lewis

February 1969

The year of 1969 found Michael and his family living in the best of times. It was in that year that his
father packed all their belongings, hitched a trailer to
their old Ford Galaxy, and headed south for what was
known then as the Hub City, Compton, California.

Michael could remember that day as if it was yesterday. They had pulled in front of a house that was yellow, containing a nice front yard with real green grass, surrounded by a white steel fence that had all its parts intact. In the backyard there were two huge trees, one an apricot, and the other he never really knew what it was, but it was ideal for shade. It also became Michael's secret hideout when he was depressed or in trouble. In addition, the house had all sorts of various plants surrounding it which made everything more serene as well as pleasant.

Michael hated Compton in the beginning because everyone that he loved and trusted was back in Watts, a place where blackness and poverty were like brothers, which was the central element that brought most black urban ghetto youth together. In Compton life was a little different, but not by much. Gang warfare and poverty permeated and overwhelmed everything. The threat of crime lurked within the shadows around every corner. A person couldn't even walk into a neighborhood store without being harassed by a wino demanding small change or something more.

At night, the city took on a deadly silence as phantoms moved about under the cover of darkness in search of their prey ~ people whom they considered weak, exposed, and vulnerable; blacks, Mexicans, Samoans, and whites.

Yes, white people, and a lot of them, too.

During this time, people in Compton kept a lot of horses and chickens. There were orange groves and a whole lot of pigeons, but having pigeons was the fad among the black ghetto youth. A fad that would turn violent as the years progressed.

In fact, the first people that Michael had met in his neighborhood kept homemade cages full of pigeons in their backyard. These birds performed all sorts of air acrobatics to the command of a whistle or a handclap. Michael would stare in astonishment at the formations these birds made. Each flying in a diamond-shaped pattern and then changing to the shape of a triangle. Then, one at a time they would begin to fall toward the earth as if they'd been shot, each one spinning downwards in an erratic motion, plummeting toward the ground. Just when they were about to hit, they would straighten out and soar skywards again. He would watch these events for hours, over and over again, until he heard his sister or mother yelling to bring his little bad ass home.

At home Michael usually felt sort of out of place and in the way because everyone in his household had a special chore to perform, including certain responsibilities that were often rewarded with some pocket change or some extra playtime. It was during moments like this it appeared to his young mind that his whole family moved in unison, all of them except him.

Michael felt this way because he was the type of child who was completely resistant to Saturday house cleaning. His mother changed his negative attitude by making him stay in the house as a form of discipline. She also made him join the Double Rock Baptist Church youth choir and take piano lessons.

Michael fought hard against the rules his mother had implemented, but a child like himself could only endure a few hours of punishment, especially during those sunny days when everyone in the neighborhood would be outside playing tackle football in the middle of the street right on the cement ~ yeah, black ghetto children were straight up rough and tough.

Finally, the day had come for Michael to go to school and he dreaded it because he didn't know what to expect or how to dress. When he lived in Watts, he often wore the black tough skins jeans with the blue crooker sack tennis shoes, a purple or blue T-shirt along with a matching ball cap. But when he stepped on the playground of Caldwell Elementary School, he saw a mixture of dress styles. Some of the young men were wearing slacks with a two-inch bell-bottom cuffs, butterfly collar dress shirts, and platform shoes; he later would learn that these guys were considered the neighborhood pretty boys.

Other young men of the neighborhood were labeled as the future up and coming ghetto gangsters. They often wore the blue or gray khakis with white t-shirts, black or blue canvas crooker sack tennis shoes, or the Waller bees with the matching black or blue Pendleton jackets. Some dudes his age wore the black watch caps that they called beanies, though they were usually worn by the older guys of the neighborhood who they often referred to as their **O.G.'s.*** (Original Gangster, slang term used by ghetto youths in reference to an older, original member or founder of a gang or organization).

Stepping upon the playground for his first time, Michael was greeted by this young dude named Dinky, who lived over on Central Avenue not too far from where he lived. He was accompanied by several other mean looking cats that seemed to have only one thing on their minds ~ to see if he was a coward or a straight up ghetto warrior. This was Michael's first test, his true rite of passage, and how he performed would determine how he would be treated in the future by those whom he considered his peers.

"Where are you from dude?" shouted Dinky as he walked past.

Michael pretended not to hear him as he stepped around the school building towards the sand lot where all the recreation equipment was.

"I'm talkin' to you, fool! The one with the fat momma who dropped you off this morning," shouted Dinky once more.

Suddenly, a twinge of fear began to flow through Michael's veins as students who were standing nearby laughed at Dinky's comment. But his fear soon gave way to anger, and before he realized it, he started looking for something to hit him with. Glancing slightly to his left, Michael spotted a brick that sat against the recreation building and without thinking he picked it up and swung it toward Dinky's head.

"Damn, that nigga is crazy!" shouted one of the students.

Before Michael knew it, a large crowd had surrounded them as he and Dinky circled each other in preparation for battle. As the students looked on, Michael tried to find the best possible position to strike Dinky. At the same time Dinky was trying to find the best possible way to escape the brick that had his name on it.

"Put that brick down and fight fair!" shouted one of the students.

"Yeah, fight em' without that brick!" shouted someone else.

"That nigga shouldn't have said what he said about my momma," Michael quickly countered.

As he moved into position, Michael spotted several teachers running toward the crowd of students who moved out of the way in order to make a path for them. As they did so, Michael took advantage of the opportunity and lunged forward, pounding Dinky first with his fist, then his feet, and lastly, the brick. Michael was beating the crap out of Dinky. But that all ended once the teachers tackled him, and then drug him off, screaming all the way to the principal's office.

Going to the principal's office in Compton was something altogether new to Michael, because in Watts, children were always fighting in school, and they were never punished because fighting was looked upon as a much needed survival tool. Michael often heard other children's parents tell them that if they ever caught them running from a fight they would tear their butts up, so most black ghetto children preferred to fight it out with each other in the streets, or at school rather than run. After all, running would only label them as being cowards, and then they would get two beatings; one from their parents and another one every time they hit the streets.

Needless to say, Michael's parents lived by a whole different set of morals and the school seemed to have a standard set of morals of its own. They suspended him right on the spot, but their decision to do so was based on the fact that he refused to tell the principal how and why the fight started. *But why should he?* He was already in trouble and telling on someone would only make things worse. Besides, Michael had a bigger problem to face ~ his mother and her big black belt, which was her final judgment and sentence.

Sitting upon their old sofa, damn near scared to death of the whipping that he knew was imminent; his parents listened attentively as Michael explained the series of events that led to him being suspended from school. After concluding his account of what happened, Michael's father laughed and then said, "Boy, I'm proud of you, and…"

28

"Preston!" his mother quickly interrupted. "We can't have this boy bustin' other children in the head with bricks!"

"But honey, you can't continue to shelter him from the outside world. He's going to encounter his share of problems, and he sure can't run every time he's confronted by some thug in school."

"Why can't he?"

"Because it doesn't look good for a boy to be running every time he encounters trouble. Plus, he'll be called a sissy by the other neighborhood children and that can lead to a negative psychological effect that neither one of us would be prepared to deal with."

"And what effect is that?"

"The gay effect, and I sho' ain't raising no punks. Besides, you already know that kids have to endure their share of problems when they move into a new neighborhood, so give him a couple of weeks to earn his place among the other children, and in time, you'll see that things will be much better."

"I sure hope so," his mother replied. She then turned toward Michael, laughed, and then said, "I betcha' that boy won't be bothering you anymore."

Three weeks later Michael found himself back in school and being treated like a celebrity. Everyone acted as if they had known him for years. What was more shocking was how Dinky approached him during recess and asked, "Do you wanna play ball with us?"

Michael didn't answer right away because Dinky acted as if they never had a problem and this type of behavior caused him to be skeptical as well as cautious. He felt as if Dinky was trying to trick him, but after looking at the faces of the students that stood around them, he knew there was nothing to be afraid of; and so it began. He became one of the crew, and Dinky's most loved and trusted best friend.

After the game, Dinky asked, "Hey man, you wanna go and steal some pigeons?"

"How?"

"It's simple. We'll walk around the neighborhood until it starts getting' dark, then we'll run over to Sherm's Liquor Store and steal some big brown paper bags and some batteries for a flashlight."

"Where are we gonna get the flashlight from?"

Dinky laughed and said, "You gonna steal it."

The act of stealing wasn't unnatural for Michael because in Watts children like himself used to steal all the time. Some stole things because of a certain need, others stole to rid themselves of the physical pains of their addictions, but Michael and his counterparts stole things because it was the thing to do.

A sly smirk appeared on Michael's face as he said, "As long as you got my back, I don't have a problem with stealing the flashlight, but there's one thing I need for you to do."

"And what's that?"

"You gotta come up with a story so I can stay out past six."

"What are you talkin' 'bout?" Dinky asked, curiously.

"What I'm talkin' 'bout is if I'm not in da' house before the street lights come on, my parents will be standing at the front door waiting to separate my ass from my body."

Dinky laughed and said, "My mom don't care what I do, and if I don't ever come home it will suit her just fine because it means more food for the rest of them."

"What about your father?"

"What about that punk! All he care about is standing in front of a liquor sto' beggin' for quarters and shit, so he can get himself some of that ole' Silver Satin wine, and if he's lucky, he'll score himself some of that *dog food (slang for heroin), so basically it's me against the world; and I like it like that."

"Damn, I'm sorry," Michael quickly said.

"Sorry for what?"

"For the way you have to live."

"Man, are you crazy? Being able to live this way prepares me for the world as is. I call my own shots, plus I'm able to hustle and fend for myself, and if it wasn't for my little sisters and brothers, I would have been gone a long time ago."

"Where would you go? How would you survive?"

"I just told you ~ hustling."

Michael knew a lot about hustling because in Watts many children his age were out in the streets living by any and all means. Some were pushed out into the streets by the pains of hunger, drugs, or peer pressure. Others were out there hustling simply for the thrill of it.

"What's up, man?" Dinky suddenly asked, "What are you thinkin' 'bout?"

"I was just thinking about what you said about hustling, and where I used to live, my homies and I would hustle all the time, but some of the other people I saw hustling done it because it was exciting."

"Where did you live?"

"I lived in Watts."

"Damn!" exclaimed Dinky.

"What's wrong with Watts?"

"Man, you don't know?"

"Naw," Michael replied with anticipation.

"Man, Watts is the city where the hardest gangsta's roam; and not even the mighty-ass Slauson Gang want to tangle with the niggas of Watts," he stated. "Now I understand why yo' ass is so fuckin crazy!"

Changing the subject, Michael asked, "How are we going to get my mom to let me stay out past my curfew?"

"We'll just tell her that my mom has invited you over for dinner, and you'll be back home by seven-thirty."

"Man, I sho' hope it works."

"Don't worry, it will."

Michael's mother fell for Dinky's lie like a fish grabbing at a fat red worm. She took the bait, hook-line-and-sinker. At first, Michael thought they were going to get caught in their lie because Michael's mother asked Dinky for his mom's phone number, but when Dinky went into his sad story about how poor his family was and how they couldn't afford a phone, Michael's mother just waved her hand in the air until they both fell silent. She then turned toward Michael, and said, "You better have yo' ass back here by seven thirty, and don't let me have to come looking for you either."

"You won't," he replied as they jetted out the door and up the block.

"That was close," Michael said, as they reached Central Avenue.

Dinky smiled, and said, "Let's go!"

Once they arrived at the store, it took them only twenty minutes to steal the paper bags, the batteries, and the flashlight. Michael also snatched himself a big bag of Lay's Potato chips while Dinky took two bottles of something he couldn't quite see from where he stood.

"Now we're ready," stated Dinky as they quietly eased their way out of the store, crossed over Central Avenue, and headed east toward a neighborhood known as the Richmond Farms.

"What do we do now?" Michael asked as they stood on the corner of Alondra and Wilmington Boulevard.

"First, we'll drink these," he answered, holding up two bottles labeled Malt Duck.

"What's that?" Michael asked stupidly.

"You ain't ever had any Malt Duck?'

Trying to conceal the truth, Michael answered by saying, "They don't sell that stuff in my old neighborhood."

"Well, man, this stuff is gonna give us the power to creep-n-run our asses off," he said as he twisted the cap off the bottle with his teeth, and then took a long gulp.

Attempting to play his part, Michael grabbed the other bottle and did just what Dinky had done. Soon as the liquid hit his stomach, it felt like someone had lit a fire up inside of him, and it was rapidly spreading throughout his whole body. The taste was something awful.

Dinky started laughing at Michael uncontrollably.

"What's wrong?" Michael quickly asked.

"Man, I can tell that this is yo' first time."

"How is that?" he asked.

"The way your left eye started spinning, then the other eye tried to do the same thing but it couldn't keep up, so it just sat there jumping while yo' other eye did its own damn thing."

After hearing that, Michael couldn't help but laugh too. It was the only way to take the sting off the sudden embarrassment he felt.

Once they caught a hold of themselves, Dinky said, "Let's move."

They traveled until the sidewalk they were on disappeared and was replaced by a dirt road which ran over a small cement bridge that was suspended over a canal, which they later learned was called *The Los Angeles River.*

There they stopped, turned left and darted into the darkness along the side of a ranch style house next to the canal.

"Look," Dinky said, pointing. "The cages are over there."

As he looked on, Michael saw three large wooden structures that contained what appeared to be an unlimited number of pigeons. He could hear their soft cooing sounds from where he sat.

"What do we do now?"

"Just follow my lead," said Dinky as he darted from one dark shadow to another until he was positioned directly behind the pigeon cages.

He then motioned Michael from where he sat and without hesitating Michael moved forward mimicking the exact movements Dinky had made. He felt like a soldier running deep behind enemy lines.

"Now peep this," Dinky said, as he made his way next to Michael.

"All you have to do is tear a couple of holes in the paper bag so the birds can breathe, then shine the flashlight in their face and grab em' around their body and shove em' into the sack as fast as you can."

"What if they peck me?"

"They won't, plus the light will act as a hypnotizing agent that will freeze em' in motion."

"Alright then, let's do it," Michael whispered.

Dinky quickly opened the cages and they both stepped inside grabbing as many birds as they could. At first, Michael was afraid, but the combination of Malt Duck and the thrill of stealing turned him into a fearless ghetto warrior. That feeling ended when the backyard floodlights came on, illuminating everything in the yard, including them.

"Run!" shouted Dinky.

Michael dropped the flashlight and took off running right behind Dinky. As they approached the fence that enclosed the backyard, a blast rang out that sounded like a shotgun. After hearing that, they hit the fence like two escaped convicts, holding onto the bag of pigeons along the way. They climbed fence after fence, with the sounds of dogs chasing them in the background, but nothing was going to stop them. They kept running until they crossed Wilmington Boulevard. There they ducked into some nearby bushes and fell flat on their backs until they caught their breath.

"Wanna go and do it again?" Dinky asked as he started to laugh.

Michael didn't reply because somewhere down the road his soul had run straight out of his body, and it was still running; and his heart was running right behind it.

Suddenly looking at Michael's face, Dinky asked, "What's wrong with you, I know you ain't afraid of a little ole' gun?"

Regaining his composure, he replied, "Nah, but let's git' back before my mother comes round here shootin' at us too."

Dinky laughed, and then said, "I betcha' yo' mother is a much better shot than that fool back there."

"I don't think we wanna find out," he said as they left the safety of the bushes.

That one experience paved the way for many more. As they grew older, the experiences that they shared became more breathtaking and dangerous ~ so dangerous that Michael would witness the loss of his best friend to a force that would become his worst nightmare, as well as his lifelong enemy ~ Compton's Leuders Park Piru Street Gang, a ghetto rival known for their constant pursuit in the hope of killing Crips.

4

The Rise of the Blue Empire

For the urban warrior, death has its own calling card,
everyone is welcome and no one is ever barred. It's a
twenty-four hour operation that sees no end; and from
around every corner, and from within every shadow
the voice of Satan seductively whispers...keep them
coming for hell is not yet full.

—K.R.D.

October 1972-1976

From 1972 to 1976 dramatic changes began to take place in the City of Angels or what is commonly known as Los Angeles, California. For minorities, these changes signaled an onslaught of death and destruction at the hands of others.

During this time, drugs seemed to flow into the minority community like ice cream. Neighborhood organizations within the city seemed to be at war with each other. Black leaders were rising and falling rapidly. Neighborhood preachers were stealing from the only place that provided hope, their congregations ~ while at the same time, President Richard Nixon, Governor Ronald Reagan, and the head of the FBI, J. Edgar Hoover, targeted minority organizations as a "threat to national security." They began using undercover informants, unauthorized wiretaps, media manipulations, and other questionable techniques in order to sow dissension among the members of these organizations, hoping to prevent the rise of other Black Messiah figures like Dr. Martin Luther King and Malcolm X.

This plot, which was known by only a few as the King Alfred Plan and initiated by secret forces within the state department, included a directive (see Elaine Brown, *A Taste of Power*, page 177, and a Mary A. Fischer, article in *GQ Magazine*, pages 203-210). J. Edgar Hoover's team outlined a plan, not only to prevent the natural emergence of a black political leader, but to empower a "puppet" leader of their own choosing.

At the same time, they sought to undermine the stability of the minority communities, and to further reduce the chances that an influential leader could be produced from their midst by making sure that the most addictive and destructive drugs were readily available within the minority neighborhoods.

Once the minority communities were destabilized, they were contained within their boundaries by the domestic caretakers of violence ~ the police ~ whose announced function 'to protect and serve' became a grotesque caricature of protecting and preserving the interest of society's elite. Serving the minority communities injustice still goes on today in some areas of the United States. The police patrol the black communities for the purpose of intimidating the minority sub-culture in order to persuade them with their violence that they are powerless to alter the conditions of their lives. As a result, many black, Mexican, and other minority youth of the community become defeated inwardly and succumb to the lure of drugs, gangs, and intraracial crime.

Those who were strong enough not to succumb to the social conditioning of the urban ghetto were frequently arrested on whims. Bullets from the police guns murder human beings with little or no pretext; aside from the universal intimidation they are charged with carrying out.

It also goes without saying that some of the police would be unable to set in motion their racist machinery if they were not sanctioned and supported by an unbalanced judicial system. The court system of this nation not only consistently abstains from prosecuting criminal behavior on the part of the suspected police, but it convict countless minority men and women on the basis of biased police testimony.

Court-appointed attorneys, acting in the twisted interest of overcrowded courts, convince 85% of the defendants to plead guilty. The innocent are advised to cop a plea so that the lengthy process and cost of a jury trial is avoided. This method summarily railroads a countless number of minorities into jails nationwide.

Therefore, it should not be surprising for those outside looking in, to see that the pattern of self-destruction within the minority community is perpetuated by the conditions of police corruption, capitalism, racism, and hatred. The gatekeeper or what those of the seventies would call the oppressor, knows as long as minorities continue to dwell in such substandard conditions, they will never bond together to build a successful change in their lives.

What started as a peaceful political movement with Dr. Martin Luther King had turned violent for the urban ghetto soldiers who made an honest attempt to wage a constructive revolutionary war against the corrupted forces within the United States. They fell short of their goal due to a measure that was implemented within the higher echelons of the Federal Bureau of Investigation.

The measure implemented was a tactic outlined by COINTELPRO ~ the FBI'S covert counterintelligence program, "to neutralize" the Panthers and other domestic groups it deemed too radical (see the Church Select Committee Report, and Mary A. Fischer article, "The Wrong Man," *GQ Magazine*.) Under this plan, informants were used as a tool to infiltrate targeted organizations. Their job was to plant-incriminating evidence that would cause the targeted organization to become divided within as well as without. Once the seeds of 'divide and conquer' were planted, all hell broke loose, which was the case when the United Slaves (US), a cultural nationalist group headed by Ron Karenga and allegedly supported by the FBI, mounted an attack upon members of the Black Panther Party that occurred January 17, 1969, on the campus of UCLA. It was an attack that left two Black Panthers dead, one being Bunchy Carter (see Elaine Brown, *A Taste of Power*, page 118) who was considered the mighty lion from the streets of Los Angeles, the former head of the Slauson Gang, five thousand strong, and the originator of its feared hardcore, the Slauson Renegades. He was also considered the most dangerous black man in Los Angeles. Murdered along with him in the UCLA attack was John Huggins, a soldier of equal reputation. Many other ghetto soldiers died before and after the significant changes were brought about including George and Jonathan Jackson, Little Bobby Hutton,

Willie Tate, Fred Hampton, Cleveland Edwards and a whole lot more. Those who weren't killed were sent to the penitentiary for years on false charges. One such person who fell under this scheme was the new head of the Los Angeles chapter of the Black Panther Party, Elmer "Geronimo" Pratt, who was imprisoned for twenty-seven years for a murder he didn't commit.

Many political and gang organizations fell prey to this method of deception. This was a very trying period in the history of the black revolutionary. It seemed that the four hundred year cycle of what Pharaoh had done to the children of Israel, what Hitler had done to the Jews, and what the so-called 'white pioneers' had done to the Native Americans was happening all over again amongst the ghetto blacks, but with one significant difference: *The urban black youth were now assisting others in the destruction of themselves by the killing of one another.*

In order to understand this concept a person first must look at the real origins of street gangs, poverty, and intraracial violence.

The first origins of Los Angeles street gangs were documented in the early 1920's and 1930's. They were known as the Kelleys, Boozies, Goodlows, and a few others. These gangs were actually considered organizations or clubs. Most were family oriented (like clans) and their activities were centered on the petty theft of automobile accessories and bicycles. It wasn't until the 1940's that the first appearance of major gangs surfaced upon the streets of Los Angeles, on the Eastside.

These groups initially emerged in the late 1940's and 1950's as a self-defense organization formulated to combat the violence that they had been experiencing at the hands of nearby white residents. This violence against blacks had been occurring for several years and continued to grow as the black population increased.

The white residents of the surrounding neighborhoods of Huntington Park, Lynwood, Southgate, and a few more communities that were located near the black enclave were dissatisfied with the black occupation of the area, and they were totally against any and all forms of integration. This was clearly shown by the creation of laws that prevented neighboring blacks from purchasing property within the white settlements and attending white public schools.

These tactics were originally established in 1922, and were designed to maintain social and racial homogeneity of neighborhoods by denying non-whites access to property ownership. However, the black residents didn't succumb to the pressure placed upon them by the white residents; instead, they launched a counter measure of their own by attacking the system through the courts. But this only led to more bloodshed and violence.

During the 1940's the black population continued to rise, thus making it harder for the white residents to perpetuate their exclusionary practices against the blacks. The white residents fought hard, and the black residents fought back by using the only means they knew ~ the courts ~ which they knew would result in more violence, but they continued to invoke the system all the same.

Also during this time many savings and loan associations had a reputation of practicing segregation as rigidly as the real estate brokers. Some multiple developers made a practice of separate-but-equal-housing ~ they kept one sub-division open exclusively for blacks. No matter which subdivision a black person went to, he always ended up at the one reserved for him ~ the salesman assuring him that this would be the one more convenient, nearer to schools and shopping centers, and a better deal all around.

In Northern California the picture, if anything, was worse. Of 350,000 houses built since World War II, only about 100 had been sold to blacks as of 1965. A survey of 62 brokers conducted in 1965 by Milton Gordon, chairman of the California Real Estate Commission, showed that not one would agree to sell a home, in an all-white neighborhood, to a black.

Los Angeles had no demonstrations of mass indignation by white residents upset at black encroachment, because the police authorities indicated they would not tolerate them. Nevertheless, there were hundreds of incidents of petty and no-so-petty harassment of blacks moving into previously white neighborhoods, ranging from broken windows and swastikas smeared on doors, to the beating-up of black children by white children, the setting off of firecrackers, and the firing of shots in the middle of the night. These incidents went almost totally unreported in the community's mass circulation newspapers, so that the average white person was never aware of them (see *Rivers of Blood, Years of Darkness*, page 105).

By the middle 1940's the younger white residents of Huntington Park, Southgate, and Lynwood, grew dissatisfied with their older white counterparts and began to take matters in their own hands. They formed a white club called the Spookhunters, which was one of the most infamous clubs at the time. Their objective was to annihilate many of the black youth within the surrounding areas. They attacked them as often and as much as they could. If blacks were seen outside of the black neighborhoods they were attacked with extreme malice, and as a result of this violence, black youth begin to form clubs of their own in order to protect themselves.

The first of these clubs was called the Businessmen, which was founded by Raymond Wright, and located on the Eastside near South Park between Slauson Avenue and Vernon Avenue. Another club that formed in response to the Spookhunters was called the Devil Hunters and they were located in the Eastside Projects of Aliso Village. They, as well as other black residents, fought back against white violence with their own form of violence. Other black youths joined the violence as a result of being dissatisfied with the job situation that was occurring at the time. These youths who numbered in the hundreds in 1944, had become thoroughly frustrated when they were denied employment within the city's streetcar system. In anger, they attacked a nearby passing streetcar and assaulted several white passengers. Subsequently, during the latter 1940's and the early 1950's, other neighborhood organizations rose up to combat the existing threat that the white establishment posed upon the black community.

Another battle was also occurring within Los Angeles that caused the white power structure to become weakened in regards to their aggression. The white youth gangs had allowed themselves to take on too much when they started a second street war with the Mexicans, who had already begun to rebel against American values and lifestyles during the late 1930's and early 1940's. The white gangs had foolishly underestimated the courage of the Mexican youth, and like their black counterparts, these Mexicans, who were also members of the second generation (the principle figures in this rebellion), had expressed their estrangement from American society by forming cliques or gangs. The reason for this occurrence was that these

individuals were rebuffed in schools and the community. They were made to feel that they didn't belong,
that they were Mexicans, not Americans, and that they
would never be equals.

Poor schooling and problems with law enforcement
kept many out of the military, and prejudice denied
them equal opportunity in the work sector.

America saw these youths as the original gang members and they were recognized by their dress style,
use of English, slang words, and tattoos. In the 1940's,
many of the Mexicans wore zoot suits, long ducktail
haircuts, and pointed shoes. They were known as the
"Pachuco's," chuco for short, but the police and the
media preferred to call them hoodlums or zoot suiters.

In 1944, a major conflict broke out with sailors
who were looking for a fight with the Mexican gang
members, and they attacked them near a dance hall in
Venice Beach. Rumors circulated that the Mexicans had
started the fight that ended with hundreds of sailors
and marines going to battle with the Mexicans within
the barrio. The next day blacks and Filipinos were attacked when a mob of marines and sailors went in
search of the zoot suiters, and this led to more bloodshed and continued violence.

In Watts, during the same time period, several black
organizations were organized geographically by the
housing projects in the area. The projects were originally built for war workers in the 1940's, and were
intended to be interracial, but that plan changed as the
black population increased. The first public housing
project of Watts was the Hacienda Village that was built
in 1942. Then, in May of 1944, Imperial Courts was
established, and in September of the same year Jordan
Downs was erected. After that, in 1955, Nickerson
Gardens, which was the largest of all the public housing

projects in Watts, was finally established. Along with the erection of these housing projects rose more black organizations that formed to combat the existing violence perpetuated by the white groups of the time. These black organizations were known as the Huns and the Farmers, and they were very active within the projects. In fact, they were so successful in their endeavors that the white residents and gangs within the area begin to relocate as black families began to integrate their communities. This was a moral victory for the black residents of the area, but this victory was short lived due to a new threat that began to surface among the black population. This threat was known as intraracial violence or what most people of today refer to as black on black crime.

Intraracial violence among blacks started when many of the white residents left the area; thus leaving the city areas of south Los Angeles as a primarily black enclave, with blacks accounting for 71 percent of the inner-city population (Brunn et al. 1993: 53). By 1960, the separate communities of Watts, Central Avenue, and West Adams Boulevard had formulated into one large continuous black enclave where the low class, middle class, and upper class neighborhoods were adjoined into one single community.

It was also during the 1960's when the black organizations began to move from interracial violence to intraracial violence. In fact, the Gladiators, one of the largest black organizations located on the Westside around 54th Street and Vermont Avenue, had fallen into conflict with other black organizations that were located on the Eastside, which at the time were the Slausons, Businessmen, Huns, Sir Valiants, Volkswagoners, Farmers, Del Vikings, Gladiators, the Swamp men, and a few other street organizations that existed at the time.

During this period, disputes among the above-mentioned organizations were handled by *coming from the shoulders (slang for hand to hand combat) and by the use of street weapons such as tire irons, brass knuckles, knives, and even sticks. Murders among these organizations were very rare.

As a gang member from the second generation of Crips, Michael had no knowledge of the events that had led to the intraracial violence between the organizations that existed before his time. He wanted to know; therefore, through his personal research he learned that the earlier disputes occurring between the aforementioned Eastside and Westside organizations started as a result of altercations on the football fields, over females, and over disagreements at parties. But moreover, he learned that most of their clashes were rooted in the socioeconomic differences that separated the two groups.

Through further research, Michael learned that the Eastside organizations resented the upwardly mobile Westside youths because the Eastside blacks and the organizations that they were associated with saw themselves as being inferior and less economically sound than those who resided on the Westside. The black youths and the organizations that they were associated with were considered less intimidating and lacking the skills to be street smart and hardcore. So, in order to demonstrate that they were equally callous as those on the Eastside, the Westside black youths got together and engaged themselves in a long standing battle with the Eastside black youths during the 1960's. It continued until the 1965 Watts riots.

For the black youths of the era, the Watts Rebellion served to be significant turning point in their lives. New leadership arose among them that eradicated the rivalry existing between the two groups and their organizations. Youths who were ignorant of their present situations were now moving towards being more politically conscious and showing greater concern for the social problems that plagued their community in general.

One person noted for effecting change among the black youths was Alprentice "Bunchy" Carter, a member of the Slausons Gang, who had successfully transformed the inner city black youths into revolutionary soldiers who fought against corruption and police brutality. Several other organizations at the time were also contributing to this change.

The Watts Rebellion of 1965 was also credited for bringing the community together as one big family. Neighborhood organizations that were once in conflict with each other had dismissed their old rivalries and supported each other against the Los Angeles Police Department which was despised by almost everyone within the black community (Baker 1988: 28; Davis 1990: 297).

It was even said that, for nearly five years, beginning in 1965, there were almost no active street gangs operating within the city of Los Angeles. Gang activity among the black juveniles was scarcely visible to the public at large and of minimal concern to south-central residents (Cohen 1972). The reason for this sudden change among the black youths was that the new movements occurring within and around the city of Los Angeles offered them a vehicle of positive identification and self-affirmation that occupied the time and energies that might have been spent in gang activity. A sense of cohesiveness began to form, along with self-worth and positive identification, as pride pervaded the black community (*Los Angeles Times* 3/19/72).

At this point, black organizations now felt that it was their responsibility to stand up and protect their communities. They began to organize neighborhood political groups in order to monitor the Los Angeles Police Department and document their treatment towards blacks. One of the first groups created for this purpose was the Community Action Patrol (CAP) founded by Ron Wilkins (ex-member of the Slausons). Other groups began to form around this time as well, groups such as the Sons of Watts, founded by Gerald Aubry, (an ex-member of the Orientals), and the Black Panther Party, founded in 1966, by Huey P. Newton, and the United Slaves (US), a cultural nationalist group founded by Ron "Maulana" Karenga. There were other political groups that formed as well, and each of their endeavors gravitated around the "policing of the police" (Baker 1988: 28; Davis 1990: 297; Obtola 1972: 7).

These political groups brought hope to their community. They were revered as a vanguard for the black citizens of Los Angeles, but in the eyes of the local and federal law enforcement, these groups posed a serious threat to the establishment that they were sworn to protect, and to the nation as a whole.

The fear of the black political groups of the 1960's caused the law enforcement to create new police tactics that would readily prepare them for confrontations with these groups. By 1967, the Panthers were one of the strongest black political groups in the nation; and by November 1968, J. Edgar Hoover dispatched a memorandum calling his field agents to "Exploit all avenues of creating...dissension within the ranks of the Black Panther Party" (Churchill and Wall 1990:

63). From 1968-1971, these tactics were used against the Black Panther Party to control and neutralize what was believed to be "a dangerous black political group." The most vicious and unrestrained application of COINTELPRO techniques during the 1960's and early 1970's, was clearly reserved for the Black Panther Party (Churchill & Wall 1990: 61; Home 1995:13), but other political groups, and even civil activists such as Dr. Martin Luther King and Malcolm X were eventually targeted by COINTELPRO.

During this period it was alleged that the United Slaves, a cultural naturalist organization, headed by Maulana Ron Karenga was being manipulated and used by the FBI in their efforts to bring about the demise of the Black Panther Party. Evidence of this was clearly shown by the incident that occurred January 17, 1969, on the campus of UCLA, which left two Black Panthers Party members dead, (see Elaine Brown, A Taste of Power, pages 156-170), Alprentice Bunchy Carter, and John Huggins. These incidents alone-created major fractures within the black power pyramid. The black political organizations of Los Angeles were now cautiously observing the behavior and attitudes of each other for signs of infiltration, dissention, and police incursion. Trust among these organizations was at an all-time low and some members within these organizations began to become disenfranchised with the whole ideology of revolution.

As a result of all this, political organizations such as the Black Panthers Party suffered major setbacks due to counter measures and tactics that were being implemented by a special task force within the FBI. These tactics eventually crippled the Black Panthers Party, thus rendering them helpless, and other black political organizations had fallen prey to these same tactics. This created a large void for the black youths who looked upon the leaders of these political organizations as their role models, role models who were decimated at the hands of the police, right before their eyes. In viewing this, the new generation of black youth within the city of Los Angeles lost all hope and trust in the system. Immediately they began to hate what they saw as a corrupted model of authority, the police. They hated things that they couldn't change, they hated poverty and the system that kept them subdued within it, and they even began to hate themselves, which caused them to rebel against their own kind, and in turn; this resulted in the resurgence of neighborhood street gangs.

During this time most black youths in the city of Los Angeles were fascinated by and attracted to the ideology of the Black Panther Party. They were impressed by their militant style, how they dealt with the police, and by the Black Panther dress code which was black leather coats, pants, boots, and the revolutionary style berets that were worn slightly to the side. Almost every black youth within the urban area seemed to have had an aspiration to be a Black Panther or something similar. One such youth who openly displayed his affection for the Black Panther Party was Raymond Washington (see Appendix, *Blood Rising*, last paragraph), a 15-year-old student at Fremont High School, who in 1969, started the Baby Avenues; the first new street gang after the fall of the Black Panther Party.

When the Black Panther Party was in operation Raymond Washington was too young to join, but that didn't deter his efforts to emulate their practices. Even though he was known as a neighborhood bully, he made an attempt to fashion his gang into somewhat of a political organization that was supposed to provide protection for the community as well as acting as a security force against the racist assaults brought on by the police. Raymond Washington and his group never obtained their goal as being a political group. They were too immature, violent, and they lacked the knowledge that would have been needed in order to develop an efficient political agenda that would have brought social change to their community. So in turn, over a short period of time, Raymond Washington and his organization became the nation's most violent street gang ~ the Baby Avenue Cribs

The name Baby Avenues wasn't altogether original; Raymond Washington copied the name from another organization, "The Avenues," that he admired while growing up. The Avenues was an old political organization that remained active throughout the sixties. They had seen their days of riots, street battles, and glory; now their name, 'The Avenues,' which was once revered and respected, represented something altogether different. In fact, within a small duration, Raymond Washington's organization, the Baby Avenues would become known as the Baby Avenue Cribs ~ an organization composed of street youths who sought notoriety and prestige through the senseless acts of intraracial violence.

In 1971, after adopting the dress style of the Black Panther Party, (*black leather jackets, black berets, and army boots*), the Baby Avenue Cribs began to venture into their own criminal behavior by committing robberies and assaults. It was even said, that in the same year several Baby Avenues Crib members had assaulted an elderly Japanese woman. When the victim was asked to describe her attackers, she described them as being "*young cripples that carried canes.*" This description was made because Raymond Washington's gang had adopted the walking cane as part of their dress style. The local media also picked up on this description, and referred to this group of deviants as the Crips (*Los Angeles Times* 2/8/72 and the *Los Angeles Sentinel* 2/10/72). The print media first introduced the term Crip, and those who were involved in a life of crime were considered to be 'Cripping' by other Crip members who were still trying to be revolutionary, with the same political thinking that the organization of the 1960's represented.

As Michael grew older, he often thought about how the Crips and the violence that was associated with them had started. He saw the bloodshed, he witnessed the killings, and he was so much a part of this process that he came to the realization that if he didn't make an honest attempt to break the dangerous cycle of his own negative conditioning, he wouldn't live to see the age of twenty.

Michael believed this to be true because the changes that were occurring within the city of Los Angeles among street gangs were also affecting its suburb of Compton, California.

The transformation within the city of Compton seemed to have occurred overnight. The children with whom Michael was raised were now callous, nefarious, and deadly. Neighborhood bullies began to form dangerous street gangs ~ street gangs such as the Crips, and their formidable rivals, Pirus and Bloods.

When Michael was younger, his older cousin told him that the Crips (see Appendix, *Blood Rising*) were at first one large organization that started in West Los Angeles and spanned deep into the suburbs of Watts and Compton. He also said the founder of the Crips was Raymond Washington and not Stanley "Tookie" Williams, as most people believed (see Appendix). The early big-shot members of the Crips included Mack

Thomas of the original Compton Crips, Michael "Shaft" Concepcion, Jimel "Godfather" Barnes, Greg "Batman" Davis, Stanley "Tookie" Williams, Monkey Man, Bogart, Gregory "Batman" Davis, Godfather, and Mad Dog. His cousin also informed him that in Compton it was never quite clear as to who its earliest founders were, but many were led to believe it was Big Huncho, Mac Thomas, Michael "Salty" Leblanc, Bitter Dog Burno, and a couple of other hardcore characters who were all legends in their time, and were known for their ability to come from their shoulders, taking no prisoners in hand to hand combat.

Michael was also told that in the beginning these gangs had positive intentions. They were the vanguards of their communities and both groups had aligned or patterned themselves after other neighborhood organizations. For instance, the Bloods were supposed to be a subsidiary of a culture nationalist's organization called the United Slaves, which was founded by Maulana Ron Karenga, but in Compton the Bloods were originally called Pirus or Piru boys, which derived their name from Piru Street. They were founded by Sylvester Scott (nickname Puddin') and Vincent Owens. The Crips were supposed to be patterned after the Black Panther Party; in fact, many that chose to stay on the political plight had said that the Crips were first known as the California Revolutionary Independent Party, and also as the Community Response to Inner City Poverty. But there was no evidence of the Crips ever standing in as political group. Instead, the Crips mostly pursued behaviors and lifestyles that embarked upon a deviant nature. This group of Crips preferred to call themselves Crazy Rowdy and Insane People. It was also said by some of their earliest founders known as O.G.'s, that their rivals, the Pirus, had once stood for The Political

Independent Unity of Soldiers. At one time the Pirus had been a part of the Crip organization, but they broke off and formed the Piru Boys after a bitter disagreement and violation of group standards. Nonetheless, both groups had been said to foster positive intentions, but all that changed when these groups began to wage war against each other.

From Michael's standpoint, violence seemed to play a major role in the lives of minority youth growing up in and around the ghettos of Compton, California. Violence had become their shield, their rite of passage, and their way of saying that only the strong can survive conditions of the urban concrete jungle. In their eyes, they were the strong ones. They believed that they were the only survivors who didn't succumb to the conditions of helplessness brought on by negative influences of the ghetto. They thought they were setting things straight, but in reality they were being groomed to be the next frontline of statistics that would be compiled over the years to come.

Michael's indoctrination into this deadly belief and behaviorism began the very day after Michael "Salty" Leblanc was tragically killed ~ a day that would haunt most original founders and cofounders of the Crip organization, and a day that will not be easily forgotten.

Michael could remember that day like one remembers their birthday. For it was on that day when he was busy in his backyard trying to create a tree house so Dinky and the rest of their homies could have a secret place to lay low; especially after those times when they made successful raids on the Piru gang, shooting up their neighborhoods and bouncing back to the safety of their own neighborhood which had now changed from being known as the Original Grandees to the Hundred Sixty Fifth Neighborhood Block Crips. As time passed, their neighborhood would take on a new title which was more notorious. They would be known as the Nutty Block Crips.

Michael was just about to climb the tree with a big piece of wood in his hands when Dinky and his other homie, Knuckles, came climbing over his back fence and into his yard. "Hey man, guess what?" Dinky said, damn nearly out of breath.

"What's up?" Michael replied, feeling somewhat agitated.

"Salty was gunned down today!"

Stunned, he asked, "By who?"

"No one has the full story yet," Knuckles volunteered, "But from what I gathered he was washing his car in his front yard when all of sudden from out of nowhere Bang! Bang! Bang! End of story, just like that."

Michael's heart dropped, Salty was the 'hood's most beloved, a true soldier. More than that, he was their version of the Army Rangers, the Navy Seals, and the Green Berets, all wrapped in one ~ now he was dead.

Recovering from his inner thoughts, Michael asked, "Does anyone know anything?"

Dinky cleared his throat, then answered, "Well, there was this girl who was walking by and she said she was just talking to Salty, when all of a sudden as she turned to leave, a Volkswagen pulled up and the next thing she knew there was a lot of shooting."

"Did you say the shootin' came from a Volkswagen?"

"Yeah, some people were saying that the Volkswagen belonged to that *rooster-ass nigga (a term Crips use to deface Bloods) they call Pudding, and others were saying it belonged to that other rooster nigga name Icky Dawson, but it's just all talk at this point."

"Ain't Icky from Leuders' Park?"

"Yeah," answered Dinky.

"Then let's roll on them niggas in the name of Salty," Michael replied.

"Naw, we can't do anything right now," stated Knuckles.

"And why is that?"

"Because soon as I heard about the news regarding Salty, me and a couple of niggas from *Lantana (a subsidiary branch of Crips) rode down to Piru street, and when we got there the police had the whole area blocked off."

"Why would they do that?" Michael asked.

"Because they were ordered to protect those rooster-ass punks," interjected Dinky angrily.

"Then they must be doing the same thing for all them punks," Michael replied more so to himself than to anyone else. "This is the first time in my whole life that I heard of white policemen protecting niggas from their own violence."

"Yeah, man it's like that all over," stated Dinky.

"Man if this shit is true, then the *K9's (slang for police) might have a part in this too," added Knuckles.

Confused, Dinky asked, "Why would the K9's want to see someone knock Salty off and then turn around and protect the very people behind it?"

"Fucking job security," Michael answered.

"If that's the truth, why are we riding down on the Pirus?" asked Dinky. "Shit, we should be out there fuckin' up the police."

For a moment no one spoke. Each man was caught-up in his own thoughts, pondering that very question that was laid before them ~ a question with no simple answer, and a question that has been asked by each and every passing generation. For years, African Americans who were caught in the middle of their revolutionary plight have asked this same question, and for years black people had been falling for the same old divide and conquer scheme ~ a tactic that was once well hidden and disguised was now in full view. The question now was, what were they going to do about it?

Breaking the silence, Michael said, "Ain't nuthin' new 'bout what those K9's are doing, and we can't waste our time worrying 'bout it now. We'll address the situation later. After all, there's a time and place for everything."

"So, we're still going after the Pirus?" Dinky asked.

"Of course, they're the ones who pulled the trigga, not the K9's. But we'll wait until after they have Salty's funeral, then we'll hit those roosters hard ~ very hard."

Knuckles smiled devilishly and said, "Man, I'm gonna kill me a rooster every year 'bout this time."

"I am too!" Dinky shouted.

"I think every Crip that is loyal to the cause will be doing the same thing."

Dinky and Knuckles looked at Michael for a long moment and then said, "Listen man, we're Crips and that makes us all like one big family, all related like cousins, so whatever we do, we do it together."

"I'm down with' that," he replied.

"Alright cuz, we'll meet up later during the funeral," said Knuckles and Dinky in unison, as they turned and proceeded back over Michael's fence.

"Yeah cuz, we'll do just that," Michael said softly.

Later that night as Michael lay in bed, his mind roamed over the events that had occurred throughout the week, and as he pondered, he found that two things were foremost in his mind. One, he desperately needed a gun, and two, how could they take care of the Bloods and then turn the table over on the police? First, he had to address the gun issue. *Who could be trusted to hold it? Where could he hide it if he couldn't find someone he trusted?* He sure couldn't keep it at home because his mother cleaned and searched around their house like a prison guard. It was bad enough that he saw his room as no more than a jail cell ~ subjected to search at any given moment.

Troubled, Michael got up and grabbed a book that he had recently obtained from the school's library. Michael often read a lot when things troubled him. He kept his interest in books hidden from his homies because most of them couldn't read, and they didn't care about the world outside of the neighborhood. For them, the neighborhood was their world, their ghetto paradise, and a series of false hopes by which they gained glory and prestige as well as self-worth. They all coexisted for one reason and one reason only ~ to live and die for the neighborhood, a place they would never truly own, nor belong.

For Michael there was life outside of the neighborhood, there were places to be seen and explored, visions to be expanded upon, businesses to be created; but mostly, in his mind, there was a big debt to be paid. Michael believed that America had owed them, and they were way past due on their promise to African Americans ~ a promise that was unknown to most of his counterparts.

Michael found out about this promise from a book he was reading on the Emancipation Proclamation, which President Abraham Lincoln created. This promise was supposed to be effective on January 1, 1863, freeing all slaves and allocating African Americans forty acres and one mule to work the land. He couldn't have achieved such knowledge without continuous reading and searching for what he thought was the truth.

At the time Michael thought the answer was simple. He felt he knew the truth and that the truth was America had purposely involved itself in a capitalistic scheme that discouraged people of color as well as other men from cooperating with each other in favor of competition. Under this scheme, one ruthless man, or a small conglomeration of such men were encouraged to grab all, or nearly all of the very land of this nation, all of its waterways, crops, gas and oil and mineral deposits, its communication and transportation networks. Then these same men extracted from the minorities the highest price possible for the use of these things.

Under this capitalistic scheme the added social ills of racism, discrimination, and prejudice developed and thrived. The capitalistic dog-eat-dog philosophy generated and cultivated disharmony and distrust among human beings, especially among minorities, thus leaving them in a poverty stricken situation where they had to battle it out with each other for jobs that barely contributed to their primary needs ~ needs that usually lead to crime or worse.

At the moment, Michael couldn't afford to dwell upon that fact, nor could he dwell upon the past, especially when he had a job to complete; and he did have a plan to get compensated, but only after he completed his purpose. Michael planned to be the brother that sets things straight. First, he had a funeral to attend, and with that thought in mind, he sat the book down and went to sleep.

Salty's funeral was to Michael what Martin Luther King's funeral had been to all of black America. Crips had come from every section of the city and from every neighborhood to pay their final respects to their fallen comrade. There were so many, that Michael couldn't even count them all. There were Crips from neighborhoods that he had never even heard of, such neighborhoods as the Harlem Rollin' 30's, Undergrounds, School Yards, Gear Gang, Venice Shoreline, and Playboy Gangsters, and a host of others.

As the funeral procession proceeded up Central Avenue, Michael witnessed the largest blue Crip rag ever displayed, hoisted up like the American flag, and it was accompanied by some of the finest low riders he ever saw. To him it was more like a parade than a funeral, but the look that was displayed upon the faces around him told a different a story altogether. These faces were callous, unmoved, and nefarious. They were joined together by one common bond ~ death before dishonor, a solidarity that projected their common purpose, and this was seen among all the Crip organizations that were in attendance, especially the Grape Street Crips.

Upon closer inspection, Michael saw that everyone was decked-out in purple, blue, and gray, and there wasn't a dry eye in the whole place. There were even some brothers from his neighborhood and beyond that he recognized, but had no idea they were Crips. They were also dressed down in gang colors and ready for war. Also in attendance was Salty's closest comrade, Frostie, along with some of the hardest Piru killers ever known to the city of Compton, California; killers like Big Huncho, King Rat, Bitter Dog Burno, Woodrat, Cosmo, Big Mac, Volcano, Roscoe, Frog Dog, Grasshopper, Michael Scott, Big Ben, Fatso, and so many others. Michael knew from that very moment he wasn't even close to being in the league that they were in. They were the elite, straight up major league players. Michael's little crew were minor league players, but as the years passed, some of them would graduate into the elite, some would fall victim to an assassin's bullet, while many others would fall victim to an old and new enemy ~ alcohol, PCP, crack cocaine, and the California State Penitentiary.

5

The Big Payback

"The urban warrior is a unique organism, always mimicking and ever changing. Like a phantom he blends into his environment, taking on the character- istics of a chameleon. Moving about unseen; focusing upon the weak, waiting for the precise moment to strike, thus fulfilling his need. After all, the purpose of the urban warrior is none other than to live, and then die again..."

—For Jaqunta 'Budda' Lewis

October 1977-79

From 1977 through 1979, every neighborhood Crip set within South Central Los Angeles began to form special cliques, and within these cliques were certain comrades that felt more comfortable with each other. Therefore, when it came time to handle business, they preferred to do it alone, or with those of their special group, which was of a chosen few.

In Michael's neighborhood it was no different, because many of his homeboys who he had once been close with, had now fallen into the pattern of forming their own cliques. As a result, Michael's neighborhood was now known as "Nutty Block" (usually spelled as Nutty Blocc, because Crips never use the letters "ck" next to each other, for it a sign of disrespect), which was broken into several large sections. There is lower Nutty Block that is located near Wilmington Boulevard and upper Nutty Block that is located near the Compton Airport between Central Avenue and Alondra Boulevard. Another section of Nutty Block ran behind Longfellow Elementary School, down Tichenor Street, with Northwood, Harlen, Tajuata, and Nester Street crossing over at intervals. Finally there is the heart of the whole neighborhood ~ One Hundred and Sixty Fifth Street ~ the block from which the name Nutty Block was derived.

One Hundred Sixty Fifth Street is where Nutty Block's most feared congregated. On any given day you could see all sort of gangsters in various moods, sizes, and shapes, playing concrete football one moment, then testing each other's chins the next. Don't come from upper or lower Nutty Block showing signs of weakness, because if you did, brothers on the block would stomp your ass into tomorrow; and would continue to do so until you improved upon your fighting skills.

It was about coming from the shoulders in those days, and Michael was living proof of that. In fact, he had to fight one of the neighborhood's best gunslingers, 'Big B', who was a master from the shoulders. Michael was definitely no match for his skills and didn't want to be labeled a coward, so he kept on fighting. He was fed up, and tired of getting his butt kicked, besides, he felt he had proved beyond a shadow of doubt that he was good enough to represent the neighborhood. So one day in the lunch area of Walton Jr. High School, Michael approached Big B, and without warning, he struck him with a hard left to the jaw, and for the first time in Michael's life he was winning a fight against one of the neighborhood's best. That quickly changed when Big B recovered and delivered a three-piece combination that sent Michael sprawling over a lunch bench and out for the count ~ but it was worth it. For Michael, this meant no more inter-neighborhood fighting; he was finally accepted as one of the neighborhood's elite, a title that was well earned.

There were other brothers from the neighborhood who were known for their superior fighting skills or for their respectable status among the hardcore, brothers like Big Mac, Blacc Jacc, Outledge, Sweet Pea, Trent Booker, Michael T., and Peter Gunn, who himself was known for more than being superior. He was the master, and he also had assisted Michael from the wrath of the other homies on more than one occasion. They had a lot of respect for each other and Peter Gunn knew that Michael was the type of individual who preferred to do things alone. He also knew about the dangers of involving others when it came to illicit endeavors and that Michael was a person who chose to keep his illegal activities to himself and maybe one other person; therefore, the risk of getting caught would be much less. After all, Michael wasn't a person who would publicize his evil deeds. He was a firm believer in the adage, "Loose lips sink ships." In his neighborhood there were some brothers whose lips were so loose that they alone could sink an entire aircraft carrier. Michael couldn't afford to have his ship sunk, especially when Dinky and the rest of them were so close to launching their secret assault on their deadliest enemy.

Three months after "Salty's" death, Michael and his crew were actually ready to put in some real *work (*slang term used in reference to illegal activity*). They didn't want to just go into enemy territory and shoot things up because that didn't make sense to them. What they endeavored, was to assassinate one of their enemies major leaders. Since Salty's funeral, the Pirus and Bloods had gone into hiding, but their efforts were in vain because they were still getting killed. In fact, one of their homies from a Crip set called Lantana Blocc had safely crept behind enemy lines and into a popular club known as Dotoes, located on Central Avenue that was frequented by Pirus. He boldly stepped inside of the club, took aim, and killed one of their dearly beloved comrades known as 'The Bartender.' That one single act sent out a very serious message that said, "*No matter where you run, no matter where you hide; somewhere deep in the shadows is a Crip waiting to inflict the punishment of a homicide.*"

Sitting in his backyard, Michael and his comrades were going over the last stages of their plan. They had been at it for hours and it seemed that they were finally on the same page. "Okay, cuz, let's go over everything in order," said Knuckles as he looked upon some pictures of three major Piru *Shot-callers (*slang for leaders*) that they had taken earlier in the week.

Knuckles was the oldest of the three by two years. He was also the most dangerous due to his calculative and defiant nature. He earned the name Knuckles from the many fights he had gotten involved in because of his light-skinned complexion. He hated for someone to address him as being yellow or half-breed. When someone did, the fight was on right then and there.

Many years later, Michael learned that in the ghetto most black youth were conditioned to use verbal racial overtones to injure one another in order to ease the hate that they felt for themselves. Subliminally, most African Americans were ashamed of being black. Their parents, grandparents, and those they came in contact with on a daily basis instilled this belief and behavior in them. Often, it was the grandparents who would tell their grandchildren whose skin was light in color that they were not like other colored children in the neighborhood because other black children had skin that was too dark and facial features that were too African and their hair wasn't good. This negative image of being black was even projected in church through the picture of Jesus, whose hair was long and blond, whose face was white, who wore sandals and a robe, and was usually depicted sitting among his flock of white children. Even in the movies the image of what black represented was distorted. Black actors were always the pimps, hustlers, and dope dealers. Those who were portrayed as black heroes wore long perms and had faces that were light in color, wore expensive jewelry, and displayed an aura of whiteness.

African Americans saw in themselves what was projected by others. Being poor and black was depicted as evil, and enforced the negative stereotype of themselves in their everyday dealings with each other. It was depicted in the way they lived, how carelessly they killed one another with little or no remorse, and was shown in their grammar when they refer to themselves as being niggers: This was just another element of conditioning that would affect most ghetto blacks for years to come.

Snapping back to the present, Michael turned to Knuckles and asked, "What did you say?"

"I said; let's go over the whole plan once more to make sure we have everything in order."

Smiling, Michael responded, "You want us to run down each individual part, or just what we have to do?"

"It would be good if we all knew each other's roles that way nothing will get fucked up," answered Knuckles.

Still smiling, Michael said, "The first thing we have to do is to make sure that everything we need in order to pull off this shit off is inside each *G-ride (*slang for stolen car*) that we'll be using."

"And what are those things?" Knuckles asked, turning toward Dinky.

"Red bandanna, belt, gloves, dark brown khakis, and white and red converse tennis shoes," answered Dinky.

"What's next?"

"Then each of us is to drive to a specific location that we already agreed upon, change clothes inside of the car, and then proceed to our target on foot."

"And what's next after that?"

"We all supposed to meet up in the back parking lot of Sears, where your sister will be waiting for us in a black van," Michael answered, correctly.

"And what do we do if she's not there?" Knuckles asked.

"We are to assume that something went wrong and then each man is on his own at that point."

Everyone fell silent on that note. They all knew the risks that were involved and they knew that there was no margin for error. They were going on foot behind enemy lines, driven by one desire ~ revenge, which was the sweetest jot next to getting pussy.

"I don't like it!" Dinky suddenly said, breaking the silence.

"Why?" Knuckles asked, sarcastically.

"I don't like it because there are too many holes in the plan."

"Too many holes...What the fuck do you mean by that?"

"What I mean is that we should already be dressed in red, and the red clothes should be worn over our getaway clothes."

"He has a good point," Michael said, interrupting. "And since we're going to be making our move at night, we should git' us some of those walkie-talkies so we'll be in touch with' each other while we're motion."

Michael thought Knuckles was going to blow his cool when they made these suggestions, but instead, he grabbed Dinky by his stocky shoulders and said, "Nigga you've been doing your ghetto homework, huh?"

Dinky nervously laughed, then answered, "To be truthful cuz, I'm scared, and I just don't want none of us to git' caught slipping by one of those *Roosta's (*a derogatory slang term Crips used in the 70's to deface Pirus and Bloods*).

"That's why we have these," Knuckles replied as he pulled out an old long-barreled .44 magnum.

"That's just it cuz, you two niggas feel comfortable with the guns you have, but I need something better than this ole'ass .32 auto," Dinky said, seriously.

"What is it that you want?" They both asked in unison.

Dinky smiled deviously, and then answered, "A sawed-off twelve gauge street sweeper."

They both were awestruck as they stared upon Dinky. They knew he wouldn't have a problem handling such a weapon due to his short frame and stocky build, but they never fathomed the thought that he would be the type that would prefer such power, especially on a mission like this.

Breaking out of their inner thoughts, Knuckles asked, "Where are we supposed to git' a gun like that from?"

"I already have one," Dinky answered, smiling. "And there's more from where that came from."

"Where...and how did you git that?" Michael asked, excitedly.

Dinky took a step forward, then gestured with his hands, and answered, "Remember that National Guard building on the corner of Rosecrans and Willowbrook?"

"The place by the railroad tracks?" asked Knuckles.

"That's the place," answered Dinky. "And there's another one behind Centennial High School."

"Yeah cuz, I remember them places," said Knuckles.

Thinking out-loud, Michael asked, "Why would they put a National Guard center in the middle of the 'hood?"

"They put them there right after the riots," answered Dinky.

"What riots?" Michael asked.

"The Watts Riots," Knuckles answered.

"But for what reason did they put them here?" Michael asked, once again.

Smiling, Knuckles answered, "Well, it's like this cuz, during the Watts Riot the National Guards were strategically placed in Compton to prevent Watts' angry blacks from reaching the white section of the neighborhood."

"That's crazy, cuz. There ain't any peckerwoods living out here in Compton; besides, there's nothing here that's worth protecting."

Dinky laughed for a moment, and then said, "Cuz, Compton wasn't always like this."

"What do you mean?"

Dinky took a deep breath, then continued, "Cuz, the history of Compton is very different from that of Watts because at that time there was a lot of rich land that was owned by whites, and it's centrally located around oil wells and refineries. There was a growing aircraft industry and a big college was even built nearby in the city of Carson. This gave rise to Compton being nick-named "The Hub City," and everything that's important is either in Compton or around Compton."

"Things like what?" Michael asked.

Knuckles pondered for a moment and then an-swered, "In the beginning, a lot of farmers resided in Compton. They had orange crops, farm animals, and other things, and those who weren't into agriculture, worked in the fields surrounding Compton. Most of the people lived right here in the city while others lived in the surrounding areas of Lynwood, Gardena, Paramount, Downey, and so forth. And remember, these people were white, and during the Watts Riots they saw us blacks as a threat ~ especially since we had the whole city of Watts on fire."

"So, are you saying that those National Guard places were built to protect Compton?" Michael asked.

"Not just Compton, but every white neighborhood that surrounded and bordered Compton."

Everyone fell silent until Michael said, "Cuz, what does this history bullshit have to do with the guns Dinky wants?"

"Nuthin'," Dinky answered. "But you should be in-terested that these National Guard places contain an unlimited amount of weapons ~ weapons that are in our 'hood and at our very disposal."

With that said, they all begin to smile deviously. They knew that if they could obtain the very weapons that were used by the United States military, they then would have the upper hand on their rivals as well as the police.

After pondering the situation for moment, they knew they had to put their original plan on hold. There was a whole new mission in mind now, a mission that could get them weapons, and ammunition, as well as some fast hot cash.

"Say cuz," they all said, damn near simultaneously.

"I'm sorry, go on," Michael said, feeling as if he had interrupted the flow of the conversation.

"Nah cuz, you go on," said Knuckles.

"Alright then, cuz, check this shit out. Ya'll know we're gonna' have to put our original plan on hold for a moment."

"I was just thinkin' the same thing!" Knuckles said, excitedly.

"Hold on a minute!" Dinky interrupted.

"What's up?" they both said in unison.

"Cuz, I know you're not planning on hitting the National Guard place!"

"Why not, you did it!"

"But with me, I had inside help, plus it wasn't even my idea."

"Then whose idea was it?"

"It was one of the homies from Park Village who put me up on it."

"And you didn't tell us about this?"

"Cuz, it was just one those spur of the moment things," Dinky said. "And like I said before, it was an inside job."

"What do you mean?" Michael asked.

"It's just like I told you, cuz, the homie from Park Village put me up on it. He has a cousin that's in the National Guard and works at the one on Willowbrook.

He's the one who provided us with the information on how to get the guns."

"Do the people he work for know they been got?" asked Knuckles.

"That's just it, cuz. Everything was set up so cool that they don't even know they been got."

"How did ya'll manage to do that?" Knuckles asked.

"It was easy because the guns we stole were kept inside of crates that were at the warehouse, and they kept them there until they were shipped out to combat units in training. If the receiving unit finds that there is a shortage in one of the crates, then the loss would be blamed on one of the shipping employees at the warehouse."

"Damn cuz, that's a good idea."

"Yeah cuz, that's real cool." Michael added. "Plus, it makes it easier for us to hit the place as well."

"It's not that easy," Dinky said.

"Why is that?"

"Because the inside man did all the work. All I had to do was retrieve the weapons from a trash dumpster, and we won't have that advantage."

"You might be right, but that shouldn't stop us from trying."

"He's right, cuz," said Knuckles. "Don't you know what we could do if we can git our hands on some guns like that?"

Dinky stared at the ground for a moment, gestured about his head with his hands and then said, "Cuz, you know I don't have any problem with' hittin' a *lick (*slang for committing an illegal act such as robbery, burglary, etc.*), but if we're going to do it, we have to do it right."

"What's different 'bout this lick than all the others we've done?" Michael asked.

"There's more at stake, and a whole lot more to lose."

"Like what?" Knuckles asked.

"Like our freedom as well as our lives," answered Dinky.

"Cuz, you act as if we're about to storm Fort Knox."

Michael laughed at Knuckle's comment, but his laughter was short lived when Dinky said, "You both think we can just roll down to the National Guard spot, break in, grab a bunch of weapons, and ride out into the sunset."

"That's right!" Michael said, believingly.

"Well, you're wrong, cuz. That place has a complex silent alarm system, plus the police patrol the area every forty-five minutes, and even if we were to gain entry we still wouldn't know how to get inside the vault."

"They have a fuckin' vault?" asked Knuckles.

"Well it's not exactly a vault. It's an old fashioned armory, where they store all their weapons, but it's built exactly like a bank vault."

Knuckles fell silent for a moment, and then said, "We'll find a way. After all, everything has a weakness."

They both laughed at Knuckles' worn out logic, and then after their laughter subsided, Michael said, "Let's get together and check this place out tomorrow."

"I down with' that, cuz," said Knuckles.

"Alright then, let's meet up around eight."

"Wait a minute, cuz. How you niggas going to make plans without me being in agreement with' this shit."

"I thought you were in?" Michael said.

"Yeah cuz, I'm in, but I don't think it's a good idea for us all to meet up together in the same place."

"Why you say that?"

"Because we should all go there alone at different times, that way no one will become suspicious of us."

"That makes a lot of sense, cuz," Knuckles said, and then added, "Lately, you niggas been showing that you do have some knowledge in those fat heads of yours."

"Cuz, that's not knowledge, that's fuckin' common sense," Michael replied.

"You're both wrong," said Dinky.

"Then what would you call it?" They both asked.

"I call it the fear of knowing what can happen if you don't plan your shit right."

There was no laughter for that comment. Reality spoke loud and clear. They all knew that every time they stepped from the confines of their own homes ~ plotting and planning ~ death was around the corner, silently waiting.

Michael didn't know which was worse, the constant threat of knowing he could get killed at any given place and time, or the constant nagging and interrogation that was inflicted upon him by his parents. Every day Michael had to face a barrage of questions: *Who was that? Where've you've been? And where are you going?* Today was no exception.

As he stepped into the living room of his home, Michael felt as if he had entered into the jungles of Vietnam. He was a prisoner of war, and his parents were his captors.

"Where you think you going!" said his mother as he tried to sneak past her and his father.

"To my room," Michael answered, looking upon his father's index finger that was motioning him toward a chair that was positioned right across from him.

"Check this out, son. There have been some serious allegations concerning you that've been brought to our attention."

"Like what?"

"Well first off, we were told that Dinky, you, and that other boy have been involved in setting fires and committing burglaries around the neighborhood."

"Who told you that?"

"Don't worry 'bout that, is it true?"

Michael hesitated for a long moment before answering. He needed the time in order to search his inner thoughts. He had no idea as to who was running their mouth, and he knew from past experiences that if he lied, his parents would know soon as he opened his mouth. Therefore, instead of lying he answered, "Yeah, I was there."

Surprised by his sudden truthfulness, all Michael's father could do was ask, "Why did you do that? Don't we give you damn near everything you ask for?"

"It's not like what you think, Dad... I had to do it."

"You had to do it! You didn't have to do a damn thing!" His father shouted.

"You did it to prove yourself for those gang guys, didn't you?" asked his mother, interrupting.

Before Michael could answer, he saw his sister hiding just beyond the entrance of their living room, and she was shaking her head in conjunction to the question his mother had asked. Upon seeing that, he said, "You can't go by what Marie says! She don't know nuthin' 'bout me and what I do."

"Who said Marie told us anything?"

"I'm not stupid; I can see her right there trying to hide."

"Come here, girl!" Michael's father shouted.

Reluctantly, Marie emerged from where she was hiding and stepped into the living room with a sly smirk on her face. She seemed to be enjoying the torment that Michael was going through.

"What did I tell yo' ass to do?"

"To stay outside and play with the rest of the kids."

"Then why ain't you out there!" screamed her father once again.

"I dunno."

Michael's father sighed, then said, "You better do what I told ya' to do before I tear into your ass like a ripe watermelon, or do you think you're too old for me to do that?"

"No."

"No what?"

"No, Daddy."

"Now git' yo ass outta here!"

The interruption gave Michael enough time to put his thoughts and words together, so before his father could ask anything else, Michael said, "Daddy, I'm not actually in a gang. The whole neighborhood we live in is considered a gang, regardless if you *bang (*slang for the actual participation of being involved in a street gang*) or not. We have to protect ourselves and each other, especially when we're out walking to school or headed to the store with the other kids in the neighborhood. It's during these times when something often jumps off, and when it does you have to participate or things can turn out bad for you later on down the road."

"What do you mean by things jumping off?" asked both his parents.

"Bad things like other kids from other neighborhoods who suddenly drive up and challenge us right there on the spot, and we can't run, so our only choice is to fight 'em.'"

"Why haven't you told us about this before?"

"I haven't told you because it's really nuthin'."

"Really nothing my ass...do you think it was nothing when that boy got beat to death at the park the other day?" asked his mother, angrily.

Michael didn't have an answer for that question, nor did he care. He knew about the incident, but it wasn't his problem. The boy was known throughout the neighborhood as a hard-core villain and it was just a matter of time before the odds caught up with him, which happened when he took his little brother to the park. He should have been packing *heat (*slang for gun*), but he didn't, and he knew better. After all, in Compton, one of the main ghetto rules was that you don't go anywhere without a gun, and you should always take a few brothers along just for added protection.

"Are you going to answer my question?" asked his mother, breaking through his inner thoughts.

"Mom, it's too hard to explain, plus I'm telling the truth. I'm not in a gang," he said, lying.

"Then if you're not in a gang, what is this?" asked his mother as she held up a blue bandana.

"It's just a rag," he answered.

"That's not what we been told. In fact, your father and I have taken it upon ourselves to drive around several of the neighborhoods in Compton, and you know what we found?"

"What?"

"We found kids wearing blue rags just like this one in their back pockets, and we saw children in other neighborhoods wearing red rags. Some were even wearing black ones, so don't tell us that this is just a damn rag!"

Becoming agitated, Michael said, "It's our protection and the way we identify ourselves."

"Protection my ass!" shouted his mother. "This is the very thing that will get you killed, and we ain't raising you to be no thug. So if we catch you wearing this rag or even hear that you're wearing one, yo' ass might as well find another place to live, understand me?"

"But…"

"But nuthin', son," added his Dad. "You heard your mother, and I'm backing her up one hundred percent. This is a very serious matter, and your activities could come back to hurt us all. Now is that what you want?"

"No."

"Then do as we ask you to do!"

"Is that all?"

At the moment Michael could see that his parents were at a loss for words. It seemed to him that they lived in a vacuum ~ in a world where they confused facts with that of fiction ~ in a place separate from the place he inhabited. When things became unbearable within their world, they could turn to God for comfort and support, but in Michael's world things were different. There were no rules, no morals, and no regulations. The animalistic law of survival was the course of nature that he was inclined to. He was in a place where the strong devours the weak, ignorance is held in praise, and self-hate is a festering wound that everyone wears like a medal of honor.

These elements were set in motion by the negative influences that were found within their environment. Subliminally, ghetto blacks had succumbed to the unknown variables that had confirmed certain theories from the mindset of Charles Darwin, which were *Survival of the Fittest, Punctuated Equilibrium,* and *Adaptation.* The most important of those theories for black children was that of adaptation. It was the main factor of their lives, a reality at best ~ and the child who fails to adapt to the conditions of the ghetto was the one who dies first, and Michael wasn't about to be that one.

Michael's mother interrupted his inner thoughts by saying, "If you're going to be in a gang, you can't live here, so you better choose what you're going to do... now git' outta my face!"

At that very moment Michael felt crushed. It seemed as if his parents were deaf, dumb, and blind. They couldn't see the forest for the trees, or maybe they saw only what they wanted to see. But he knew one thing that was for certain, surviving life in the streets was real. He wasn't about to jeopardize his life by punking out, so he decided right then and there that it would be best if he took off on his own. *But where would he go? How would he survive?* These were mind blowing decisions of life that he had to ponder ~ decisions that would have to wait until morning, because he was too tired to think any further.

"Damn cuz, where you been? We've been calling your house and coming by for the last three days only to hear your folks say you ain't been home."

"That's my fault, cuz. I had a big argument with' my parents, so I sort of moved out."

"C'mon cuz, be real. Everyone knows that you ran away," said Dinky.

"How you know that?" He asked.

"You know your sister's mouth is like the *Los Angeles Times* newspaper."

Michael laughed for a moment and then said, "Yeah cuz, it's true, I did run away."

"But where have you been staying?" asked Knuckles.

Michael was too embarrassed to tell them the truth, so he tried to lie, but it was of no avail. "I stayed with my cousin."

"C'mon cuz, we just seen yo' ass come out the back-door of that church."

Michael was now truly embarrassed, especially knowing that they had seen him coming out of the church. This was a big blow to his pride, so he tried to counter the ill effects he felt by saying, "You two nig-gas can clown all you want, but there's no other place better than a church."

"Why you say that?" asked Dinky.

"I say this because it's the only place that has run-ning water, a shower, a kitchen, and plenty of food."

"Fuck that, cuz. I'm moving in with' you!" Knuckles exclaimed.

His sudden comment was followed by a burst of laughter that allowed him to feel better than he had in the last past seventy-two hours.

"Say cuz," Michael said, as he looked toward Dinky.

"What's up?"

"When you went to my house, did my parents act as if they were worried 'bout me?"

Dinky scratched his head for a moment and then said, "Your sister seems to be happy that you're gone, but I can tell that your mother is kinda worried."

"And how can you tell that?"

"Because when we went by your house for the third time, she asked us had we heard from you before we could even open our mouths, and when we told her that we were just about to ask her the same question, she told us to please let her know as soon as we got word from you."

Upon hearing that Michael felt kind of bad because he knew his parents loved him despite what he did in life, so he said, "Go on and tell her I'm alright."

"You tell her!"

"Why?"

"Man, that's your mother, cuz, and we ain't trying to git' caught in the middle." Knuckles said. "And anyway, what happened between you two?"

"I thought my sister told you."

"She only ran her mouth about you running 'way, so tell us, what happened?"

"The little bitch snitched on me!"

"Your sister?" asked Dinky.

"Cuz, who else would I be talkin' 'bout?"

"When you said the little bitch, I thought you were talkin' 'bout someone altogether different from your sister."

"Nah cuz, that bitch told my parents that I had been puttin' in *work (*slang for illegal activity*) wit' you guys, plus she told my mom that I was bangin'."

"I thought your parents already knew that you were bangin'," said Dinky.

"Nah cuz, I keep what I do in the street separated from what I do at home."

"That shit would drive me crazy, cuz."

"Why you say that?" Michael asked, curiously.

"Because that's like playin' two damn roles, cuz, and you have to be equally good at them both. Like me, I can't do that shit. I'm a Crip twenty four hours a day ~ no rest, no play, down to spray, chili-chili-bang-bang, Crip-n-things!"

"Are you sayin' I'm not always down?"

"Nah cuz, I'm not sayin' that."

"Then what are you sayin'?" Michael asked.

"What I'm saying is this, cuz. If one of us niggas got shot while you were at home and we needed your help right then and there, you couldn't provide. You would have to git' past your parents, but for us, we don't have to go through that shit. Our parents know we're bangin', and they know they better not make us choose between them and our homies."

"And it's the same way for me!" Michael said angrily. "Cripping comes first, and if any one of you niggas get shot or even shot at, I will be the first to be at your side...even if I had to climb out the fuckin' window. So know for sure that I'll be there for the both of you, understand?"

For a moment they just stood there looking. Each in their own separate thoughts until Dinky broke the silence, turned to Knuckles and said, "Cuz, you know he ain't no *buster," (*slang for punk, and a weak minded person*).

"I never said that, cuz. What I meant is that when it comes to putting in work, Cripping comes before God, family, and even friends."

"I feel the same way, cuz, and even if one of my family members was a blood, his ass would have to die. After all, it's death before dishonor." Michael stated, strongly.

"You got that right, cuz!" Knuckles added, sinisterly.

"Say cuz, since we all have an understanding about this shit, let's git' the fuck outta' here and git' into something more worthwhile," suggested Dinky.

"Where you wanna go?" Michael asked.

"Nigga, I know you haven't forgotten about our plans to hit the National Guard place."

"But cuz, I haven't even..."

"Don't worry, everything is set in motion," said Dinky, cutting Michael off in mid-sentence. "Cuz, it's gonna' be a piece of cake."

"I sure hope so," he said quietly to himself as he followed his comrades to a car that was parked nearby.

6

Real Soldiers, Real G'S

"For the urban warrior, life, love, and women hold no
purpose or value, for death is his only reward, which is
a door into another dimension of reality, and a guar-
anteed promise to the end of all his pain...."
— For Jonathan Lewis

February 1973-1976

Everything went off like a charm. It was like they were professionals at the game of deception, implemented in the art of war. Intentionally, they set two buildings on fire, shot up a gas station, and placed three phony 911 calls to the Compton Police Department that created a diversion long enough for them to break into the National Guard armory and make off with the weapons of their choice. They were some smooth criminals for sure.

"Don't point that thing at me!" shouted Dinky.

"Cuz, this isn't just a thing, it's a mothafuckin' .45 caliber submachine gun that most niggas call a grease gun," said Knuckles, with the pride of a ghetto gun scholar.

"But it's no match for what I got," stated Dinky as he held the stock of a HK91 up in the air.

"Damn!" Michael exclaimed as he grabbed the HK91 from Dinky. The rifle felt like a woman in his hands, a body of fine precision, with perfect curves here and there. She wasn't too heavy, nor was she too light, and she was all a man could ask for. It was also said that she had an effective range of a thousand yards, with enough strength to slam through a concrete wall, through a tree trunk, and still have enough power to kill a man ~ *what a woman*, Michael thought.

"Give me back my bitch!" said Dinky after a moment.

Laughing, Michael gave him back his rifle as he looked over the rest of the arsenal that lay before him. It was composed of M1's, M14's, M16's, Colt .45's, automatics and ammunition for all. There were also fragmentation, smoke and tear gas grenades, grenade launchers, gas masks, four Springfield .03 sniper rifles, five HK91's, five .308 rifles, complete with scopes and ammo for them, C4's, dynamite, *A.P. rounds (armor piercing), claymores, and a loose assortment of other weapons that weren't American made.

"Damn cuz, this is just like fuckin' Christmas!" he said, and then added, "Better yet, this is a fuckin' ghetto paradise."

"That's no bullshit, cuz!" Knuckles said.

Dinky looked at Michael sinisterly, and then said, "C'mon cuz, pick yourself out a damn weapon."

Carefully, Michael looked over each weapon until his eyes settled upon a Remington .22 long-range sniper rifle, with threaded barrel, sound suppressor, complete with twelve-inch infrared night and day vision scope.

Knuckles and Dinky laughed as Michael picked up the Remington rifle. "What are you gonna do with that, shoot birds at a thousand yards away?" Dinky asked.

"You must think the gun you have is better than all the others," Michael said quickly.

"It is, look at this fuckin' bullet, cuz," Dinky said, proudly. "See how big it is, and see what it says on the bottom."

Michael grabbed the bullet and peered at the inscription, which read NATO 7.62mm. After that he handed him back the bullet and said, "So what, it's a 7.62mm."

"Well, it's bigger than the shit you have, and I know for a fact that this bullet would put a hole in your ass the size of a fuckin' tennis ball."

"Ya'll niggas don't know shit when it comes to guns and bullets."

"Cuz, I know you're not saying the gun you have is more powerful than the shit we have."

"I'm not saying that my gun is more powerful than yours, cuz, but from what I've read in the magazines that my daddy has layin' around da' house, it states that the .22 caliber bullet has more penetrating power than a fuckin' .45."

"I don't give a fucc 'bout what some book says, all I care about is puttin' one of these big mothafucca's into a roosta (*a slang derogatory term that Crips use to deface members of the Blood gang*) nigga's head," Dinky replied, irritably.

"C'mon cuz, it don't make sense in having you two niggas here arguing over who has the baddest guns, especially when we successfully scored these mothafucca's without receiving one scratch."

"Yeah cuz, you're right," Michael said. "We shouldn't be arguing over this shit, especially when it can bring attention to us, and we don't want that."

"Why you say that, cuz?" asked Dinky.

"Because what we have in our possession should stay in our possession, plus we can't even tell the homies about what we got."

"Why is that, cuz?" asked Knuckles.

"Because I feel no one outside of us should know, at least not yet."

"But that still doesn't answer my question, cuz."

Michael paused for a moment in order to gather his thoughts. He clearly needed to convey the importance of this matter. He didn't want his comrades to feel as if he were trying to keep them from climbing up in status among the homies. Having such power in their grasps would give them that, especially when they would be known as the ones who supplied the neighborhood with new weapons ~ a commodity that is praised and ranked along with silver, pussy, and gold.

Turning his thoughts back to the situation at hand, Michael turned toward his homies and said, "Cuz, the only homies that can know about this are the ones who have a reputation for keeping special things under the table, especially where these weapons are concerned."

"Damn cuz, it shouldn't be any big deal as to how and where we got these weapons," said Dinky.

"But it is, cuz," Michael countered. "In fact, these guns are so hot at the moment, that every 'hood within a radius of five miles is going to be swarming with the FBI, ATF, and maybe the fuckin' CIA, and we sure don't need that type of heat."

"He's right, cuz." Knuckles said after a long moment, "Especially about some of the niggas from the 'hood. You know they be up running their lips like broke-ass bitches with their legs gapped wide, and a big-ass mouth to match."

Dinky and Michael laughed for a moment. It felt good knowing that they were now all on the same page and working for the same cause. Michael also knew that for them to continue to be successful in their endeavors, they had to know who they could trust ~ failure to do so meant the instant termination of one's freedom and maybe life as well. Michael knew this to be true because in every neighborhood, there is at least one or two *player haters (*slang for a jealous person or persons*) waiting among the shadows to bring a person down, like crabs in a bucket.

Later that night, Michael struggled to get himself to sleep like night struggles to keep its sole possession over day. He tossed and turned, and fought and fought with himself throughout the stillness of the night, and for the life of him, Michael couldn't sleep despite lying in the darkness of Dinky's garage. His conscience kept bothering him in regards to his parents. He missed them a great deal, and for some strange reason, he even missed his smart-mouthed sister.

Michael had been away from home for two weeks now. He knew his family was extremely worried about him. At least he hoped that was the case, and for some reason, he knew it was true. After all, Michael and his parents had always been close. He never stayed anywhere long without letting them know that he was okay. *But what was he to do? How could he express the fact that he loved them without losing his pride in the process? And what would Dinky and Knuckles think of him if he were to coward-out and go back home? Would he be considered weak?* Who cares, *I'm out of here*, he finally thought.

As Michael fumbled around in the darkness for his pants, his mind began to drift to those special times he had shared with his family. He smiled inwardly as he remembered how his Dad used to take him fishing, bowling, and to those Dodgers' baseball games where he would buy him those long Dodgers' dogs and point out all the major league baseball players.

Michael even remembered one time during the drive home after being taken to a Dodgers' game, his father had turned to him and said, "Son, I'm so proud of you just for the fact that you are my son, and nothing in this world could ever change that fact. So whatever you decide to do in your life, make sure you be the best at it, understand?" Those were his father's words, and he loved him and his mother regardless of what came between them.

Michael hadn't noticed that he had begun to cry until he hit the cold streets of Compton. The last time he could ever remember feeling this way was when he was eleven. The tears he now shed were altogether different; these tears resulted from the bad decisions that he was making in his life ~ decisions that were causing his family a great deal of grief and pain. Just the thought of his problems had his mind in turmoil. He felt like a young man attempting to please two masters and this was driving him crazy. *How could he separate the things that his parents had taught him from that which he had learned in the streets?* He didn't have the answer at the moment, but he sure knew where to find it: twenty blocks away in the wisdom of the only person who he really knew and trusted ~ his father.

It took Michael twenty minutes to gather up enough courage to ring the doorbell of his parents' home and it would have taken him longer if it weren't for the constant wind that was sending chills throughout his body.

The thought of turning back was quite inconceivable, so Michael stepped forward, pressed the doorbell and waited.

After a few minutes, the person he needed most answered the door. "Come on in, Son," said his father after looking Michael over closely.

Michael could feel that his father was fighting the urge to hug him, and he too had to resist the urge of running into his arms, so instead, he followed him into the den where they both elected to sit in silence. It was like they were at a loss for words.

After a few moments Michael's father looked towards him and said, "Son, your mother and I have been worried to death about you."

"I'm alright, Daddy."

"How were we to know that? You didn't call, send a message, or nothing, and every time the phone rang, your mother felt that it would be the police calling to tell her that you were dead."

"But Dad," Michael began. "I left because I didn't want to cause you and mom any more pain due to the things that my friends and I do."

"And what are those things, if you don't mind me asking?"

"Gang banging," Michael answered.

Michael's father sighed for a moment and then said, "Son, why do you feel the need to belong to a gang?"

Michael didn't answer right away because he couldn't find the right words to convey the reason for him being in a gang. Truthfully, he didn't have an answer, so he tried to reverse the question by asking, "Why do you think I'm in a gang?"

"Maybe it's for respect, protection, drugs, or maybe women. I really don't know because I'm not the one who's living in the streets day-by-day and night-by-night. That's why I asked you."

"Well, I'm sure not in a gang for the need of protection."

"Then tell me something, Son. Why would someone like yourself who is intelligent beyond his years, want to live the life of a ghetto hoodlum?"

"It gives me a purpose, a reason for being and living. Plus I love my 'hood, it's all I have."

"What about us? Don't you love your family?"

"Of course I do, but tell me this. Daddy, did you ever have something that you loved so much that you had to defend it at all cost?"

"Yes."

"And what was it?"

"This family and that's my gang, my motivation and my reason for getting up every day at four o'clock in the morning. And if something ever threatened the stability of this family, I would put my life in direct danger to ensure that you were all safe and well provided for, do you understand?"

"But Dad, that's different, that's your job as a father."

"So you really think so, huh? Well, let me tell you this, Son. I don't have to do a damn thing for you or this family. I could be just like the rest of your friends' fathers, hanging out in front of liquor stores, begging for quarters; or worse, I could be a dope fiend father who comes around only once a month in order to beat down your mother and take her money and use it toward my addiction. Now, is that what you want in your life?"

"No," Michael replied, as he thought about what his father had just said. He was actually right in his adducement of his friends' fathers. Michael had seen time and time again how the fathers of some of his closest comrades would show up at their wife's or girlfriend's house on the first and fifteenth unannounced, talking big and bad, brandishing weapons in order to scare them into giving them money for dope and other negative means. In fact, there was a time when Michael and Knuckles had gone over to his mother's house only to find that his father was in the act of beating Knuckle's mother. They had intervened by pistol whipping him beyond recognition. Yeah, his father was right, but in Michael's mind, that's the only thing he was right about.

Michael's father suddenly stood up and started pacing back and forth; he often did this when he was about to hit Michael with some cold, hard facts of life.

"Son," his father began, "I understand that we're born into a system where a fair chance has not been afforded to people of color. On top of that, we're being reduced, one by one, into homicidal, psychopathic killing machines. Through this behavior, we lost the love that we once had for ourselves, and this makes it easier for us to kill each other. The only panacea that I can see for our people is that we have to bond together spiritually in order to break down the negative social conditioning that causes so many of us to commit genocide among ourselves."

"Dad," Michael said after a moment of contemplation.

"Yeah, Son?"

"Can you break it down so a little ole' sixteen year-old black child like me who resides here on earth can understand what you just said?"

Michael's father laughed for a long moment and then said, "Son, I'm sorry, sometimes I get carried away when I'm trying to press upon a point, especially when it comes to blackness and the killing of our own people. You might not believe this, but Son, this type of negative behavior is perpetuated in more ways than one."

"But Dad, haven't our people been killing each other since day one?"

"Son, you of all people know better than that. I taught you very well when it comes to black on black killing. In fact, I remember how badly it affected you when you witnessed the beating of that little boy by the police. You were so upset that you wanted to go out there and fight all the police; and you were only eight at the time."

"But things have changed now. Dad, racist white people ain't killin' us no mo', it's our own people."

"Who do you think is behind all of this?" His father asked.

"It can't be any white people; they don't live n' the 'hood."

"They don't have to because they provided you with the tools for your destruction, and these tools are right here in the neighborhood."

"What tools are you talkin' 'bout?"

"Tools like alcohol, guns, and drugs, the same tools that's been created by them but used by us for our own annihilation, and what makes matters worse is that you street youths are so damn blind you can't even see the plot when its placed right before you in full view."

"But Dad, ya'll made the same mistakes. Ya'll had gangs!" he countered.

"You're very wrong son. We had organizations that were created for the benefit of our people and other minorities as well. And the purpose of most of these organizations was to unite us all under a common cause and goal. Goals that provided breakfast programs for children in need, free shoes and clothing, legal assistance for needy families, Medicare, free busing that enabled the elderly to make it to and from medical appointments and grocery shopping, free intercommunal news service, and the betterment of the minority community as a whole. If you were in need, there was always an organization that would assist you no matter what the need was."

"But Daddy, what about those groups that were in Watts when I was little?"

"What groups?" his father asked curiously.

Now it was Michael's turn to convey some facts of his own, and since he had the floor, he was going to make use of it.

"Daddy, when we lived in Watts, there were a lot of groups and gangs that were located in our neighborhood. I remember them very clearly. There were such groups as The Businessmen, Slausons, Volkswagoners, Sir Valiants, Farmers, Gladiators, Boozies, Slausonettes, and the United Slaves who had their very own special flag whose colors were red, black, and green. The red represented the blood that was shed both in war and in racial confrontations, the black represented our culture, the green represented youth and new ideas, but over-all, most of their words was nothing but a bunch of hot steam and bull..."

"Why do you say that, son?"

"Because I remember what their leader had done to the Black Panthers. I used to read about it every night before I went to bed, and I have the whole event memorized."

"What leader and event are you talking about?"

"I'm talkin' 'bout a man who went by the name of Ronald Everett, but he changed his name to Maulana Ron Karenga which is a Swahili term that loosely translates as "great teacher." (See Elaine Brown, *A Taste of Power*, page 113). He formed a black organization called the United Slaves. It was rumored that his organization was in the back pockets of the FBI who saw the Black Panther Party as a major threat to the national security of the United States. The Black Panthers were no match for United Slaves because of the rumored support by the police, the FBI, and everyone who played a part in the plot (see Elaine Brown, *A Taste of Power*, page 176-177).

"Son, how did you come across all this information?"

"Dad, can I finish first?"

"I'm sorry, Son, go on."

Michael paused for a moment, searching his mind for where he had left off. After a few seconds, his recollection came back to him and he began by saying, "Dad, there was a lot of evidence that led many to believe that Karenga and his followers were the principle figures behind a plot to bring about an end to the Black Panther Party."

"A plot?" asked his father.

"Not so much as that, but there was an incident that occurred between Karenga, the black student union of UCLA, and a few members of the Black Panther Party that sparked rumors and suspicions among many."

"What was this incident, and when did it happen?"

"It happened between January 15, 1969 and January 17, 1969. This is when Maulana Ron Karenga appeared on the campus of UCLA to speak at a meeting that was being held in Campbell Hall by the Black Student Union. He created tension among the students when he tried to force-feed them his rhetoric and beliefs. Many students were afraid of him and they dared not speak, but there was one student who had no such fear. He stood up and said, 'We are the students here, and we alone will determined our destinies!' Not only were there Black Student Union members in attendance, but a few members of the Black Panther Party were there as well who stood up along with students and applauded after hearing the bold statement of the Black Student Union member. The students then demanded that Karenga leave and when he was ushered out of the meeting, the Black Student Union made a decision that they would no longer have any dealings with Karenga or anyone else that represented his organization. They scheduled another meeting for January 17, 1969 ~ a day for which Karenga would exact his revenge."

"Revenge on who?" asked his father with keen interest.

"I'm getting to that."

"Alright, go on."

"Ok, on January 17, 1969, just minutes after the Black Student Union meeting had ended, one of Karenga's soldiers showed up and started an argument with a woman name Elaine Brown, who later became the first and only female head of the Black Panther Party. This particular soldier had overheard the leader of the Los Angeles chapter of the Black Panther Party, Bunchy Carter tell Elaine Brown, not to take any shit off of any United Slave punk. After that was said, she walked away and the shooting began, shooting that left two Black Panther Party members dead, John Huggins and Bunchy Carter. They died from the trigger that was pulled by a brother who represented an organization that had proclaimed to be down for the rights of black people ~ now Dad, how absurd and blind can one be when it comes to our people?"

Michael's father was stunned. He never knew that his son had possessed such knowledge, and this wasn't knowledge gained by reading. This knowledge was acquired from years of observance, listening, and living the life of a curious street thug.

After a few minutes of contemplation, Michael's father said, "Son, you do have a valid point, and I applaud your knowledge. Plus, I have to admit that you know more than I do when it comes to street affairs, and I'm going to tell you something, but first let me grab something for you."

Michael's father left the room for a moment and then returned with a sealed envelope. "Here," he said, handing the envelope over to Michael. "Don't open this until you wish to know more about the truth and other things that may not be clear to you at this time."

"Dad, I don't understand."

"Don't worry. You will in time, and like I said before, you do have a valid point, but there's one thing that underlines the whole scheme of things."

"And what's that?"

Michael's father paused for a moment, cleared his throat, and then said, "Even though blacks are out there killing each other every day, the strings that are tied to these killings are being pulled by people who live comfortably in their own homes. They watch what happens to us like they watch a movie. They get their enjoyment by seeing us destroy ourselves, and they can afford to laugh at us because they're so far removed from our violence that they know it will never affect them totally as a whole. In fact, they benefit from it. They reap the rewards of our violence through our incarceration, which provides jobs for them as well as their children. These people also know that as a result of our negative behavior that brings about our violence, the neighborhoods in which we live will be run down and poor thus perpetuating a condition of helplessness that is often associated with violence and dependency. Dwelling in such conditions means that we can be easily manipulated and controlled, thus making them our puppet masters. The world is their stage and we're the puppets putting on an everyday show. You can't see this for yourself, or you refuse to see it. I don't know which is which, but I do know one thing for sure."

"And what's that?"

"I know the gang that you're in, isn't going to make things any better. In fact, all you're doing is destroying another mother's son, and another person's brother or sister who will in turn feel just as you do when you lose a loved one. They view their families just as you view yours, and as I view mine. We're going to protect our families at all cost, even in the name of vengeance, so think about that when you're about to pull that trigger of yours. There's also another thing you need to remember."

"And what's that?"

"That there's always going to be another person on the other end of that same trigger, trying hard to cancel your Christmas and the other ten major holidays of the year."

"You make it seem as if I have a death wish."

"When you live the lifestyle that you're attempting to live, you'll find that you and everyone else that you hang with will have a death wish in the form of a bullet with all your names on it."

"That's not always true," Michael said, defensively.

"Just read the contents of the envelope before you decide to do something that you'll later regret."

Michael hated when his father tapped into his conscious mind. He always had a way of throwing the truth against falsehood. When he did so, this often left Michael confused and shaken, just like now.

Turning his back on his father, Michael got up and peered out of the window, and as he did so, his mind began to ponder several questions such as: *If what my*

father said was true, how could I alone change any-
thing? What was I to do? If I stopped gang banging,
wouldn't there be another person to take my place?
Michael knew these questions needed answers, but at
the moment there were none to give because he was
way too consumed with the lifestyle of gang banging. It
gave him power, a purpose, and a reason to live.

Michael suddenly turned from the window and
walked over to his Dad and reached out and drew him
into his arms. They held each other as if they knew that
one would eventually lose the other.

After a moment, Michael stepped back, looked into
his father's eyes, and said, "Dad, I have to live my life as
I see it. You have to allow me to make my own choices.
I'm still attending school, and I promise not to bring
harm to any member of our family. If I feel that things
are getting to be too much for me, I'll quit the gang
altogether, but please don't ask me to turn my back on
my homies. They're my family, too."

Michael could see from the look that was present
in his father eyes, that he understood, but at the same
time, he saw what he perceived as a hint of fear; and
the fear was for Michael.

"Son," he began. "I love you no matter what, and
I will always be here for you, but please come to me
before you do something stupid."

"I will," Michael said, smiling for the first time since
he came home.

"Oh, one more thing before I forget," Michael's father said.

"And what's that?"

"If you get caught doing something illegal, you ride
your own beef. Don't expect your mother and me to
involve ourselves in any of your endeavors. We won't
be your mouthpiece or your get-away drivers. That's

what your friends are for. If you get into trouble, we'll come to court to make sure you get a fair deal, but we're not putting up our home, car, or anything to get your ass out of jail. Again, that's your friends' responsibility, after all. Like you said, they're your family, too. So do we have an understanding?"

"Yeah, Dad, I understand."

"Okay then, now go get yourself something to eat... and get some sleep, too. Lord knows you'll need it."

7

The Point of No Return

"The Urban Warrior fights many battles, he fights against family, foes, society, and friends, but the greatest battle he faces is the battle of self."

—For "Alvin Jackson"

March 1, 1973

Sleepless nights were beginning to be a common occurrence with Michael. Tonight was no exception. He felt like a crackhead who'd taken a hit and then journeyed beyond the cosmos in search of a wet dream in the middle of a barren desert. A journey that was full of apprehension, excitement, chaos, and mind-blowing decisions.

Michael's head was really messed up, and there was only one person to blame ~ his father. He always had a way of knowing when he was about to do something devious, and like always, he would intervene by planting subliminal messages of reality within his subconscious mind; messages that made it hard for him to sleep, think, and respond to the negative behaviors that he so often desired.

Looking up at the clock, Michael could see that it was going to be daylight soon, and he knew this was the day that he and his comrades had chosen to put in work. With that thought in mind, he threw off the blankets and raced to the kitchen to get him something to eat.

Three hours passed since Michael had left his parents' home and made his way back to Dinky's garage. Stepping inside, he was surprised to find Knuckles there along with another comrade of theirs whom they called Bitter Child.

Bitter Child was known as a ruthless ghetto assassin, so ruthless that you never knew what to expect of him. One minute he could be smiling and playing around, and the next moment he would be putting his foot deep in someone's butt. The most dangerous element he displayed was his ability to be patient. He was known to let certain things go until the time was right. When people least expected it, he would rise up and strike, like a King Cobra after its prey. What made him even more ominous was the fact that he would hit you during two special days of the year ~ days on which he knew there would be no police intervention or assistance on your behalf.

In Compton and other parts of Los Angeles, people who were in tune to the mentality of the ghetto knew that if you wanted to rob or murder someone in cold blood, the best time to do so was during those two special days of the year: *The Fourth of July* and *New Year's*. These were the nights duly known by the police as nights where the underworld had a license to kill, and the police knew that if they took a chance and patroled the hard sections of the urban ghetto then, they might as well be patrolling the streets of hell, because that's where they'd be headed.

"Where you been, cuz?" Knuckles asked as Michael entered.

"Nowhere really," he answered; noticing the weapons they had stolen, sprawled all over the garage.

"Yeah cuz, where you been hiding at?" Dinky added.

"I went over to my parent's house to set things straight."

"And how did things go?" Knuckles asked.

"Cuz, you know how parents are. They're always tryin' to hit a nigga' with' that ole' song and dance guilt trip, and I've been there and done that shit... and we all know that shit ain't true."

"Why you say that, cuz?"

"I say that because ain't none of our parents put in any work for the 'hood."

"Speak for yourself, cuz. My Daddy put in a lot of work," said Dinky.

"Yeah, on the other end of a Silver Satin wine bottle," Knuckles added.

Everyone laughed for a moment, and Michael was glad because he didn't want to be reminded of his father's lecture or of the envelope he had given him.

"Say cuz, what about this one?" Bitter Child asked, breaking Michael's chain of thoughts.

Looking in his direction, Michael saw that Bitter Child was holding a Soviet RPD, which was a light machine gun that fires a 7.62mm NATO round. "It's okay with me, if it's okay with everyone else," Dinky answered.

"I got no problem with it," Knuckles added.

At that point, everyone turned toward Michael. "Why is everyone looking at me like that? I don't even know what's going on."

"Cuz, we're sorry 'bout that, but Bitter Child ran into some problems with those roosta' nigga's the other night."

"Where did this happen?" Michael asked

"At a party over on Aranbe and Elm," he answered.

"Ain't nuthin' but Bloods over there, cuz," Michael said.

"That doesn't mean nuthin, cuz. I go where I want to go, plus one of the homies' grandmother lives over there."

Michael had no choice but to agree with Bitter Child in reference to his statement because most Crips did journey above and beyond their own neighborhoods. Some ventured out hoping to catch one of their rivals *slipping (*slang for not being on guard or prepared*). Others ventured out for the purpose of showing off their cars, jewelry, and other material possessions, while the rest ventured out in pursuit of the most treasured and prized ghetto commodity ~ black pussy.

Snapping back to the present, Michael asked, "What's the plan?"

Bitter Child just smiled and replied, "You know me, cuz. When the feeling hits me, I just roll with' the punches."

"I guess that means you don't need any help?"

"You already helped me by letting me have this beautiful black bitch."

Again they laughed as Bitter Child grabbed some ammunition for his weapon and stepped out into the early morning sunshine.

"Bitter Child is a straight-up fool for real."

"You're damn right about that," Michael added.

A sudden ominous silence fell over each man in the garage. They knew this was the day they had been waiting for ~ a moment in time where boys would become men by killing those who they deemed their enemies. This would be the day when they would earn their ghetto strip ~ or better yet, martyrdom. This also would become a day for mourning.

Breaking the silence, Knuckles turned toward Michael and asked, "Are you ready for tonight?"

"I'm ready if the rest of ya'll are ready," he answered wearily.

"What's wrong, cuz?" Dinky asked curiously.

"Why you ask me that?" Michael quickly countered.

"Cuz, I can always tell when something is bothering you, especially now ~ so what's up?"

Dinky was right, something was bothering Michael, and he couldn't quite shake the feeling that it had to do with the envelope that was in his back pocket.

All of a sudden, Michael pulled the envelope from his pocket and tore the end off.

"What's that?" Knuckles asked.

"It's something that my father gave me before I left the house," he answered, as he pulled the contents out of the envelope.

Everyone drew close to Michael as he began to read what seemed to be some old worthless newspaper articles.

"Damn!" he exclaimed as he read each article.

"What's wrong, cuz?" Knuckles and Dinky asked excitedly.

Slowly looking up from the articles, Michael said, "Cuz we're fighting the wrong mothafuccin' battle."

"Why you say that?" asked Dinky.

"Because according to what I just read, the police, the FBI, the government, and even some of our own weak-ass people have been playin' a key role in plotting our destruction."

"How, and when did that shit happen?" Dinky asked.

"Well, it's like this, cuz; some of those weak-ass nigga's of our past were used as double agents or provocateurs to infiltrate our black organizations and gangs. Soon as they were accepted within the ranks of the targeted organizations, they would take vital information, illegal guns, and even drugs provided to them by the police and plant it in certain locations within these organizational headquarters or meeting places. Once this was done, the police would be called, the media would be alerted, and the rest is history. They would also take information that they personally gathered back to the police and inform them on everything that they saw or heard, and there's more."

"Go on, tell us cuz," Dinky said, anxiously.

"Well, you might not believe this cuz, but I think the government is behind the violence between the Bloods and Crips."

"C'mon cuz, I don't believe that shit," Dinky said.

"Me neither," said Knuckles as he stepped away from Michael, then turned around and abruptly added, "How can you come up with that just from reading a paper?"

Angry, Michael answered, "You can read, can't you!"

"Yeah, nigga, I can read," Knuckles answered, in a tone that hinted danger.

Michael knew he was treading upon dangerous waters. He also knew that Knuckles wouldn't hesitate to fight when he felt his pride was being tested. And with all these weapons lying out and about, a fight between them could easily escalate into murder.

"Cuz," Michael finally said, "I didn't mean anything by asking can you read. What I meant was read these articles for yourself."

Knuckles didn't say anything; instead he stared at Michael for a very long moment. Michael knew Knuckles was debating on whether to punch him or read the articles first-hand. Whichever way he decided, Michael was prepared.

After a two-minute stare-down, he reached out and Michael gave him the articles, which read:

[NEW YORK CITY, 1965] Police and FBI agents uncovered a plot to dynamite the Statue, Liberty Bell, and Washington Monument. Master-minded by a six-month old group known as the Black Liberation Front, the terrorist plan also included a surprise air attack on the White House and simultaneous nationwide assault on police stations, airfields and industrial plants. A police informant who had infiltrated the Black Liberation Front later testified that the leader of B.L.F. had received training in guerilla tactics and weapons construction from a North Vietnamese Army major stationed in Cuba.

[PHILADELPHIA, 1967] Informants told police that members of the Revolution Action Movement were in possession of nearly 300 grams of potassium cyanide and had tried unsuccessfully to initiate a riot on July 29. Had they succeeded, the Cyanide would have been placed in the food and distributed to police assigned to quell the disturbance. An FBI analyst reported that the dosage could have killed as many as 4,500 people. Earlier raids on RAM units had uncovered numerous weapons (including a machine gun and steel tip arrows), literature on guerrilla warfare, and plans to assassinate moderate civil rights leaders, blame the murders on whites, and thereby spurring nationwide racial uprisings. Police also speculated that RAM members were acting as advisors to ghetto youth gangs. J Edgar Hoover encapsulated the nature of the RAM threat by information to a House Subcommittee on appropriations that the "highly secret all-Negro" organization had units in several cities and was "dedicated" to thwart the capitalist system in the United States, by violence if necessary.

[**NEW YORK CITY**, 1969] Twenty-one Black Panthers were charged with conspiring to blow up police stations, department stores, and other buildings in the city. The accused circulated an open letter through the underground press praising "righteous urban guerilla actions" and criticizing the national leadership for tripping out, sowing seeds of confusion and being insufficiently militant. They claimed that mere readiness to die for the cause ~ to commit "revolutionary suicide" ~ would only make martyrs. The Panthers desperately needed more revolutionists who were completely willing and ready at all times to kill to change conditions. Only continuous confrontation and armed struggles would destroy the Amerikkklan machine and its economy.

[**CHICAGO**, 1972] Six young blacks were arrested and accused of taking part in nine recent murders throughout Illinois. At their arraignment, the suspects appeared with arms extended in the Black Power salute. Police told reporters that they were part of a nationwide league of embittered black combats, veterans who had to "kill a whitey to get into the gang." Cook County officials claimed that the arrests thwarted the group's plan to begin a systematic cop-killing spree. Dashing any sense of relief this news may have encouraged, Tribune headlines screamed: "MURDER GANG 3,000 STRONG DE MAU MAU TAKING OVER FOR THE PANTHERS."

"Say cuz, what does this entire shit mean?" Knuckles asked as he handed the articles to Dinky.

"It means that the FBI, working along with independent police agencies and the media, were at the time initiating bogus newspaper articles with the intent to start street wars between the neighborhood organizations and gangs. Even some of our own people got caught up in the scheme."

"Our people?" Knuckles asked, surprised.

"Yeah cuz, our people, and you'll be surprised what a nigga' would do in order to keep his ass out of jail or for some money."

"Fuck that shit, I'm not snitching on nobody and I'm definitely not going to talk to the police," said Dinky.

"Not all black people are as strong as us and we must also keep in mind that there's weak-minded niggas everywhere and in every organization and gang."

"If I find one, his ass is gonna git' smoked," Knuckles stated.

Looking up from the articles, Dinky said, "Believe it or not, cuz, my grandfather use to collect a lot of shit like this. In fact, I have some of his old articles right here in this garage."

"Where?" They both asked.

"Over here," he answered, as he climbed up on a bench in order to reach a shelf that contained a black shoebox and other items.

As he sat the box upon an old workbench and prepared to open it, they surrounded him like hungry dope fiends waiting for their turn to get a hit.

"Git outta' my light!" screamed Knuckles as he peered at the countless newspaper clippings. The articles were so old that they had turned yellow, but they contained valuable news stories that occurred before their time. Stories with headlines that read: Education v. Brown, Jim Crow Strikes again, the Scottsborough Boys Get the Death Sentence, and there were other articles as well. But the article that caught their attention the most was the one that read:

Informant Turns the Tables on the Los Angeles Police Department and Other Organizations

According to agent/provocateur, Louis Tackwood; The Los Angeles police department operated the three most dangerous intelligence units used to damage the Black Panthers. Operatives for those units were sent on missions nationwide. Tackwood who passed all tests administered by investigative journalists to establish his credibility, says that the units engage to destroy not only the Panthers, but also other black and white radical groups "through any means necessary." Tackwood worked for two of those divisions, infiltrating both the Panthers and the Los Angeles militant group, United Slaves. The intelligence divisions were so secret that not even rank-and-file Los Angeles police officers were aware of them (*see Hugh Peterson, the Shadow of the Panther, pages 180-81, and the Glasshouse Tapes by Louis Tackwood, and the citizen's research committee on police tactics*).

"Damn cuz, this shit is really something!" exclaimed Knuckles.

"It's more than that, Cuz," Michael replied. "It's a straight-up conspiracy, and we're all caught in the middle."

"What I don't understand is how Crips and Bloods play a part in all of this. There isn't any article that shows a conspiracy between the police, Crips, Bloods, and other street gangs of our era, so the only thing I could gather from all of this is that the FBI and others had executed a clever game of infiltration, divide, and conquer among those niggas of the past."

"And you don't think the police are using the same practices on us today?"

"Naw cuz, I don't," Knuckles answered, confidently.

"I feel the same way," Dinky added.

Michael paused for a moment to gather his thoughts. He knew there had to be a plot that was causing blacks to kill one another, but he couldn't find the proof to convey it, so he said, "Cuz, I remember you both sayin' that you respected my father and his knowledge 'bout certain things, right?"

"Yeah, we do, but what's that got to do with us?"

"A whole lot, cuz," Michael answered. "We can go to him and see if he thinks there's a conspiracy between the Crips, the Bloods, and the police."

"Fuck that shit, cuz! Let's just do what we planned to do!" Dinky stated, angrily.

"Yeah cuz, it don't make any sense in us going to your father when we know ain't no police doing any drive-by shootin's. Plus, they're not the ones who murdered Salty. The fuckin' Pirus done it, and that's who we're going after. Now if you got beef wit' the police, you can handle that shit on your own, but after we finish smoking a few Bloods. Understand?" asked Knuckles.

Michael lowered his head slightly, and answered, "Yah cuz, I understand."

"Now, that's what I'm talkin' 'bout!" Dinky said, excitedly.

"We wasted enough time, so let's git' our shit together," stated Knuckles as he picked one of the *straps (*slang for guns*) that was lying on the table.

Michael was angry as hell. *How could his own homeboys be so naïve? Couldn't they see the plot? Couldn't they see they were playing directly into the hands of their unseen enemy ~ an enemy who'd been successfully planning their annihilation since day one? What was the use?* Michael knew at that very moment it would be better if he kept what he felt suppressed. He knew from past experiences that once those brothers had their minds made up, there was no turning back. For Michael, it was the point of no return. He had to ride with his comrades regardless of how he felt. Not doing so would be viewed as a crime of treason, and everyone knew that the crime of treason within the ghetto was punishable by death ~ a death that Michael wasn't about to bring upon himself. After all, he loved life better than he loved himself. And he wasn't the type to be suicidal.

8

A Time for War

*"The life of an Urban Ghetto Warrior is unlike any
other. He fights not for the sake of glory or a flag for he
has no country. He fights not for a city, for he belongs
to no state. He fights not for a color for he has no
substance, pride, or honor. The Urban Ghetto Warrior
fights for only one reason ~ preserving himself..."*
                                                    —K.R.D.

The night of March 1, 1973

Rare as it may be for Southern California, dark threatening rain clouds began to appear on the horizon as darkness slowly crept in, pushing the last remnants of daylight aside. It was during these times when the most vile and deadliest phantoms would emerge from the cloak of darkness, and this is when Compton took on a more ominous appearance. During these moments the underworld would awaken, proliferating chaos while pursing victim after victim, extinguishing the very essence of life in a world that was controlled by street gangs, ghetto thugs, and government and police corruption.

"Luck must be on our side," Michael said into the walkie-talkie as a light mist of rain began to fall upon the car he was in.

"Call it luck, or call it the Crip god, but whatever it is we can sure use it to cover our tracks, 'cause once the shootin' starts, it will make it much harder for the police to respond," stated Knuckles.

"But it can also work against us," Dinky added as he keyed in on his mic.

"Not if we follow the game plan, cuz," Michael said.

Michael and his comrades had been sitting in their strategic positions for over thirty minutes, and there wasn't a Piru or Blood in sight. Like herds of sheep sensing the moment just before they were brought in to be slaughtered, it seemed as if the Pirus, too, knew that their death was imminent.

"Say cuz," Michael began. "It seems that the weather is going to keep them niggas off the streets for tonight."

"Just be patient, cuz. We'll spot one of them niggas real soon," stated Knuckles.

As if on cue, a burgundy 1964 Chevy pulled into the gas station right across the street from where Michael had positioned himself. He wasn't surprised to see that the occupants who had exited the car were all Pirus. He knew that to be true by the red bandanas that a couple of them were wearing from their back pockets along with the red golf hats to match. There were four people in all, two of them hung around the car casually talking, while the other two walked over to the cashier's window.

"It's on!" Michael excitedly screamed into his walkie-talkie.

"Where are they?" Knuckles asked.

"They're in a burgundy sixty-four-Chevy right across the street from me at the gas station."

"Hittin' them in their car wasn't what we planned," said Dinky.

"With the weather the way it is we have to take what comes to us," countered Knuckles.

"So what you want me to do?" Michael asked.

"Nuthin' yet," Knuckles answered, and then added, "Follow 'em when they leave, and we'll follow you at a distance. And wherever they go, they're bound to meet up with more of their homies, and that's where we'll hit 'em."

"But there's one thing that you forgot about, cuz," said Dinky.

"And what's that?"

"You forgot about the cars that we're in. They got to show up sooner or later on the hot list."

"Well, that's a chance we gotta take, cuz," said Knuckles, after a moment.

"We been lucky so far," Michael suddenly said in effort ease the rising tension.

"Well, let's just hope that luck stays on our side," Dinky finally said.

It wasn't long before the Pirus had piled back into their car. They pulled out of the gas station and headed east on Rosecrans Boulevard. Michael waited for a few seconds before following closely behind. The Boulevard was busy with people trying to make their way home after a hard day's work. Michael and his comrades couldn't be more thankful for the congestion. The traffic provided the concealment that they all needed, and if everything stayed in their favor, the weather, along with the traffic, would make their getaway that much easier.

"Say cuz," Michael quickly said into the walkie-talkie. "They just turned right on Harris Street, and parked just a few houses down from a pink church."

"I know exactly where that's at," Dinky said, excitedly.

"All right cuz, find yourself somewhere to park, but don't lose sight of them," said Knuckles.

"You don't have to worry 'bout that because I just passed em' as they exited their car and went inside a green colored house right across from where their car is parked."

"That's good, cuz, now change into your blood out-fit and we'll be in position in two minutes."

"Consider it done," Michael said.

The rain had stopped momentarily as they contem-plated their next move. Each man chose his avenue of escape by parking close to the boulevard as one possibly could. Michael had the longest route to take on foot because he parked his G-ride near Compton Boulevard. Michael believed that it didn't make sense for all them to make their getaway on the same street because if by chance someone was to see them, they wouldn't be able to give an accurate account of who went where due to them running in different directions.

After a moment, Michael spoke into the walkie-talkie saying, "Peep this cuz, I just remembered something."

"What is it, cuz?" Dinky asked.

"Well, when those fools first parked, they got out of their car and started walking towards the house when all of a sudden one of them went back to the car and reached under the front wheel base for something."

"He might have stashed a strap (*slang for gun*)," said Dinky.

KEVIN LEWIS

"I don't think that's it," Knuckles began. "I think he went back to turn on his alarm system since his Chevy is kinda *tight (*slang for looking good*).

"That's it!" Michael quickly said. "If there's an alarm I'm going to set it off. Then, I'll walk away from the car real slowly. Once ya'll see the front door open, take off blasting and I'll swing around and let em' have it from my position. After that, I'm outta there, like Casper the friendly ghost."

"Let's do it then, cuz!" both Dinky and Knuckles said simultaneously.

"I'm in motion, cuz," Michael stated as he proceeded slowly down the block.

Dressed in all red, Michael cautiously approached the Chevy as he looked for a sign showing that it did have an alarm. To his surprise there was a key face affixed slightly above the chrome sliding that outlined the front wheel base. Without losing a step, Michael quickly moved towards the car and gave it a big shove. The alarm went off instantly as he stepped back, and made his way up the block.

Two of the Pirus that Michael had seen earlier rushed out of the door like a nest of angry bees and ran toward the car, but they never made it because they ran directly into a hot swarm of 7.62 Piru killers.

The first couple of slugs caught the taller of the two Pirus directly in the chest, sending a spray of bone, flesh, and blood out the middle of his back. The other Piru didn't fare any better as bullets pulverized his face into a crimson mass of bone and bloody flesh.

Suddenly more Pirus emerged from the house and started firing wildly into the pre-darkness of the night. Screams of fright and shouts of rage pierced the cold night air as sirens wailed away in the distance.

116

At that point, Michael raised his rifle to fire upon the group of Pirus who had gathered upon the porch, but nothing happened. He tried again to fire but to no avail. Something was wrong with his gun. Fear suddenly fell over Michael as someone fired off a shot in his direction.

"Get that nigga'!" someone shouted.

Block after block Michael ran as footsteps followed closely behind. His mind switched to autopilot as he cut through a side gate that led into a backyard. He threw his rifle over a fence, and without hesitating he pulled himself over as well.

Landing in a dirty back alley, Michael quickly hid himself behind a dumpster and sat in silence. As he pondered his situation, prickles of apprehension broke out over his body. The hand that was holding his rifle trembled, though that could have been caused by the sudden tenseness of his muscles. Michael was on guard with his back against the wall and he was frightened, but he told himself, *I'm a Crip*, so he stood his ground. *Or was it that he was so consumed by fear that he couldn't move, even if it was to save his life?* He didn't know.

Michael was no longer alone. Something or someone was now in the alley with him. Now the predator had become the prey, and Michael had to find some way to reverse that situation, and he had to do it fast.

Quickly, he picked up his rifle and inspected it. After a few seconds he located the problem. Unconsciously, in the heat of the moment Michael had forgotten to take his rifle off safety. *How could I have been so fucking careless?* He told himself as he scanned the darkness of the alley for the slightest movement.

Two ghostly images suddenly appeared at the mouth of the alley while he was slowly inching his way westward, or *was it southward?* He didn't know. Michael completely lost his sense of direction while running for his life. Once again Michael's life was being threatened, only this time he wasn't running.

As the two images proceeded deeper into the alley, Michael reached into his pocket and pulled out a sound suppressor for his rifle and carefully screwed it into the threaded part of the barrel. He then peered through the scope that turned night into day, and instantly, the two ghostly images were recognized as being among the Pirus that he had seen earlier while at the gas station.

Quietly, he took aim, but not to kill. Michael just wanted to wound them bad enough to halt their forward progress so he could escape.

After a few moments, Michael took a deep breath and squeezed off three short bursts that whispered silently in the cold night air. The first round missed the first Piru by only inches, but the shot wasn't wasted because the other Piru that was following closely behind had clumsily stepped directly into its path. The .22 caliber bullet drilled itself through the fleshy part of his neck, missing his carotid artery by less than a centimeter. The other two bullets found their mark as they buried themselves deep into the shoulder of the first Piru. The power of the bullets was so intense that they ricocheted off his shoulder bone, and then traveled throughout his body, causing him to jerk involuntarily, looking as if he was break dancing.

Michael didn't waste any time after witnessing that action. He discarded the clothes that he was wearing and carefully concealed his rifle at his side. Michael then made his way out of the alley and back onto the residential block. Once back on the street it took him only a few minutes to find the car and gather his senses.

Reaching under the seat he removed the ignition key and started the car. Glancing briefly behind him, he slipped the car into gear and slowly cruised up White Street until he reached Greenleaf Avenue. There he turned right and traveled westward until he saw the outskirts of his beloved neighborhood.

Upon entering his neighborhood, Michael quickly stashed the car behind a plant nursery that was located across the street from Walton Jr. High School. He then set the car on fire and took a shortcut route that led through the populated area of his neighborhood. Everyone who lived in this particular section of Nutty Block also used this route to and from school.

It took Michael fifteen minutes to reach the sanctuary of his parents' home, and he was exhausted, physically as well as mentally. He was also so afraid that he couldn't think, nor could he feel. His mind kept acting as if it was a video recorder, continuously replaying the earlier events of the night.

There was no pleasure in what he felt; only anguish and regret combined with the knowledge that he had partaken in the senseless act of taking the life of another. *How could we commit such crimes so easily, and then bask in the pleasure of ghetto glory?* He thought inwardly.

Struggling to shake what he was feeling Michael had silently slipped by one of the rooms where his siblings were sleeping peacefully. Pausing briefly at the entrance of one of their doors, He pondered about the aspirations of his brothers and sisters. *What did they dream about during the course of the night? What would they accomplish in life? And what would he do if someone suddenly attempted to extinguish the very life that flowed through their veins?* Michael didn't have any answers at the moment, but he did know this: his siblings were not like him, and for that reason alone, he knew he had to protect them from the dark reality of the ghetto streets.

Immediately, Michael sensed that he wasn't alone as he stepped into the darkness of his room. He stood motionless for a moment wondering what to do next when suddenly the lamp that sat upon his night stand came on, illuminating his father who was quietly sitting in a chair next to his bed.

"Do you know what time it is?" he calmly asked.

"No," Michael honestly answered, and then added, "What's time is it?"

"It is 3:30 in the morning, and your friends have been calling here since ten-thirty last night, so where have you been?"

Michael hated being caught off guard, especially at those times when he had no way of knowing what the mindset of the opposition was. Therefore, the only choice for him was to play this episode out by ear.

Breaking his chain of thought, he answered, "Dinky and the rest of my friends kinda' had an argument, so we all split up and went our separate ways."

"Split up where?" his father asked quickly as he could. Michael's father always used the method of quick question and answer in an effort to catch him lying. But tonight he was quicker on the draw as he answered, "We went our separate ways after going to this little get-together in North Long Beach."

"Where in North Long Beach?"

"In them apartments that sit over on the right side of Long Beach Boulevard, after you cross Greenleaf."

"And what time was it when you all left?"

"I dunno really."

"So why did you get split up?"

"We split up because after having a few drinks, everyone started tripping."

"So you're drinking now, huh?"

"Daddy, you know better than that."

"I'm just asking you to make sure. After all, you children change like the weather."

Michael tried to change the subject so he asked, "What are you doing up so late?"

"Boy, you know I get up every morning at this time to go to work."

"Oh, I forgot."

"Look, Son," his father said after a moment. "I really don't know what's going with you and your friends, but things are going to change as far as this family is concerned, understand?"

"Not really, Dad," he said.

"That's good because I'm going to explain it to you right here and now. Starting today you're going to be in the house by eleven. No longer will you have us up at all hours of the night worrying 'bout your black-ass like we did tonight."

"Why were you worried?" he asked, seriously.

"You don't know?"

"Know what?"

"Last night between the hours of ten-thirty and twelve midnight a major gun battle broke out which left three people dead and two critically injured. And all of this was going on while you were out there in the streets."

For a moment Michael was at a loss for words because he was confused by the number of people who his father said were dead. He knew for a fact that his homies had gunned down the first two Pirus, *but who was the third? Did one of those Pirus die that I shot?* His father must have his facts mixed up. At any rate, he knew he had to keep his cool.

Turning to face his father Michael asked, "How did you find out about this?"

"It was on the news. In fact, your mother and I were watching a movie when it was interrupted with one of those special bulletins saying that a gun battle had just occurred in the four-hundred block of Harris Street which left three dead; two black males and a little nine-year-old girl. They found two more black youths who were critically wounded in an alley several blocks away. The police that were called to the scene believe that the shooter or shooters were still in the vicinity. They blocked off the whole neighborhood, searching house-to-house, and block-to-block with dogs. That's all I know for now, but I'm pretty sure, by sunrise we'll know a whole lot more."

All Michael could think of at the moment was how? They couldn't have killed a little girl. There had to be a mistake, somehow it had to be.

"What's wrong?" his father asked.

"It's nothing, I was just thinking."

"About what?"

"About me having to be in the house by eleven, now I understand why."

"I hope so, Son," his father said solemnly. "Also, there won't be any more spending nights at your friends' house during the week, and soon as your mother and I get a chance, we're pulling you out of Compton High and sending you Lynwood."

"But Dad, why are you taking me outta Compton? All my friends are there."

"That's just it, there's too much trouble going on at that school ~ trouble that will get you sent to jail or worse."

"But…"

"But nothing son, that's our decision, now get yourself some sleep. You got school to get to in a few hours."

As Michael's father exited the room, his mind went wild. *How could this be happening? I told the homies this wasn't cool, or did I tell them that?* Shit, he couldn't remember, but he did know this. The heat was sure going to be on now, and he was going to lay low, so low that the homies would have to look for him in the daytime with a flashlight.

9

Ghetto Retaliation

"In the ghetto, hate and love run like a river, each crossing the other at perfect intervals. Love sometimes comes disguised as a foe, while hate often comes as one's friend. Together they work intricately to form the perfect balance between good and evil..."
—For Jennifer Molina

March 1973, Continued

Even though it was the dawn of a new day, Michael was still haunted by the events of the previous night. A night that left an innocent nine-year-old girl dead, and a whole community in mourning ~ a community now divided by poverty, illicit drugs, and gang violence.

Michael began to feel sick at the thought of all of it. As he pondered the situation, he wondered how anyone could celebrate the killing of another human being without first thinking about the consequences of his actions. Though the killings were done out of vengeance, the killing of an innocent child didn't sit well with Michael. It left him feeling numb and out of place, while his counterparts celebrated the affair with quarts of Old English, marijuana, and loud ghetto music.

"What's wrong, cuz?" Dinky asked, drunkenly, cutting through the fog of Michael's mind.

"Oh, it's nothing, cuz," he lied.

"C'mon cuz, I know when something's bothering you…It's the girl, ain't it?"

"Kinda," he slowly answered.

"Cuz, it's not your fault, none of us could have foreseen that anyway, that's how war is."

"And what you mean by that?" Michael asked, slightly agitated.

"Just what I said cuz, she was a casualty of war. And sittin' here tripping off it ain't gonna change a damn thing!"

"But it could have been prevented."

"How? You're not fuckin' God!"

"What's going on over here?" Knuckles asked, as he walked up interrupting.

"Aw cuz, this fool is tripping 'bout the little girl who got killed last night."

"Cuz, why you tripping 'bout that? We didn't kill her."

"How you know that?" Michael asked curiously.

"Because it's in all the papers," said Knuckles as he pulled out a fresh *Los Angeles Herald American* newspaper. "Here, read for yourself."

"Slowly, Michael reached out and grabbed the newspaper which contained an article about the shooting which read:

Los Angeles Sentinel, March 2, 1973 "Five black youths who are members of the Compton Piru gang were jailed last night on charges of murder after a fierce gun battle with unknown assailants, which left three dead and two injured, one a nine-year-old girl, killed in her own living room while eating dinner with her parents. According to reports, the girl was apparently shot by the retaliatory fire of one Piru member who had suspected one of their own members was attempting to steal one of their cars. A detective closely involved in the case disclosed that the Pirus were at home when one of their own associates attempted to steal their car; but failed when the car alarm went off, sparking immediate gunfire from the assailants who fired upon two members of their own as they burst from their house to investigate. Pirus who were still in the house retaliated with a shower of bullets that penetrated several houses on the block, including the one in which the little girl was killed. The FBI has also become involved because the weapons used in the gun battle are believed to be of military origin." (*See Appendix, Blood Rising, subsection 8 for information on Crip and Blood rivalry and the article Gang Grief for teen killings*). [Note: Date, year, time and actual names have been changed in this article in order to protect the privacy of victims' families.]

After reading the article, Michael couldn't believe how they had tricked the Pirus as well as the police. It was like they had used the police's own method of deception against them. Now the Pirus would have to go through the experience of being victims of the police old scheme of 'divide and conquer'.

Looking up from the article, Michael said, "I can't believe how we pulled that off."

"Yeah cuz, everything is working in our favor, and the Pirus is gonna be catching hell for real…from murder-one to community ostracism."

"What's that?" Dinky asked.

"What's what?" Knuckles asked, slightly confused.

"What's ostracism?"

"Oh, that's when everybody disowns you."

"Shit, if that's the case, I was ostracized since the day my mom kicked me off the nipple."

"You too," Knuckles said, laughing.

"Hell yeah, in my family everyone is ostracized, each nigga' for his own damn self."

As Knuckles laughed at Dinky's comment, Michael began to dwell upon the fact that the whole Black Community in itself was ostracized in one way or another from the rest of humanity. *They were despised, hated, and envied, and for what reason? What was the cause of such hatred? What crime did black people commit upon being born? Why were they so feared? What was the purpose of the hate that was directed toward black people? Why did black people hate themselves? Was being black a crime that should warrant ostracism and death?* Michael sure didn't know, but what he did know was this, he wasn't going out like some of those sell-out's of the past, emulating and submitting to white society just so he could be accepted by them.

Michael wasn't going to tap dance for anyone in that respect. *He had faith* and he truly believed that one day the killing between people of color would cease, but that day hadn't arrived, and he didn't think he be living to see it. So with that thought in mind, he'd turned to Knuckles and Dinky and said, "Nigga, give me a drink."

"What did you say?" They both asked in unison.

"You heard me."

"Damn cuz, you really must be feeling good now."

Michael laughed and then said, "It wouldn't make sense to let ya'll celebrate by yourselves."

"Now that's what I'm talkin' 'bout cuz!" Dinky said as he handed Michael a quart of Old English beer.

September 1975

Two years had passed and summer had come and gone twice over. With the passage of time came another struggle, new faces and a brand new school ~ *Lynwood High*. This school would prove to be the greatest challenge Michael ever faced. Lynwood High School was a school of many things. It was a school of affluence, proud academics, and multiculturalism. But it was also a school that was predominantly inhabited by members of the Compton Piru Gang.

During this time the gangs within Los Angeles had grown at a rapid rate. With this growth came new gang *sets (*slang for a subsidiary or branch that originates from a larger Crip organization or group*). These were more violent than their predecessors. In fact, these gangs began to show mafia-like features such as threatening and killing potential witnesses who were scheduled to appear in court against them. (*For a recent example, see the Appendix*). Even the police began to become gang-like in nature, and as the years would follow, many will learn that the Los Angeles Police department would fall prey to their own form of corruption (*see Appendix*).

In the city of Lynwood you rarely heard about police corruption or violence, but that doesn't mean it didn't exist. Things in Lynwood were different because the community was more affluent, cohesive, and ethnically more diverse. Therefore, the Police Department, which was operated by the Lynwood Sheriff's Department, patrolled the streets more frequently. There were community patrols and organizations that kept a tighter lid on things, and because of this, gangs who operated within the area had to be more sophisticated in their illicit and illegal endeavors. This was especially true for the Crips who were few in number and low in ghetto status. (*In the early 80's Crips outnumbered the Bloods in the city of Lynwood.*)

Michael's first day at Lynwood High was sort of strange. Everyone from the teachers to the students seemed to be sizing him up. At five feet eleven, he had grown into a nice, muscular 190 pound wrecking machine. He knew from the look upon people's faces that they were asking themselves: *Who is that nigga?*

Stepping around the onlookers, he proceeded to find his locker when someone called out to him from behind saying, "What's up, cuz?"

At first, he thought it was one of the Pirus trying to trick him into responding in order to see if he was a Crip or if he was one of them. When Michael turned, he saw it was his homeboy, Barry Cunningham, who lived in the same neighborhood as he back in Compton.

"What are you doing here, cuz?" he asked as Michael gave him a big hug.

"Ah cuz, I was gonna ask you the same thing."

"Man, I'm here because my parents started trippin' 'bout me getting into trouble at Compton High."

"Don't even trip, cuz. My parents got so scared of Compton that they moved the whole family right here in Lynwood."

"You gotta be bullshittin' me, cuz!"

"No I ain't, we live right here in Lynwood over on Palm Street."

"Is your crazy-ass brother livin' out here, too?"

"Yeah that nigga is out here, plus there's a lot of *down-ass (slang for fearless)* homies out here from Compton, and we all kick it over on Palm and Oak Street."

"Which niggas from Compton are you talking about?"

"Turtle, The Twins, Angelee' and Angelo, Robert Franklin, Poppin' Freddie, Bullet (Kim Tate), and Tiny Man, but he's originally from Los Angeles (*most of these characters are dead*)."

"Shit, those niggas is from Santana Blocc."

"I know," Barry said.

"I thought you said there were other niggas from Compton who hung around here, also."

"Oh, I forgot about Tweedy Bird and Fat Ike from Atlantic Drive, plus there's some niggas who live right on Palm and Oak that is also down, and you have to give them niggas of lot of credit."

"Why is that?"

"Because their 'hood is completely surrounded by *Pirus (*see gang territorial map below*). They have the Mob Piru just across Bullis Road, then there's Lueders' Park Pirus which isn't faraway, then there's a loose outfit of Pirus who live discreetly and very close to Palm and Oak, but the 'Palm and Oak' niggas be lettin' them *slobs (*a slang term Crips use to verbally deface their rivals*) have it on sight."

Black Gang Territories in Compton and Vicinity 2000

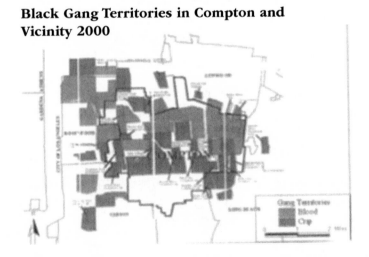

Blood and Crip gang territories were in Compton and surrounding unincorporated areas of Willowbrook, Athens, Rosewood and the areas of Carson, Lynwood and North Long Beach. Notice Blood gangs dominate the northern part of Compton while the southern portion of Compton had a greater Crip presence.

"Even here at school?"

"Nah, because there's a lot of security guards who be carrying *straps (*slang for guns*) and shit, so school is like a neutral zone, although we do have our share of one-on-one fights between each other. But when school is out, it's a whole different story."

"What do the Crips in Lynwood call themselves?"

"We call ourselves Palm and Oak steet Crips."

"We?"

Barry smiled and then said, "Listen cuz, I know we're from Nutty Blocc, but Nutty Blocc is in Compton. You're in Lynwood now, and once you learn your way around this campus you'll realize that Crips are outnumbered five to one. Without the help of the Palm and Oak niggas, and the rest of the homies who aligned themselves along with them in this war, we'd be headed straight to hell in a blue body bag. So out here in Lynwood, we're all Palm and Oak's, understand?"

"I understand cuz, I can't argue with that," Michael said. "By the way, do Turtle and the rest of the homies from Compton go to school here as well?"

"Nah, they just show up after school to make sure that most of the homies make it back to the 'hood safely."

"Is that much drama jumping off here?"

"Hell yes, cuz, every day. In fact, remember that nigga name Freight Train?"

"That *buster-ass (*slang for weak-minded and physically weak person*) Piru nigga from Stevenson Village."

"Yeah cuz, that's the nigga."

"What about him?"

"Well, that nigga got these fools out here thinkin' he's real big shit."

"He goes to school here?"

"Yeap."

Michael smiled sinisterly and then said, "I been wanting to beat that nigga's ass for a long time."

"Don't worry, you'll git' your chance real soon, but there's other slobs who come here from Dominguez High School in order to help their homies, and those niggas ain't no punks."

With that statement, Michael's mind drifted back to the very reason why he was transferred from Compton. His parents thought they were placing him in a good environment, but what they did was put him directly on the front lines, deep within enemy territory. As he pondered his situation, one of the Isley Brothers' songs, '*The Heat Is On*,' came to the forefront of his mind, and everyone knows from experience, where there's heat, there has to be fire, and Michael sure wasn't about to get burnt. (See Appendix for lyrics.)

Snapping out of his reverie, Michael turned to Barry and asked, "Which Piru niggas from Dominguez be comin' up here?"

"Some of their hardest G's (slang for gangsters) like China Dog, Stanley Pitts, Jeffrey Chisom, Part-Time, Stutter Box, Little George, and a whole lot more."

"Damn cuz, those niggas are the Piru's elite."

"Yeah they are, but we be giving them niggas the blues."

"I hope so," Michael said as he stared down the hall at this big giant who was coming towards him.

"Who's that, cuz?" Michael asked, nodding in the direction of the oncoming giant.

"Oh, that's the homie."

"What's up cuz?" asked the giant as he shook Barry's hand.

"Ain't nuthin much, cuz," Barry answered, and then said, "This is another homie of mines from my old 'hood."

"What's up, cuz . . . they call me Big Juney," he stated as he shook Michael's hand.

"And they call me "Wheatgerm," he lied.

"What!" Barry exclaimed. "When did you git that name?"

Laughing, Michael answered, "I got this handle when I started driving iron and eating nothing but wheat germ morning, noon, and night. Plus, it gives me the energy to stay 'n a slob's ass."

For a moment everyone laughed until a large group of Pirus walked by, each staring at the other as if they were looking for a weakness.

"Damn cuz, those niggas are deep," Michael said as they passed by.

"Cuz, they ain't nuthin but a bunch of busters trying to gain a little rep' in order to impress these little bitches 'round here."

"He's right cuz; you'll see the real slobs' right after school."

"We all laughed once again, and then Big Juney turned to Michael and said, "C'mon cuz, let me introduce you to the rest of the homies."

For Michael, the city of Lynwood was a lot of things that Compton was not. People who lived in the area seemed to have more pride about themselves and the things they possessed. The community in general even displayed a form of solidarity that could never be found in Compton. He guessed this can be credited to higher property values, thriving businesses, and most of all, a dedicated Police Department who demanded a lot from the community.

Another thing about Lynwood was that such crimes as murder were easily solved within the first 48 hours because there wasn't a great fear of gang reprisal within the community (*that's long since changed*), and the least violation of the law would bring down the sheriff ~ hard and fast. But still, this didn't stop the gangs from growing and expanding. Nor did it stop their violence. It just served to keep their activities confined to an area where most of the minority community lived. In this case, the area in question was located right off Long Beach Boulevard, on Palm and Oak Streets, just a few blocks from the notorious city of Compton, California.

Michael was shocked when he stepped into the territory of Palm and Oak. He thought their neighborhood would be like the neighborhoods in Compton, where one gang territory extended as far as two or three miles, and if a territory was smaller, the gang occupying that territory would make up what they lacked in size by having members that were absolutely more deadly, as well as callous.

Some neighborhoods in Compton had gangs that consisted of at least two to three hundred members. But in Lynwood, the territory of Palm and Oak was just two small back streets that intersected each other, one running north and south, and the other running east and west.

Their membership, from what he saw, consisted of about thirty strong, but by no means were any of these youngsters weak. In fact, the Palm and Oak Street Crip gang had straight-up killers who believed that being outnumbered was a major advantage.

"So what do we think about the 'hood, cuz?" asked Big Juney as they walked up a driveway that led to some apartments, hidden behind a big house.

"I like it, cuz, especially over here."

"What you mean by that?"

"What I mean is if this is the place where all the homies hang out, then it's cool because no one can do a drive-by or walk-up without us seeing them first."

Big Juney laughed and then said, "I see that cuz be really observing everything."

"What did you expect? The nigga just finished doing a tour of duty in Compton," said Barry.

Big Juney fell silent for a moment. It seemed as if his face took on a whole new expression while he struggled with something inwardly. After a few moments, he cleared his throat and said, "Listen cuz, don't take this shit wrong. I know Compton is considered to be hard, and niggas out there be puttin' in a lot of work, but don't think for one minute that we're not just as hard if not harder."

Looking at Barry, Michael could see that he didn't want what started as a peaceful moment blown into something big and personal, so he interrupted the conversation by saying, "Cuz, we're all down for the same cause, plus our enemies and your enemies are the same. It's Cripping with all of us and it will be that way until the day we die."

Big Juney looked at Michael, then at Barry and said, "The only reason I said anything is because a lot of Compton niggas think they're harder than everyone else, and that attitude creates a lot of bullshit at times."

"I understand that, cuz. I feel the same way you feel with some of my own homeboys, but can I ask you one question without you taking it the wrong way?"

"Go on cuz, ask."

"What makes Palm and Oak as hard as the 'hoods in Compton?"

"In the way we deal with' those slobs, which is on an everyday basis. We live damn near on top of them, and it's constant pressure, twenty-four hours. We're out manned, outgunned, and they have way more fire-power. But we got heart, plus when those slobs see us, they know it's no love; just murder in the making. And when you're out here dealing with us, protection of the chest is mandatory. So if they get caught slipping, they'll find a mad-ass Crip in the mode of *bullet flip-ping (*slang for gunfire*)."

Turning to Barry, Michael said, "Cuz, this must be the heart of Vietnam, and you know why I'm sayin' this?"

"Why?"

"Because in Compton, the Pirus ain't got the heart to drive from their 'hood to make a hit on us, therefore we're not under a constant threat. But on the other hand, these Palm and Oak niggas got to sleep with' a strap and a full extra clip."

They all laughed for a moment and as they did so, the tension that was in the air dissipated.

"C'mon cuz, let's go take you to meet the rest of the homies," Barry said.

Looking at his watch, Michael quickly asked, "When does the last bus leave for Compton?"

"You are riding the bus?" Big Juney asked.

"Yeah cuz, I be catching the bus from Compton ev-ery morning just to make it to school."

"I thought you lived out here."

"Nah, my parents hooked it up for me to attend Lynwood. They thought by sending me here, I wouldn't be getting in trouble like I did at Compton High."

"Oh, I see. Well, don't worry 'bout the bus; I'll get you a ride back to the 'hood."

"In that case, let's check out the rest of the homies…"

10

The Land of the Dead

"In the ghetto, gangs form like the plague, each fight-
ing for a piece of territory they'll never own, each
struggling for a status never gained, and each destroy-
ing the other for reasons unknown."
— Chasity Ann Lewis

September 1975

Gangbanging is an extreme occupational hazard that many failed to consider. It's not something you venture into part-time or half-heartedly, nor could you treat it like a sporting event where you can ask for a time out. Real gangbanging is like being in the military. Once enlisted, you're in for the duration. The set you represent is the branch of service you signed up for. Your neighborhood is where boot camp is held. Tattoos are rewarded for successful completion of certain tasks. But there is one major difference between gangbanging and the military service. In the military one has the option to enlist for a period of two or more years, but with gangbanging, there are no such options, once enlisted, you are in for life, and that's the part many fail to consider.

In every neighborhood there are those who take the abovementioned facts as a joke. They live their life as if they never enlisted into a gang. They travel about carelessly, in the lustful pursuit of pussy ~ a pursuit that usually leads them on a dangerous journey behind enemy lines. Some do it knowingly, and some unconsciously, but a vast majority do it out of stupidity and blind infatuation. Those are the ones who end up dead as a result.

"How did it go?" Michael's father asked.

"How did what go?"

"School," he answered. "You did go?"

"Yeah, I went."

"How many classes do you have?"

"Way too many," Michael said, as he thought about all the stupid classes they put him in.

"Well, that's good, son. Now you'll be busier and you won't have so much time to get in trouble."

Michael laughed, not because he thought what his father had said was funny. He laughed because his father had no idea as to how much trouble Michael was going to find himself in at Lynwood High. If he knew, Michael would be out of there at a moment's notice, and then he would be attending Catholic school or something worse.

Suddenly the phone rang, and looking at his father's face, he knew it was for him.

He handed him the phone and said, "Don't be too long, I'm waiting for a call."

"I won't," Michael said as he grabbed the phone. "What's up, cuz?" he asked, realizing it was Knuckles.

"Say cuz, I need you to come by as quickly as you can."

"Why? What's up?"

"That nigga, Dinky, is stuck over in Piru territory again."

"What he's doing over there?"

"He probably chasing after that stupid-ass Piru bitch!"

"Cuz, I forgot about that ho.'"

"Well, he hasn't. Damn near every night the nigga been sneaking over there. And check this out, the bitch called em' up to come over there and he vacated the premises like a dog in heat."

"That nigga went into Piru territory in broad daylight?"

"Yeah, cuz, he did."

"That bitch may be tryin' to set him up," Michael said.

"That's what I told him," Knuckles added.

Michael paused for a moment and then said, "Alright cuz, I'll be there in ten minutes."

It had taken Michael more than ten minutes to reach Knuckles' pad due to his parents constant questioning of: *Where you going? How long are you going to be? And when will you be back?* Michael hated that stuff for real. He felt like they treated him as if he was some snot-nosed teenager who didn't know his butt from a hole in the ground.

When Michael finally made his escape, he raced down to Knuckles' house where he found him patiently waiting inside of a car that he obtained through the sales of marijuana.

"What took you so long?" he asked as he pulled the car from away the curb and proceeded East, down Alondra Boulevard.

"Cuz, you know how my parent is, always giving a nigga the third degree while at the same time, asking a thousand and one questions."

Knuckles smiled for a moment and then said, "Better you than me."

Michael laughed at his comment and then said, "I'm not doing this shit no more, cuz."

"You always say that, and every time Dinky gits' into a bind, you come to his rescue."

"Well, this is the last time for sure."

"Cuz, don't be too hard on the nigga, he just a sucka for a big fat ass and a side-dish of pussy."

"Shit, if that's the case, he can find plenty of that right here in the 'hood."

"With cuz, it's not the same, he feels like it's a victory on his behalf when he gits to fuck a slob bitch. Plus, it makes them slob niggas mad as hell, especially when they know they'll never be able to swing their dicks around our hood and fuck our bitches."

"Cuz, I don't give a damn about these chicken-head ho's in da 'hood. All of em' ain't nuthin but trouble."

"C'mon cuz, you be getting yo' dick wet just like everyone else."

"That may be so, but I don't fall n' love with these bitches...once I get mine, it's back in traffic for me. Michael laughed and then said, "I know what you're saying, cuz. It's really hard to trust a bitch."

"Especially, if she's not a Crip and down for the 'hood," added Knuckles.

As Michael pondered upon Knuckles' statement, he began to realize that there were a lot of females who were just as hardcore as their male counterparts. Then there were those who were just *fuck me on's ~ females who gave up their bodies in order to be accepted and respected. Then you had females who hung around their male counterparts, hoping to earn some type of ghetto status and protection. In the ghetto, these were the females who were the most trouble. If something serious ever occurred, they'd be the first ones to break under pressure. And there were a few males who possessed the same bitch-made characteristics.

"Damn," Knuckles exclaimed, snapping Michael out of his reverie. "I'm always gettin' held-up by a mothafuckin train!"

"It won't be too long," Michael said as they both fell silent.

"Is they still out there?" Dinky asked the female who had slipped back into the bedroom.

"Yeah, but they won't come in here."

"How you know that?" Dinky whispered.

"I know because my brother and his friends are not allowed to come into my bedroom."

"Fuck that, I ain't takin' any chances, I'm outta here."

"Baby, please don't go."

"Bitch, you must be crazy. Your brother is out there with' a whole room full of slobs and you say, don't worry, everything` is cool...fuck that shit."

Anger quickly appeared into the eyes of the female as she said, "I'm not going to sit here and keep letting you disrespect me like that. Do you understand me, nigga?"

Dinky was caught completely off guard by the sudden change in the female. Being quick tempered, he reached out and started choking the female while at the same time punching her about the face with his free hand. His mind went blank, and in one fluid motion he let go of his grip as he propelled himself through her open bedroom window, landing almost feet first in her backyard. Dinky didn't waste any time getting to his feet because he knew he had only a few seconds before the female would alert her brother and his crew about who he was and what just happened.

Feeling around in his pockets for his gun, Dinky quickly found cover in the safety of some bushes. There he waited until he saw what he had expected. Two Pirus had carelessly poked their heads out of the opened bedroom window that he had just escaped, and caught death in the form of four neatly placed, .38 hollow points, which drilled a hole in the first Piru making him seem as if he had three eyes instead of two. The second Piru took three slugs in the chest and flipped out the window like a raggedy old doll.

Wasting no time, Dinky scaled the fence and made his way from backyard to backyard until he reached a yard that led to a side street. He quickly walked up the block trying to reach Compton Boulevard, which would place him near Crip territory, a place where he knew he would be safe. But that was not to be because as he turned to cross a back-street intersection, a car suddenly pulled out of an alley to his right, and before he could react, one of the occupants of the car yelled, "That's the nigga. Blood, over there!"

Dinky immediately started to run but his steps were in vain as the occupants of the car opened fire, including the Piru female that he was with earlier. It sounded like children popping fireworks on a fourth of July evening as bullets riddled Dinky's body. His eyes rolled skyward as his body hit the ground.

Lying in a pool of blood, people began to gather as the car slowly pulled off. It was like they were making sure he was dead; and dead he was.

"Damn cuz! I thought this fuckin' train would never end," said Knuckles as they pulled off. "Next time I'm gonna' take Central Avenue straight to Rosecrans."

"Now we both know ain't no Crip in his right mind gonna ride down Rosecrans wit' all them slobs livin' on one side of the boulevard, and in some areas of the street they are on both sides."

"Yeah cuz, you're right. That would be too risky." Knuckles said, as they turned left on Bullis Road.

Riding once again in silence, Michael began to think about all the times Dinky and he had come close to death. Each time, they cheated death and embraced life only to try their chances at death again. After a while, they felt like they were invincible, two ghetto hoodlums straight up immune to death. There were a lot of times when Knuckles would share the same experiences with them. But, Dinky was the glue that tied the three together. Also, there were some things Michael could share with Dinky that he could never come to Knuckles with, and Dinky did the same with Michael.

Knuckles was special too. He was an essential part of their trio, being the oldest. But the comradeship and love that Dinky and Michael shared was formed that very day they came to blows; a day way back in their beginning, on the campus of Caldwell Elementary school ~ a day when hate turned into mutual respect and unconditional love.

Michael's mind suddenly snapped back to reality as the sound of sirens pierced the air.

"Damn cuz, somebody must've had an accident." Knuckles stated as they watched an ambulance, and several police cruisers turn off Compton Boulevard onto Ward Lane traveling south."

"It's probably one of those Mexicans, you know how they be drinking and driving around this mothafuckin' 'hood," Michael said.

Knuckles took the same route the ambulance had taken. As they proceeded, it didn't take long for them to learn what they perceived as an accident was actually more than what they were prepared for. "I wonder what happened," Michael said as they approached a cordoned-off crime scene filled with police, ambulance, onlookers, and yellow tape.

"Whatever it is, it sho' ain't no accident," Knuckles said as he pulled into an unknown driveway.

"What ya' doing?" Michael asked.

"Turning the car around so we can go git' the homie...you know the nigga been waiting on us."

"First, let's see what's happening."

"Cuz, you know we don't know this territory too good, and if we run into the wrong niggas, we're gonna' be the ones needing an ambulance and police assistance, plus you know Dinky's situation, we can't keep him waiting like that."

"He waited this long, what's a few more minutes? Besides, ain't no niggas gonna be trippin' off us with all these police running around."

"Alright cuz, let's see what's up, but soon as we see what's going on, we're outta here."

"Okay, let's go."

Quickly, Knuckles parked the car, and then proceeded up the block towards the crowd. The closer they came, the more Michael began to feel as if something wasn't right. His heart pounded with each step. His pulse raced. His breathing quickened as they made their way through the curious onlookers.

"What happened?" Michael asked a woman as he tried to push his way through the crowd.

"Some kid was gunned down by some gang members," the old woman answered.

"How long ago did this happen?"

"Thirty... maybe forty minutes ago."

"Thanks," Michael said.

"C'mon cuz, let's go," Knuckles said as he pulled Michael towards his direction.

"Wait cuz; let me see who it is."

"Cuz, we don't know any of these people who live over here," said Knuckles, irritably.

A few people in the crowd suddenly shifted in position which gave them clear sight as to who was killed.

"Oh my God, cuz…it's Dinky," Michael said unbelievably.

"Let's get outta' here," Knuckles quickly whispered.

"We can't leave him here like this, cuz."

"Do you want to take a trip down to the police station and hear questions you don't have answers for?"

For a moment Michael didn't know what to do. His best friend was dead, all alone, lying in the street, in a pool of blood with his eyes staring into what was now another world.

"C'mon cuz," Knuckles said for a second time.

Reluctantly, Michael quickly followed him back to the car where they got in and slowly drove back to the neighborhood in silence.

For hours, Michael lay wide awake in the darkness of his bedroom trying desperately to figure out what he could have done in order to prevent Dinky's death. Together over the past few years they had overcome pains of hunger, racism, and addiction. Each day they fought against the unseen forces of nature while they struggled about aimlessly trying to understand their true direction in life. They often questioned the purpose of God, wondering if God was as strong as he said he is. Why were they as a product of his creation, so weak, especially if they were created in his image? *Why didn't God warn them of death before it came?* It seemed so unfair the way Dinky had to die; and Michael wasn't even given the chance to say goodbye.

Now he had no one. He was now a lone soldier with no purpose and no desire. He no longer wished to wage war against the Bloods or anyone one else that was black. That desire was now over ~ without Dinky, nothing mattered. For Michael, Dinky was the neighborhood, and the neighborhood would never be the same without him.

His thoughts were suddenly interrupted by a knock upon his bedroom door.

"Come in," Michael whispered.

Switching on his night light, Michael saw that it was his father, and with him at his side was his mother. They both appeared concerned about something as they sat next to him on his bed.

"Son," Michael's father began. "We just learned about what happened to your friend."

"How did you find out?" Michael asked tearfully.

"It was on the news, and the police are looking for two young adults who they think may have information about the murder."

Looking into his father's eyes, Michael knew he wanted to know if he was there or involved in some sort of way, so instead of going through what he knew would be another interrogation, Michael said, "Dad they may be looking for Knuckles and me."

"Why would they be looking for ya'll?" his mother asked.

"Because we were there after he got killed."

"Who killed him?" his mother asked, damn near hysterically.

Michael answered, "I don't know," as he stared at a picture of Dinky and himself that was sitting in a frame upon his dresser. "We were just on our way to pick him up from an area near Leuders Park when we suddenly decided to take a back street. It was there that we saw the police, the ambulance, and a large crowd. We wanted to know was happening so we got out of the car, and that's when we found out it was Dinky."

"I'm sorry 'bout your friend, son. But we're worried about you and your state of mind."

Michael really didn't feel like discussing it anymore, but at the same time he was hurting. The pain he felt was so bad that he couldn't control the tears that started flowing uncontrollably down his cheeks. From past experiences, his parents knew that when he was hurting like this, it was best to let him work out the pain in his own way.

They waited patiently for Michael's tears to subside, and when they did, his father said, "Son, this is the very reason why we took you out of Compton High School and sent you to Lynwood. We want you to have a chance in life. We want you to live. It could have been you out there lying in the street today, but thank God it wasn't. I don't know what I would have done if it was. And I'm not going to sit here and say that I know what you're going through because I don't, but do know this…your mother and I love you very much, and if you need us, we're here to listen."

"I love you, too, Son," said his mother as she rose to leave.

"Don't go," Michael pleaded, as tears once again filled his eyes.

His mother turned, and then said, "I'm here, Son."

"Mom," he began, "Dinky was my best friend. He was all I had…and they took him before I even had a chance to tell him how I felt."

"Life is like that, Son. Tomorrow is never promised to any of us. That's why you have to make the very best out of life while you have the chance to do so. But you young people take life for granted. You all make the wrong choices ~ decisions that you have to either live or die with. All we can give you is our advice. We can't live life for you. Dinky chose to gangbang just like you choose to do. The price of that decision was death. If you don't choose to do something better with your life, sooner or later you'll be sent to prison or killed in the streets just like Dinky. The only winner in this whole scheme of things is the people who created such conditions in order to lure you children into this explosive cycle of destruction. And this deadly cycle of destruction will continue as long as you children play the game."

This was the first time Michael ever heard his mother elaborate on a subject with such keen insight. He thought she was illiterate about life in the streets. He now knew differently. The things she spoke about were true. But nonetheless, the things she said couldn't save Dinky. He was now a part of another existence, and it seemed to Michael that he too, was doomed to follow that same dark, desolate road.

Michael slowly looked up and said, "It's everywhere."

"What's everywhere?" They both asked.

"Death…he's everywhere. Patiently waiting…in Compton, Watts, Inglewood, Carson, Long Beach, and he's even in Lynwood, just waiting. If he wants you, he'll find you. There's no escaping him."

"That may be true, Son, but there's a way to keep death at bay."

"How is that?"

"By possessing a strong will and desire to live."

"I do have the desire to live, but it's hard because of corrupted things I see before and around me. I see it every day in the streets. I see it in the faces of people I pass. I see their pain as if it's an opened book. I feel their stress. I can even sense the hunger, abandonment, and rage in every person I focus upon while in passing. Even the children are hurting. We don't have a chance. Dinky didn't have a chance. His family never cared. His father was never there, and it's like that for most of my homies."

"Son," his father interrupted, "There has to be one of your homies who has two parents living in the house together, right?"

"Dad, I'm the only one who has a mother and father who live together in love. The rest of my homies' fathers don't give a damn... truly they don't care, and long as life is like this, nothing will ever change."

The words that Michael conveyed caused his parents to fall into silence. It was like he touched something deep within their minds. For what he conveyed was the plain truth. They lived in a society where the deck was stacked against them, and Michael believed that the only way that blacks could reverse this fate was by becoming the dealer of the deck, thus commanding and shaping their own destinies. But as long as African Americans allowed the negative forces of deception to govern who they were, where they lived, ate, and worshipped, then the change they so desired would not be forthcoming.

"Listen, Son," his father finally said. "It's getting late, so if you want, we can finish talking 'bout this when I come home from work. And if you're not up for going to school to tomorrow, your mother and I understand. We know it's not easy when you lose someone close, especially a best friend.

"I'm okay, Dad. It will be better for me to go."

"Well, it's your choice."

"Thank you," Michael said as they turned to leave.

"Thank you for what?"

"Thanks for taking time to listen and being there for me."

"That's what we're here for, Son...we just want the best for you, but most of all; we want you to be careful out there in those streets."

"Don't worry, I will..."

11

Agony and Ecstasy

*"In the ghetto, one quickly learns that you'll never
know how much you love something until it's gone.
You never know how much something is truly worth
until you pay for it, and you'll never know what's on
the other side of life until you lose the one you have..."*
—Kelvin Lewis

October 1975-1983

Several weeks had passed since Dinky was laid to
rest. With his death, gang warfare seemed to be on
a dangerous rise. It seemed that every street thug who
resided within the inner ghetto was at war as neighborhoods all over the city began to compete with each
other for a position at the top of the ghetto power
pyramid.

This was a time when gangsters wanted their neighborhoods to be the hardest and most feared. The early
signs of this behavior began with three neighborhood
street gangs known as the *Rollin' 60's Crips, Eight-tray*

Gangsters Crips, and the *Hoover Crip* gang who were responsible for initiating the intra-Crip on Crip violence, or BK, CK (*Blood Killer, Crip Killer*).

This meant that the Hoover Crip gang not only saw Bloods and Pirus as being their rivals, but other Crip sets as well. As a result of this behavior, Crips were now killing Crips everywhere, and their rivals, the Pirus and Bloods rejoiced at this affair.

At one point, the killings between Crips had gotten so bad that Crip neighborhoods all over the city of Los Angeles began to form alliances with each other in order to make their neighborhoods into one large gang conglomerate. By doing so, it made it harder for other Crip gangs to launch an attack upon one of its own.

The first Crip set to form such an alliance was the Eastcoast Crips of South Central Los Angeles. They combined the streets or neighborhood sets of 1st Street, 43rd Street, 62nd Street, 66th Street, 68th Street, 69th Street, 76th Street, 89th Street, 97th Street, 102nd Street, 118th Street, 190th Street, and *SOS (*acronym for Sons of Samoa*), into one large killing conglomerate.

Each of these abovementioned gang sets pledged to ride faithfully under the banner of the Eastcoast Crips. To counter this rising threat, the Hoover Crip gang formed a conglomerate of their own consisting of 43rd Street, 52nd Street, 59th Street, 74th Street, 83rd Street, 92nd Street, 94th Street, 107th Street, and 112th Street. This neighborhood gang conglomeration made the Hoover Crips the second largest and most dangerous, unpredictable Crip gang in all of Los Angeles during the 70's.

Not all Crip gangs formed alliances due to the rising threat of other Crip gangs. Some formed alliances because of close family ties, proximity between streets, having the same numeric order of their streets, and having a street or neighborhood that occupied the same boulevard or avenue. The rest formed alliances for reasons that can't be explained due to the fear of gang reprisals.

The survival factor of a gang member depends on how well their knowledge and instincts are in reference to the gang territories of others. They must know the exact location of every Crip and Blood neighborhood, which ones are safe to travel in and which ones are in direct opposition to theirs. The same goes for parks, stores, swap meets, popular eating establishments, clubs, and much more. A gang member had to know first and foremost identifying trademarks of rival gangs, graffiti and tattoos. In knowing this, a gang member could tell what territory they were in and who represented what particular set. Gang members also had to know the complete map of the gang empire structure throughout Los Angeles.

Michael learned about this the hard way. It was during his involvement in some gang activity which caused him to be apprehended and arrested by the Los Angeles *Crash Unit (*an acronym which stood for Community Resources Against Street Hoodlums*) and placed in their custody at a substation for about six hours. After that, he was transferred to the Los Angeles County jail where he was interrogated, beaten up, and thrown into a large holding facility that was notoriously known as ninety-five hundred.

It was there, during his initial classification with a special unit of the Los Angeles Sheriff Department called Operation Safe Streets (OSS) where Michael learned about the gang territorial map. The Sheriff, along with the OSS, had compiled a complete list and map of all the gang territories within the city of Los Angeles. When Michael saw this, he became angry, so he started diverting the attention of one of the officer's by joking around while removing the documents that contained the information he needed. Michael did this because he wanted to show his gangster comrades how careless and stupid some of their homies were. To Michael, it didn't make sense in providing information to an enemy who was more dangerous than any Crip or Blood. Just doing so was treason, a violation that instantly merited death to all who participated in such endeavors.

It took Michael about fifteen minutes to remove the documents from the officer's folder that sat upon his desk. He stuffed them inside of his jail issued pants and read them when he got back to a place of semi privacy ~ the inmates' restroom, a place where every ass was exposed to all who cared.

He couldn't believe his eyes when he scanned the papers. There were Crip neighborhoods he didn't even know existed, but there they were in a memo that read:

Gangs, Names, and Location

All Crip Gangs in Los Angeles

Altadena Block Crips
47th Street Gangster Crips
48th Street Gangster Crips
Eight Tray Gangster Crips
87th Street Gangster Crips
97th Street Gangster Crips
98th Street Gangster Crips
118th Street Gangster Crips
43rd Street Hoover Crip Gang
52nd Street Hoover Crip Gang
59th Street Hoover Crip Gang
74th Street Hoover Crip Gang
83rd Street Hoover Crip Gang
92nd Street Hoover Crip Gang
94th Street Hoover Crip Gang
107th Street Hoover Crip Gang
112th Street Hoover Crip Gang
129th Gardena Pay Back Crips
134th Street Gardena Pay Back
  Crips
Pasadena Raymond Ave Crips
Avalon 40's Crips
Geer Gang Crips
Ghost Town Crips
116th Street Avalon Gangster
  Crips
76th Street East Coast Crips
68th, 69th Streets Play Boy
  Hustler Crips
Beach Town Mafia Crips
Harbor City Crips
75th Street Play Boy Hustler
  Crips
127th Street Harvard Gangster
  Crips
Boulevard Mafia Crips
102nd Street Raymond Ave
  Crips
120th Street Raymond Ave Crips
112th Street Broadway Gangster
  Crips

97th Street Holmes Town Crips
52nd Norwalk Broadway
  Gangster Crips
Rollin 20s Crips
Rollin 30s Original Harlem Crips
Rollin 40s Neighborhood
  Avenues
Playboy Gangsters Crips
Rollin 40s Neighborhood Crips
Rollin 60s Neighbor Hood Crips
Rollin 80s Westcoast Crips
Dodge City Crips
Inglewood Village Crips
Rollin 80's West Coast Crips
21st Street Insane Crips
Rollin 90's Crips
Neighbor Hood Crips
Rollin 90s Westcoast Crips
87th Street Kitchen Crip Gang
116th Street Kitchen Crips
95th Street Kitchen Crips
Du Rock Crips, Duarte,
  California
School Yard Crips
Sin Town Crips
99th Street Mafia Crips
Main Street Crips
1st Street East Coast Crips
43rd Street East Coast Crips
59th Street East Coast Crips
62nd Street East Coast Crips
66th Street East Coast Crips
68th Street East Coast Crips
69th Street East Coast Crips
76th Street East Coast Crips
89th Street East Coast Crips
97th Street East Coast Crips

102nd Street East Coast Crips
118th Street East Coast Crips
190th Street East Coast Crips
Sons of Samoa East Coast Crips
98th Main Street Mafia Crips
Stevenson Village Crips
Mansfield Gangster Crips
Marvin Gangsters Crips
Ten Line Gangster Crips
104th Avenue Tonga Crip Gang
103rd Street Menlo Gangster
  Crips
65th Street Menlo Gangster
  Crips
Mona Park Crips
103rd, 105th, 107th Street
  Underground Crips
Venice Shore Line Crips
106th Street Neighbor Hood
  Crips
111th, 112th Street Neighbor
  Hood Crips,
Water Gate Crips
Four Corner Block Crips

Neighbor Hood Crips
Four Deuce Crip Gang
  (Westside)
Four Line Drive Crips
55th Street Neighborhood Crips
57th Street Neighborhood Crips
59th Street Neighborhood Crips
67th Street Neighborhood Crips
28th Street West Boulevard Crips
64th Street West Boulevard Crips
96th Street Gangster Crips
West Covina Neighborhood
  Crips
109, 110th Neighborhood Watts
  Crips
West Side Mafia Crips
42nd Street Gangster Crips
43rd Street Gangster Crips
105th Street Gangster Crips
88 Street Avalon Garden Crips
53rd Street Avalon Gangster
  Crips
Grave Yard Crips

Compton Crips

Boot Hill Compton Crips
  (1969-1978)
Grandees Compton Crips
  (1969-1978)
Mid-Town Compton Crips
  (1969-1978)
Oaks Park Crips
Compton Boulevard Crips
Original Swap Boys Crips
Acacia Blocc Crips
Atlantic Drive Crips
Ducky Hood Crips
Farm Dog Crips
Kelly Park Crips
Lantana Blocc Crips
Neighborhood Compton Crips

Nutty Blocc Crips
Original Front Hood Crips
Mona Park Crips
Palmer Blocc Crips
Park Village Crips
Pocket Hood Crips
Santana Blocc Crips
Mayo Avenue Crips
Nester Avenue Crips
South Side Crips
Spook Town Crips
Tragnew Park Crips
Ward Lane Crips
Twilight Zone Crips
Palm & Oak Street Crips
Carver Park Crips

Long Beach Crip Gangs

Crip Gangs in Long Beach,
California Insane Crips
Brick Block Crips
Boulevard Mafia Crips
DAWGS
East Coast Crips, Sons of
Samoa

Four Corner Block Crips
Lettin' Niggas Have It
Mack Mafia Crips
Original Hood Crips
Rollin 20s Crips
Rollin 80s West Coast Crips

Watts Crip Gangs

Grape Street Watts
Hickory Street Watts
Compton Avenue Watts
Back Street Watts Crips
Holme Town Watts Crips
Beach Town Watts Crips
Fudge Town Watts Crips
Hat Gang Watts Crips
110th Street Crips

Front Street Watts Crips
99 Mafia Watts Crips
P.J. Watts Crips
7th Street Watts Crips
Watts Franklin Square Crips
(1990)

Crip Gangs in Carson California 1995-present

Don't give a fuck
East Coast Block Crips
190th Street Crips
East Side DAWGS

Stevenson Village Crips (Cold
Village Dog)
Too Many Hoes Gangs
Victoria Park Crips

Crip Gangs that formed after 1990 in various cities

Crip Gangs in Gardena, California

Dragnet Crips
Gardena Pay Back Crips
Sex Symbols Crips

Shot Gun Crips
Straight Ballers Society

Crip Gangs in Hawthorne, California

118th Street Gangsters

Water Gate Crips

Crip Gangs in Pomona, California

Pomona 357 Crips
Angelo Mafia Crips
East Coast Crips
Ghost Town Crips

Sin Town Crips
South Side Village Crips
West Side Mafia

Harbor City Area

208th Street Crips (formed to combat the threat from Mexican
gang members) ended in 2001

Crip Gangs in Inglewood, California

Legend Crips, 102nd Street
Tonga Crip Gang, 104
Inglewood Village Crips

102nd Street Raymond Ave
Crips

Blood Gangs in the City of Los Angeles

Be-Bopp Watts
Bishops
Black P Stones-City
Black P Stones-Jungles
Blood Stone Pirus, 30's
Blood Stone Villains
Bounty Hunters (Lot Boys)
Bounty Hunters, Bell Haven
Bounty Hunters, Block Boys
Circle City Piru
Dalton Gangster Bloods
Denver Lane Bloods
East Side Pain
Family Swan Bloods, 89, 92

Fruit Town Brims
Hacienda Village Bloods
Harvard Park Brims, 62
Mad Swan Bloods
Miller Gangster Bloods
Neighborhood Rollin 20s
Outlaw 20s
Pacoima Pirus
Pueblo Bloods, 52
Queen Street Bloods, 76 Block
Rollin 50s Bloods
Van Ness Gangsters, R. 50s
Water Front Pirus
Athens Park Pirus

Blood Gangs in Compton, California

Campanella Park Pirus	Elm Street Pirus
Butler Block Piru	Fruit Town Pirus
East Compton Piru	Holly Hood Pirus

Leuders Park Pirus (Formerly Leuders Park Hustlers)

Lime Hood Pirus	East Side Pirus
Tree Top Pirus	151st Original Block Pirus
145 Street Neighborhood Pirus	West Side Pirus
Cedar Block Pirus	135th Street Pirus
Cross Atlantic Pirus	

Blood Gangs in Inglewood, California

104th Avenue Piru Gang	Inglewood Family Gang
Center Park Blood	68th Street Neighborhood Piru
Centinela Park Family	Queen Street Blood
Crenshaw Mafia Gangsters	Weirdos Blood
Doty Block Gang	

Blood Gangs in Carson, California

Center View Pirus	Samoan Warrior
Calas Park Loks Pirus	Bounty Hunters Bloods
Cabbage Patch Pirus	Scottsdale Pirus

Blood Gangs in Pasadena, California

Park Nine Bloods Pasadena	Summit Street Bloods
Denver Lanes	Tip Top Bloods
Project Gangster Bloods	

Blood Gangs in Pomona, California

456 Islands	Barjug 456

The following Blood gangs that formed after 1990, or migrated from other areas within the city of Los Angeles to form subsidiaries of their own for the purpose of selling drugs and other illicit activities:

Blood Gangs in Hawthorne, California — Hawthorne Pirus
Blood Gangs in West Covina, California — West Covina Mob Pirus
Blood Gangs in Torrance, California — Down Hood Mob and Rifa Mob
Blood Gangs in Lakewood, California — 706 Bloods
Blood Gangs in Lynwood, California — Mob Piru* (also claimed Compton as a part of their territory)
Blood Gangs in Altadena, California — Squiggley Lane Gangsters
Blood Gangs in Willowbrook, Unincorporated Los Angeles County — Village Town Pirus

Michael couldn't believe the accuracy of the information the police had complied on gangs. Just the thought of it made him realize that the methods used by police and their agencies were the same methods used on the cultural nationalist and revolutionary groups of the 1960's.

In Michael's mind this simply meant that a lot of brothers who represented the lifestyle of a gangster, were going to be set-up, incarcerated, and killed because of those whom they trusted as their faithful comrades. There were nothing but FBI plants ~ double agents working secretly for the police in order to save their own butts. Some were doing it for the love of money, and others were doing it simply because it was a part of their nature, a condition developed during slavery, and a condition that threatened the very survival of those who were true to the cause, and those who were true to themselves.

At this point in Michael's life, he felt that the only way a person or organization could protect itself from betrayal was to change the conditions within that organization or self. Once this is accomplished, the people and the organizations that they represent will be able to perceive things that once were not clear. Through the eye of revelation, all falsehoods are exposed, reality magnified twofold, and turncoats are exposed and shown in their true colors.

But this was not to be, due to the fact that most of Michael's comrades and other young African Americans growing up in the ghetto preferred ignorance to intelligence. In being ignorant, they felt immune to acts of treason that were inflicted upon themselves by their very own hands. *To hurt one another was to nullify the real pain that they felt within themselves.* They thought they were invincible as long as they were dealing with people of their own cultural background, but let the police or some other foreign face appear on the scene, and those brothers would start running like escaped convicts trying to reach the Mexican border.

In Michael's mind, this was the behavior of most ghetto youth, a condition by which they all suffered, and the same condition and mindset that destroyed their role models and their self-esteem. Now this condition threatened to destroy the very thing that Michael held sacred ~ his life.

Lastly, what was so confusing to people who viewed Michael from a distance was that they saw him as a young man who came from a good home, having two parents who loved him, and instilled the proper morals of life. Still, all in all, Michael preferred to hang out with gangs. He wanted to be a part of the ghetto scene; and most of all, he wanted to be respected and feared; the only people who held such a status were the ghetto warriors ~ Crips and Bloods.

A few days after Dinky's death, Michael boarded a transit bus and headed for the city of Lynwood,

California, which was the territory of the Palm & Oak Street Crips.

"What's up, Cuz?" asked one of his new homies as he ventured around the school looking for something to get into.

"Ain't nuthin' happening," he replied as his eyes beheld one of the finest females he had seen in quite a while. This wasn't the type of girl that Michael's comrades saw as being attractive. That was because she was petite, about five feet tall, and shy, but she displayed an innocence that most of them feared. This was because they didn't like women who were academically inclined and content with themselves. They preferred women who were insecure, uneducated, ghetto bred, and ghetto led. Michael didn't want that for himself. He wanted someone whom he could love and trust. A woman who was separate from the ignorance of the ghetto, and a woman who would believe in his dreams and assist him in making them come true. Hopefully, that was the woman before him.

Walking up to her, he said, "My name is Wheat Germ, what's yours?"

Startled by Michael's sudden abruptness, she answered, "Cherianna."

"Cherianna what?"

"Cherianna Santiful," she answered, shyly.

"That's a beautiful name."

"Thanks."

"Listen, I'm new here at this school, and I want to know if you would like to git' together sometime?"

"I would love that, but like you, I'm also new to this school, and I need to take the extra time I have to familiarize myself with the things on campus."

"So you're new here to Lynwood?"

"No, I'm not new to the city of Lynwood, just to the school. I use to attend Hostler Middle School."

"Where's that at?"

"It's the school that's located near Lynwood Park. It only goes up to the eighth grade."

"There are ninth graders going to this school?"

"Yes."

"I didn't know that," Michael said, seriously. "I thought all high schools started from the tenth to the twelfth grade."

"What school did you go to before coming here?"

"Compton High," he answered.

A look of sudden fear appeared upon her face. "What's wrong?" He asked.

"Oh, it's nothing," she quickly answered.

"C'mon, I can tell when something is wrong."

"Well," she began. "I always heard that people who went to Compton High were really crazy...they were dope dealers, gang members, and a lot of other stuff."

"And what's wrong with gang members?"

The class bell suddenly rang, causing her to say, "I have to get to class."

"Can we get together at lunch time?" he quickly asked.

"Sure."

"Alright, I'll meet you in front of the big statue of the knight, around 11:30."

"Okay," she said, as she walked away...

12

Nowhere to Run

"In the ghetto millions of blacks are forced to find
hope in the playing of numbers, the use of alcohol,
the pursuit of heroin, and in the pleasure of cocaine.
Others find comfort and strength in the Malcolm X's,
the Muhummad Ali's and in the Thurgood Marshall's.
Some even find comfort and strength in the exis-
tence of God...but then there are those whose comfort
comes only in the pleasure of seeing people of color,
exterminated..."

—K.R.D.

November 1973-1983

It didn't take long for Cherianna and Michael to fall
in love with each other. They were inseparable,
although they were different in many ways. Despite being younger than Michael, Cherianna taught him things
he didn't know about himself, and the time he spent
with Cherianna made it hard for him to step back into

the realms of ignorance. It was like living two lives, serving two masters, and playing two roles. He was Doctor Jekyll by day and Mr. Hyde by night. The pressure of living such a life had begun to dangerously weigh upon him.

Even Michael's new comrades saw that he was struggling with the moral code of right and wrong. They blamed Cherianna for what was happening to him. They felt he was becoming weak as a result of her, but they were wrong. They didn't understand the type of woman she was. She was intelligent, beautiful, articulate, and fragile. Her qualities were a threat to them, but she was his girl, and he was going to keep her protected and separate from the world that he cohabited ~ at least that's what he thought.

Michael and Cherianna were walking hand in hand one day, when suddenly one of Michael's homies ran up and said, "Hey cuz, come quick!"

"What's up?" he asked, feeling irritated by his sudden invasion.

"You know that slob nigga' Freight Train?"

"Yeah, I know the nigga."

"Well cuz, the nigga' just pushed yo' sister over by the lunch area."

In the past few weeks, Freight Train had really been trying to prove himself in front of his homies, but today, he pushed his luck way too far.

Without saying a word to Cherianna, Michael let go of her hand and took off for the lunch area. There, he found his sister screaming at the top of her lungs. Standing in front of her was his prime target ~ Freight Train.

Wasting no time, Michael stepped up and drove a fast right and left combination to the head of Freight Train that quickly dropped him to the concrete. From there Michael started kicking him, and he would have killed him if it weren't for Shaft, one of the school's security officers.

Shaft grabbed Michael from behind while another security officer grabbed Freight Train. They were then escorted separately to the school's security office, where they were questioned, threatened, and suspended from school.

Even though Michael was suspended from school, the fight itself had launched him into a new level of respect among his peers. He had already acquired the status of a celebrity among the students on campus due to the number of victories he had on the school's wrestling team, and also from weight lifting. Everyone now knew he was also good from the shoulders, and surprisingly, that made Cherianna proud.

"You're really something special," Cherianna said to Michael as they made their way towards her house.

"Why you say that?" he asked.

"I say that because you're not like the rest of your homeboys. You're smart; you always go to your classes. Plus, you respect and treat me like a lady."

"I'm supposed to do that. You're my girl, plus I don't want you to get caught-up being like the other women that I hang with."

"What do you mean by that?"

"Girl, you know how my home girls act," he answered.

Looking down into the eyes of Cherianna, Michael suddenly began to realize she didn't understand the other life he led. Her actions revealed that point. Even though she didn't voice it, he knew she wasn't content with him being a gang member. He also knew if he didn't sever ties with his dangerous lifestyle, he would soon lose Cherianna and everything else he loved.

"I'm afraid for you," Cherianna said suddenly, breaking the silence that had enveloped them.

"Why you say that?" Michael asked curiously.

"I'm afraid because my friends and my parents keep telling me all these bad things 'bout people in gangs."

"What are they sayin'?"

"A lotta things"

"What kind of things?"

"You know, things like ya'll shoot people's kids for no reason. And you all are alcohol users, drug users, dealers, and hardcore gangsters. Plus they say ya'll have wild sex, and have illegitimate kids living everywhere, and there's more they be saying, but I can't remember it all."

"Do your parents be sayin' that stuff 'bout me?"

"Not really, I tell 'em you're different. I let 'em know you don't drink or smoke. Plus I told 'em that you always go to class and play sports for the school. But they still are tripping because they know you're in a gang. They feel that one day I'm going to get hurt as a result of your activities."

At that very moment Michael knew Cherianna needed some assurance. She needed to know she would always be safe, regardless if he was around or not. He also knew she needed him to give her a better understanding as to why he was in a gang. So he grabbed her hand and said, "Let's stop at the park for a moment."

They walked over to the park together and sat upon a picnic table that faced Saint Francis Hospital. Michael then turned to her, and said, "Listen baby, a lot of people is gonna be sayin' a lot of negative things 'bout me and gangs. These people don't have any idea of what they're talkin' 'bout. You must realize people always say stuff about things they don't understand and fear.

That's why white people be callin' us niggers and other mean things. It's because of the fear of not knowing who we are and what we might do that causes them to submit to their preconceived ideas they have about us."

"So you're sayin' none of this stuff about gangs and other things is true?"

"No, I'm not sayin' that," he quickly responded.

"Then what are you saying?"

"Cherianna," he began. "This is a not easy to explain. I say this because all your life you've had a mother and a father who've provided the best for you. They showed you love and sheltered you from the evils of this cruel world. But on the other side of the coin there's people like my homies, who have only one parent that's usually struggling to raise six or more children. With no father in the home, the mother is often forced into the streets to find work. When they don't find it, life for them becomes unbearable. Under this condition some mothers turn to drugs, and others turn to prostitution in order to make ends meet. Then you have those who do finds jobs, but the job takes up so much of their time that their kids end up raising themselves, all alone. After a while, these children themselves feel somewhat ostracized. They get teased and verbally abused at school. They get yelled at and abused at home, so bad that they eventually turn to the streets. And the streets are where they find love and comradeship."

"But what's your excuse? You have good parents, and they both live together at home, so tell, what's up with that?"

Pondering upon Cherianna's comment, Michael came to the sudden realization that she was right. He did have good parents; and like Cherianna, his parents had asked him the same questions, about a million times over.

Sighing heavily, he answered, "Cherianna, I live among the poor, the sick, and those who don't have. If I act as if I'm better than them, then they'll come together against me... and that won't be a pretty picture."

Cherianna slowly put her head down and then said, "Then you're not what I thought you were."

"And what did you think I was?"

"I thought you were a man who would stand up against anyone and anything."

"Are you sayin' I'm a coward?" He asked angrily.

"What do you think?" She responded, surprising him with her boldness.

Trying to control his anger, Michael said. "Listen Cheri, you just don't understand. I can't go up against a whole neighborhood. That's suicide. I live there, and I will continue to live there until I can get a job and make enough money to leave."

"That's if you live that long... plus who's going to have enough trust to hire a gang member?"

Michael suddenly turned away from Cherianna. He didn't want her to see the anger that was in his eyes. He also didn't want to say something that he would later regret. So he got up and started walking towards Century Boulevard.

"Where are you going?" she shouted.

"I'm going home."

"Wait, please!"

Stopping, Michael turned to see Cherianna running towards him. "Baby," she said as she caught up to him. "I don't want to fight with you. I'm just afraid. I don't want you to get hurt...and I don't wanna' get hurt."

Looking into those beautiful brown eyes of hers, Michael said, "Baby, I would give my life for yours, and I'll do it at any cost...please believe me."

"I believe you," she said, as they started off walking toward her house.

Surprisingly, the rest of the year went by quietly. There were no gang killings or shootings. It was like everyone was preparing for next year, and the long hot summer that would come with it; and a hot summer it would be. For most people, it would be a time for crime, love, and sex. After all, this was the ghetto, and in the ghetto, murder, sex, and money were a cycle that never ended...

13

Living In a Time of Fear

"The life of an Urban Warrior is like the waves upon the ocean. No one knows where they'll start, and no one knows where they'll end..."

—Roosevelt Lewis

June 1974-1983

A s time passed on, Michael began to lose faith in everything that he held sacred. He felt this way because life seemed so unfair and unjust towards minorities living in the ghettos of Los Angeles, California. On a daily basis, Michael witnessed black people being constantly assaulted, framed, and murdered by a system that was sworn to serve and protect. Each day it appeared as if every black father, brother, uncle, and son was being targeted. Those who found a way to escape the atrocities brought on by the men in black couldn't escape the social ills that caused alcoholism, drug addiction, and other negative elements that were associated with these problems. As a result, many of them, as well as the organizations that they represented, began to wage war against each other, and no one seemed to care.

During this time many people felt there were a lot of black political organizations within the city trying hard to effect change within their communities. With this being true, the only question of these people then would be: *Were these organizations sincere and dedicated to the cause of black people? If so, to whom did they cater? Was it the house Negro organization or was it the field Negro organization? Or was it black in name but secretly operated in the interest of whites?* Many African Americans asked this question due to the negative counter-measures launched against black political organizations in the past. Therefore, blacks would be skeptical of any organization on their behalf, especially after witnessing the long-term effects of J. Edgar Hoover and the plot of COINTELPRO.

Most African Americans were ignorant of the social changes around them, but Michael was one that was well read and gifted. He was aware of these changes, and he was aware of the goals and tactics of COINTELPRO which were as follows:

1. Prevent the coalition of militant Black Nationalist groups.

2. Prevent the rise of a 'messiah' who could unify and electrify the militant Black Nationalist movement.

3. Prevent militant Black Nationalist groups and leaders from gaining respectability by discrediting them.

4. Prevent the long-term growth of militant Black Nationalist organizations.

After learning these facts, Michael believed that it was important for African Americans to make an honest attempt to form a true black political organization that would benefit not only their people, but everyone who has been affected by corruption, lies, and manipulation brought on by the unseen forces that surround them.

He also believed that people of color collectively would be viewed in a suspicious manner regardless of what they did. If they built a sound organization for the benefit of their people, those living on the outside would view that organization as something negative, and only because they choose to work together economically. In Michael's mind, he felt that any attempts on the part of African Americans to create a sound organization equipped with a strong economic infrastructure within America would be viewed as a threat to the capitalistic system of America. No one wanted African Americans to work together collectively; instead, they preferred them to depend upon the oppressive sectors of the American government for their primary needs, like an obedient child to his mother.

So, in a sense, this is why so many African American youth have become like wayward children, moving about following no set purposes or goals, while the rest of them prostitute themselves into a system whose primary focus is to destroy as many of them as possible, and by any means necessary.

Michael read evidence of this fact which started in the late 1960's, when J. Edgar Hoover and the FBI declared a nationwide war upon the Black Panther Party, a war that started on July 28, 1968, which resulted in the following incidents:

FBI and local police agencies declare war on Black militants and their organizations

July 28, 1968: Two members of the Black Panther Party in New York City throw a Molotov cocktail at an empty police car, completely destroying it.

August 6, 1968: Police exchange gunfire at a service station with three members of the Los Angeles Black Panthers, resulting in the death of all three and the wounding of two police officers.

August 31, 1968: Three members of the Los Angeles Panthers are arrested after an alleged unsuccessful attempt to ambush police officers.

September 24, 1968: Three members of the Jersey City Black Panthers are arrested after allegedly attacking police officers that were in the process of arresting another Black Panther.

November 18, 1968: Two Black Panthers in Berkley allegedly open fire on police after their car is stopped for a traffic violation. Police returned fire, wounding one of the Panthers.

November 19, 1968: Bill Brent and seven Panthers are arrested in San Francisco after their car is stopped for a traffic violation. Police returned fire, wounding one of the Panthers.

November 29, 1968: A Black Panther in Jersey City is arrested for allegedly firing thirty-six rounds from a machine gun into the police department's fifth precinct station.

December 7, 1968: Forty-three Denver police raid the Panther office there. Panthers claim $9,000 in damage.

December 12, 1968: Twelve Chicago Panthers are arrested on weapons charges.

December 18, 1968: Local police who were looking for illegal weapons raid the Indianapolis Panther office.

December 21, 1968: Local police raid the Denver Panther office.

December 27, 1968: The local police raid the San Francisco office.

January 11, 1969: A Black Panther member in Seattle is arrested for allegedly shooting at a police department patrol car.

January 17, 1969: Two Black Panthers allegedly open fire on two New York City patrolmen investigating their parked car along the expressway.

January 17, 1969: Los Angeles police exchange gunfire with four suspects from an armed robbery, one a member of the Black Panthers. Members of the rival militant group, United Slaves, murder Black Panthers Bunchy Carter and John Huggins on the campus of UCLA, allegedly. Police then raided the home of John Huggins and arrested all twelve people there, including Huggins' widow and infant child, charging them with assault with the intent to commit murder.

April 1, 1969: The police raid the Los Angeles Panther office and two Panthers are arrested.

April 2, 1969: "New York 21" Panthers are arrested and charged with conspiracy to blow up department stores, police stations, and commuter railways.

April 26, 1969: The Des Moines Panther office is totally destroyed by a bomb. Two Panthers are injured. State police arrest several Panthers after the blast.

May 1, 1969: Local police raid the Los Angeles Panther office again, and in a two-week period the Los Angeles police arrest forty-two Black Panthers.

June 4, 1969: Detroit Panther office is raided in an attempt to find suspects in the Alex Rackley murder. The Chicago Panther office is raided for the same purpose; thirty Panthers are arrested in Chicago.

June 7, 1969: The local police raid the Indianapolis Panther office.

June 15, 1969: The local police raid the San Diego Panther office. Local police raid the Sacramento Panther office.

June 16, 1969: The police raid the Indianapolis Panther office and sixteen Panthers are arrested.

July 31, 1969: The local police raid the Chicago Panther office and three Black Panthers engage them in a forty-five minute gun battle.

September 8, 1969: The Black Panther free breakfast program in Watts is raided by armed police.

September 23, 1969: The FBI and Philadelphia police raid the Philadelphia office.

October 18, 1969: Local police raid the Los Angeles Panther office.

December 4, 1969: Chicago police raid the home of Chicago Panther leader Fred Hampton. The police alleged that Mark Clark fired a shot at them first. Others alleged that Clark fired only after the police first fired. In any case, the police blasted the apartment with ninety-four shots, killing both Clark and Fred Hampton, and seriously wounding four other Panthers.

December 8, 1969: Police again raid the Los Angeles Panther office, resulting in a four-hour gun battle in which three Panthers and three police officers are wounded. (For the facts, see Hugh Pearson, *The Shadow of the Panther*, pages 206-209)

In conclusion, from the fall of 1967 through the end of 1969 across the nation, nine police officers were killed and fifty-six wounded in confrontations with the Panthers, while ten Panthers were believed killed in such confrontations and an unknown number were wounded. In 1969 alone, 348 Panthers were arrested for a variety of crimes. Since then, the Panthers were forced to go underground. At present, the police and FBI attention is now focused upon a new threat, one that has been financed and supported by their very own hands (*Crips and Bloods*). This threat is slowly spreading nationwide into every community throughout the nation.

Looking himself over in the mirror, Michael saw the image of a true ghetto warrior. He was dressed in a pair of powder blue Khakis, matching blue belt, with a blue sweat shirt that had his gang name and the word 'Blood killa' embroidered on the back. He also was wearing a blue L.A. Dodger's cap, *murder one's locs (*slang for dark sun glasses that are favored by gang members*) and blue and white converse tennis shoes, which meant he was Cripping from head to toe.

Pleased by what he saw, Michael quickly grabbed his .32 automatic from under the mattress of his bed and concealed it within the waistband of his Khakis as he proceeded to leave his house.

"I'm gonna' tell momma'!" yelled Michael's sister as he stepped out of his room and into the living room of their house.

"Tell her what?" He asked angrily.

"About that Crip rag you got hanging from your pocket...you know momma said no gang rags are allowed in this house."

Damn, he thought as he pulled the rag from his back pocket. I should have known that my mother had left my sister, the watchdog, to oversee things while they were away.

Michael had been spending so much time in Lynwood over the past few weeks, he had completely forgotten his parents were heading out to Stockton, California to visit friends and relatives.

Turning toward his sister, he said, "I'm getting' tired of yo' snitching' ass!"

"Then do something 'bout it," his sister said, challenging him.

Being older and bigger than Michael, Marie felt he wouldn't do anything to her. For years, he had to endure her sharp tongue and the ghetto slaps to the back of his head, but today all that was about to change.

Without giving her the slightest warning, he quickly pivoted on his left foot and snapped a quick jab that caught Marie square on the jaw. The jab was so powerful that it sent her sprawling over the living room table and into a big stack of record albums.

Shocked and surprised, Marie got up and came at Michael like ten angry mountain lions. She started hitting and scratching him with things he couldn't make out. Punches seemed to come out of nowhere. She even tried to take out a piece of his throat with those big teeth of hers, and when she didn't succeed, she grabbed a brass statue, which doubled as a lamp and swung it toward him. Upon seeing that, Michael knew right then it was time for him to pull out his equalizer.

Spinning away from her incoming thrust, he reached within the waistband of his Khakis and pulled out his .32 auto and quickly said, "Bitch, if you swing that lamp at me again I'm gonna put a bunch of holes in yo' yellow-ass!"

Marie froze when she spotted the gun. It was as if someone had pressed pause, freezing everything in motion, including them. He knew right then he had done the wrong thing. Knocking his sister down on her ass was one thing, but pulling a gun on her as if she was some street thug was another thing altogether.

Slowly, Michael backed away from her until he was at the entrance of the front door. He lowered the gun and said, "I told you I was tired of yo' shit!"

His sister didn't respond. That was because her attention was still upon the gun that Michael now held at his side. He knew from past experiences that she hated guns. She was afraid of everything that signified death. She didn't even like fireworks and always stayed locked up in her room during such holidays as the Fourth of July. The day she hated the most was New

Years, but now there was something she hated even more ~ her brother.

Snapping out of her dream-like trance, Marie slowly walked over to the phone, snatched up the receiver and said, "Git' outta here!"

He didn't move.

"Git outta of here!" she said for a second time and loud enough for the whole block to hear.

Still, Michael didn't move. Instead, he held his position in front of the door in an effort to a show her he had no fear of her or anything else that was to come.

"I'm calling the police on you right now...and I'm gonna tell em' about the gun, about you and your Crip buddies, and I'm telling momma..."

The mere mentioning of calling the police was enough for Michael. He knew she would do it, so he raised the gun up once again and pointed it in her direction. Michael knew by doing this, he would buy enough time to get himself out of the house and out of the area. It worked as planned. Marie dropped the receiver and ran for her room.

Wasting no time, Michael ran over to the phone, disconnected the receiver, and hid it under the cushion of the couch in the living room. He then ran to the door of her room and said, "I'm not going anywhere until you calm yo' yellow-ass down. So I'll be out here waiting when you want to come out and talk to me with some sense."

He then turned and headed back into the living room. He straightened everything up in order to remove all evidence of the fight that had occurred between them. Once satisfied that everything was back in proper order, he turned on the television to make it seem as if he was still in the house. After that, Michael quietly eased his way out the back door, climbed over the fence, and made his getaway into the dangerous streets of Compton, California.

Three hours later, Michael found himself at Lynwood Park waiting for Cherianna to meet him. He had called her earlier from a phone booth in Compton. He told her he was in serious trouble and he desperately needed to talk to her. She was reluctant at first because they hadn't been getting along lately, due to his homegirls trying to come between them. They had been telling Michael stuff like Cherianna was much too soft, and he needed to be with one of them instead. Plus, Cherianna was slowly becoming weak from the stress of her parents who were having problems among themselves. She was also stressing over the lifestyle Michael had chosen for himself ~ a lifestyle she feared more than anything.

As Michael waited, he started to dwell upon his life and everything he had done up until that point. He thought about his parents, his brothers and sisters, and the direction his life was now taking.

Pondering upon those things caused Michael to realize he was slowly deteriorating in mind, body and soul. He didn't care about anything in life outside of being a Crip. This was the only thing that mattered to him. Cripping gave his life so much meaning and purpose. Even though his life could be taken at any given moment, he'd rather go out at the end of a smoking gun, than to go out by serving the man and chasing after his false gods. Michael wasn't with all that *turning the other cheek or things will get better* ideologies. As he saw it, black people had been waiting for a change for over four hundred years, and all they had received from waiting was a big white foot in the ass and a piece of paper saying, *you got a free kick coming next time.*

Nah, he wasn't down for that, and since life was full of choices, Michael figured that his best choice was to go straight out like a gangster, at least that's what he thought at the time.

"What's up?" Cherianna asked, startling him.

Shaking his head clear of the cobwebs of thought, he simply said, "Cherianna, I'm in trouble."

Walking up, Cherianna took his hands and placed them inside of hers. She then said, "Now tell me what happened."

"I just lost it."

"Lost what?" Cherianna asked patiently.

"My head, everything, I just lost it."

Sensing danger, Cherianna asked, "Did you shoot someone?"

"No, but I almost did."

"Who was it?"

"My sister," he answered slowly.

Shocked, Cherianna released his hands and asked, "What in the world could make you so mad that you would want to shoot your own sister?"

"She kept fuckin' wit' me...she always fucked wit' me," he answered, hysterically.

"And you almost shot her because of that?"

"It wasn't like that...we got into a fight and she came at me with a brass statue, and there was nuthin' else I could do but pull my gun on her."

Cherianna was terrified. She couldn't believe that Michael would succumb to his anger in such a way that he would reach out and try to cause harm to his own kin. She now felt that if he could do this to his sister, then he could do the same to her as well.

Cherianna looked Michael in his eyes and said, "I don't know you anymore. You need help. And as long as you choose to live your life in a destructive manner, you'll be no good to yourself or to the people who love you."

"So what are you sayin'?"

Cherianna suddenly turned, and as she did, Michael saw what caught her attention. Five police cruisers were parked strategically around the park, and at least ten policemen were converging upon the spot where they stood.

"You in the blue sweatshirt and pants, get on the ground, and do it now!" shouted a policeman on a bullhorn.

For a moment Michael hesitated. He needed to let Cherianna know that he loved her, but when he turned to say something to her, she stopped him by saying, "Do what they say, and do it now."

Michael slowly got down on his knees, and then laid his body upon the warm grass.

"Now stretch your arms out to your side with your palms facing up, and do it slowly!"

Again, Michael complied.

"Now I want the woman to do the same."

Seeing Cherianna stretched out on the grass like she was some kind of criminal made his heart drop. *How could he ever expect her to love him after putting her through this?* Michael had broken his promise to her. He told her she would never be hurt or humiliated by the actions of his hands. But now, because of him, they both were laid out upon the grass like two pieces of raw meat on display at a neighborhood meat market.

Quickly, the police converged on them with all guns drawn. They weren't taking any chances. They searched Cherianna first, and when they were satisfied she was free of weapons, they searched Michael and found his .32 automatic, a switchblade, and his wallet containing nothing but a bunch of worthless memories which at the moment was the story of his life. After that, they read him his rights and escorted him to an awaiting police car.

While sitting in the back of the police car, Michael listened while the police questioned Cherianna who was only a few feet away. He heard them tell her he was being charged with attempted assault on his sister, attempted assault with a deadly weapon, and carrying a concealed unregistered weapon. Plus they said he was a suspect in several drive-by shootings in the area.

After hearing that, he knew Cherianna was through with him. He could see it on her face as they pulled off. There was nothing he could do about it. He had made his own bed. Now he had to lay in it, but the only difference now was the bed that he was going to lie in would be surrounded by prison guards and prison bars...

14

Friends and Strangers

"In America there are many rights afforded to its citizens, but in the ghettos of America the only rights that one has are their last rites..."

—Jaqunta Lewis

July 1974-1983

If anyone tells you that jail time is easy, don't believe them because they're straight up lying. There's nothing good about being in jail, especially in Los Angeles County Jail where the inmate population easily exceeds ten thousand. Housed within are some of the most dangerous convicts ever known to a county jail system. Many people view this place as being harder than any federal or state prison, and no penal system in California compares to the confines of the L.A. County Jail. It's like a city within a city, beyond a city ~ and in this city there are two rules one must abide by. They are: *protect your ass at all times, and make sure you sleep with your eyes open and your shoes on.*

Los Angeles County Jail is also known for having the hardest, most corrupted, and meanest sheriff deputies ever. Here everyone has an attitude, and the atrocities that go on inside, never reach the eyes or ears of the public ~ and those wishing to reveal the source of these atrocities never live to do so. It's like one hand washing the other where time, racial hate, and crime are solidified partners in a world of corruption, and the buck doesn't stop there.

On a daily basis, the hardest of the hard lay in wait like vultures, each taking its turn at a free piece of meat while the weak huddle together in herds trying hard to gather strength from one another. Those who are fortunate enough to escape the game of predator and prey are those most respected; but like in all things, respect is not given, it's earned. Within the county jails of Los Angeles that's a task within itself.

This was Michael's second trip to the L.A. County Jail. The first time he was taken there he had lied about his age because he wanted to appear hard and unshaken in the presence of his homeboys and the arresting officers, but his stay only lasted about six hours. His comrades had informed his parents that he had been arrested and taken to the adult jail.

Furious, his parents contacted the L.A. County Jail and gave them his real name and date of birth, which resulted in him being transferred immediately to Central Juvenile Hall. But today, things were different. There were no lies to tell. The police knew Michael's age, which was seventeen, but that didn't matter because the crimes he was now charged with meant he would be tried as an adult. This time, there was no getting out of jail.

Sitting in a holding tank with at least three hundred strange faces, Michael sat patiently waiting to be called so he could be classified and dressed into his L.A. County Jail fatigues. This was just one of the many procedures he would face before reaching his final destination which was a concrete jail cell.

As he waited, Michael began to scan the faces of each person to make sure there weren't any enemies or unseen threats lurking about. Other inmates were also doing the same thing ~ each man using his eyes to size up the other, hoping to find a weakness or a sign that would tell him who the individual actually was.

This action alone was dangerous because no one among the ghetto culture, especially gang members, likes to be stared at and examined like some laboratory rat. Even eye-to-eye contact was dangerous because most ghetto thugs perceived eye-to-eye contact as a challenge through what is known throughout the ghetto as a *mean mug (*a facial expression one uses to instill fear*). This technique and behavior usually causes the individual more trouble than it's worth.

Finally, Michael was called out along with fifty other prisoners, and they were all made to line up against the wall. From there they were escorted to a big elevator and herded inside like sheep awaiting slaughter. Afterwards, they were taken to another area of the jail where fifteen or more officers awaited them. The scene was like a scene from a movie, where prisoners were ushered out in front of a firing squad and killed, but Michael was soon to learn that this scene was altogether different.

Without warning, an officer shouted out, "Get ya'll asses up against that wall!"

Everyone suddenly lined up against the wall as if they were about to take a picture for a police mug shot.

Clearing his throat, another Sheriff Deputy said, "Now I want everyone to step forward and place their property on the red line that's in front of them."

Again they complied, and after a few moments the sheriff deputy said, "Now remove all your clothes and place them on the line with the rest of your property."

After seeing that they had done as asked, the sheriff's deputy then said, "Now I want you all to turn around and place your hands against the wall, and if anyone here thinks he has enough nuts to turn around while my officers are searching your property, then do so now so we can boot yo' fuckin' ass to the moon!"

No one dare to move, not even Michael. These officers were crazy and they were straight up giants, each one standing at least six feet two inches or more, weighing about three hundred pounds. Only a fool would provoke these giants while being asshole butt naked.

After thirty minutes, they were ordered to turn around. As they did so, they could see that the police had purposely mixed up all their property. The look that was on their faces spoke for itself. The Sheriff Deputies were enjoying the inmate's discomfort, and there was nothing they could do about it. They were at their mercy, and Michael knew they were praying for one of the inmates to get out of hand. He, too, was praying and he was asking God not to grant any of their prayers.

After seeing they weren't about to cause them any problems, one of the sheriff's officers then ordered them to spread out at arms distance. After they complied with his order, he then said, "Now I want each of you to grab your little ass dicks with your left hand and lift them up."

They complied.

"Now do the same thing with your nuts as you did with your dicks."

Again they complied.

"Now open your mouths."

Once again they complied.

"Stick out your tongues."

And again they complied.

"Now take your left index finger and run it around the inside of your mouth right between your lips and gums."

"I ain't doing that!" said a prisoner who stood a couple of places from Michael.

Without warning, two sheriff deputies grabbed the naked prisoner and rammed his head into the concrete wall like it was a jackhammer.

Blood gushed instantly from his nose as his body dropped to the freshly waxed floor. "Oh, you wanna fuck up our floors now, huh." said one of the sheriff deputies as he moved forward to kick the prisoner.

"You can't have all the fun," added another sheriff deputy as he joined in delivering kicks and punches of his own.

"Keep your eyes and head forward!" shouted another sheriff deputy as he stepped closer to the other inmates.

The inmates instantly turned themselves to face forward. They didn't want to suffer the same punishment that was being inflicted upon the unfortunate prisoner who carelessly allowed his mouth to betray his common sense.

Suddenly the beating stopped, and the prisoner was dragged away by several sheriff deputies who were laughing and high-fiving each other as they went. As they disappeared from the inmates peripheral view, the sheriff deputy who was originally in charge of their processing stepped forward and said, "Does anyone else have any more smart-ass remarks to get off their chest?"

No one dared to answer. No one in their right mind would offer an answer after witnessing what they had seen. Michael was pretty sure that if the officer had now ordered them to stick their finger in their butts and then put the same finger in their mouths, everyone would do it with a Coke and a smile ~ including him.

After a few seconds, the officer realized that no one was about to defy his order, so he told all the inmates to bend over, spread their asses and cough. They were then dressed into their L.A. County blues and escorted up an escalator where they were housed in a section of the jail called ninety-five hundred.

Going into ninety-five hundred was like walking into enemy crossfire. There were at least three hundred or more inmates crammed inside a dorm that could have easily doubled as a warehouse garage. There was also a line of bunks positioned right next to each other with a three-foot wall that divided the dorm into four sections. Up front was a row of benches that new inmates sat upon during roll call and court call-outs. There were also about eight public telephones affixed upon a far wall. The most frightening thing that was ever present was the chaos combined with the fear that hung heavily in the air.

Stepping inside, Michael was greeted by hundreds of menacing stares and curious onlookers. Everyone seemed to be sizing him up, but that was to be expected. He was now the new fish among a sea of sharks, and if he didn't turn into a killer whale fast, he would soon be eaten up by one of the many predators that were on patrol in the dangerous waters of ninety-five hundred.

Displaying a mean mug of his own, Michael started out in search of an empty bunk, and as he did so, he ran across a scene that slightly shook him. Several hardcore looking brothers were gathered around a bunk that sat in the dark corner of the dorm. They had a long sheet that was hanging from the top bunk all the way down to the bottom. The sheet blocked the view of everyone, except those standing nearby. On the bottom bunk was a white inmate who was bent over with his ass and mouth full of black meat. The scene reminded Michael of an oil field, with oil pumps pumping away at will. Brothers were standing in line waiting to get themselves a piece of ass like heroin addicts waiting for a quick fix.

Backing away from the gruesome sight, Michael turned to find several brothers heavily engrossed in a game of blackjack where money was exchanging hands like a Las Vegas casino. A few bunks down from the blackjack game sat a couple of brothers who were selling single cigarettes at five dollars each, and another brother was selling candy bars and homemade sandwiches. The whole damn dorm was functioning like an illegal swap meet where sex, gambling, and bartering were performed around the clock, seven days a week. Everyone was on the take, the prisoners, the police, and even the damn free workers, which were people who were employed by the county to work as cooks, janitors, and commissary workers ~ how else could inmates get such things as cigarettes and other illegal things inside a county jail? Anyone could be bought or bribed if the price was right.

Finally, Michael spotted an empty bunk. As he moved forward to secure it, he stopped in his tracks because his eyes caught some suspicious movement to his left. There, he saw a group of Mexican inmates gathered around an empty bunk, passing *shanks (homemade knives) to one another. Upon seeing that, Michael knew something was about to happen and the brothers within the dorm were completely oblivious to what was going on around them. Or maybe they were too over confident, since the blacks outnumbered everyone else in the dorm five to one. From Michael's past experiences in dealing with Mexicans, he knew they didn't give a damn about being outnumbered. It was all about respect and pride with them, and they were going to get their respect, even if they had to die for it.

Moving cautiously, Michael made his way back to where the inmates were gambling, and he quickly said to a brother that was dealing the cards, "Hey cuz, something 'bout to go down."

"What did you say?" he asked, appearing slightly irritated by the interruption.

"I said, I think something is about to go down."

"Going down with who and what?"

"It seems like it's going to be going down with those Mexicans over there by the far wall."

The brother took a causal glance over in their direction, then said, "We ain't done nuthin' to those *spics," (a derogatory term that some blacks and racist whites used in reference to Mexicans).

"Well, someone did," Michael said adamantly.

Suddenly, another player who was involved in the game said, "I think cuz is right."

"Let's get the brothers together then, but do it quietly as possible."

"Okay cuz," said the brother as he slipped away.

"Where are you from?" the brother asked.

"Nutty Blocc," Michael answered.

Smiling, he said, "My name is Ricc Rocc and I'm from Grape Street Watts Crips."

Laughing slightly, Michael replied, "I'm Little Salt Rocc, I took that name in honor of my big homie who is resting in peace, and I'm from Nutty Blocc."

"Well, Salt Rocc, I hope you're down like the rest of your homies."

"You know my homies?"

"I damn near know all your crazy-ass homeboys, especially Wood Rat, Big Mac, and Peter Gunn."

"All of the names you just mentioned are my O.G.'s."

"Who do you kick it with?"

"I hang with some of the little homies, but sometimes I try to kick it with Rod Alexander and my ace homeboy who we called Knuckles."

"Yeah cuz, you're from the Blocc."

"Why did you say it like that?" Michael asked curiously.

"Because a lot of niggas be coming to jail and claiming to be from 'hoods they ain't actually from, and they do it either for protection or to be recognized, so that's why niggas like me don't take anyone's word until they prove themselves."

"I never knew niggas was doing that type of shit."

"This must be your first time down."

"Actually this is my second time down, but this is the first time I made it this far into the system."

The brother who had left earlier suddenly broke up their conversation. "Say cuz, those Mexicans are grouping up everywhere, and it seem as if all of 'em are gonna ride on us; they got shanks too."

"What you expect them to have? You know them punks can't fight," Ricc Rocc said angrily, and then added, "Do everyone know what's going on?"

"Yeah cuz, they're just waiting for us."

"Let's break this damn game up then," said Ricc Rocc. He then turned to Michael and said, "Now it's time to see what you're made of."

"You ain't got to worry 'bout me," Michael said. "Just make sure you're ready."

Ricc Rocc laughed as they cautiously made their way toward the back of the dorm.

As Michael looked around the dorm, he saw that some of the brothers seem to be treating the situation as if it were a game. He personally didn't see it that way. He knew those Mexicans meant business and nothing was going to stop them fools from being successful at their business endeavors but them; that's if they all had the heart and nerve to do so.

Standing amongst a group of gangsters for what Michael presumed were Crips from other neighborhoods, he listened as Ricc Rocc barked-off several orders to some of them that were near. As they ran off to fulfill the tasks that were asked of them, Michael carefully examined the situation before him. What he saw was this: There were at least three hundred people in the entire dorm. Blacks made up the majority while the rest were Mexicans and a few dope fiend whites. There were no guards stationed inside to protect or prevent anyone from being harmed, injured, or wronged. That task was left up to the inmates. Looking closer, he saw that there was nothing visible that they could use as weapons but the razors that were given to them for shaving. So all that was left for them to use was their fists ~ which was a God given talent blacks used when they found themselves in such situations.

"Everyone is ready cuz," said one of the brothers as he came back from fulfilling his task.

"What's the game plan?" Michael asked, confused by everything that was going on.

Turning to face Michael, Ricc Rocc said, "I'm sorry cuz, I forgot that this is your first time down."

"What's that got to do with anything?"

"A whole lot, cuz," he said as he turned to face the Crips that were standing next to him. "See these niggas here. They have been through this shit a thousand times. They know how to handle themselves in these types of situations, and they know what it would take to smash these fuckin' spics. But on the other hand, you haven't been through this type of shit, so it's my mistake for not telling you what is needed for this type of war."

"Then tell me what I need to do so we can get this shit going."

"You don't need much, cuz. Just grab yourself a blanket and a mattress, and use your bunk like a protective shield."

"Are you serious?"

"Hell yeah, I'm serious. What do you think is going to protect you from them fuckin' shanks?"

"Now I understand, cuz," he said slowly.

"Don't worry 'bout nuthin' cuz, just handle your part and we'll handle ours."

"Okay cuz; just give me a chance to get ready."

Ricc Rocc smiled and then said, "I'll see ya'll after the battle, but first I'm gonna see if there is some type of way to avoid this bullshit."

"Good luck, cuz," Michael said as he watched Ricc Rocc and three other brothers weave their way through the bunks toward the Mexicans' encampment.

As Ricc Rocc and the others made their way through the bunks, he spotted a couple of Mexicans with shanks trying to creep up on them from behind. Without saying a word, Michael and a few others took off after them.

Within a few steps Michael shouted, "Watch out, cuz!"

Ricc Rocc and the others suddenly turned in time to see the two Mexicans that were trying to sneak up on them. At that very moment, everyone and everything within the dorm seem to freeze in motion. Upon noticing this, Michael sensed that something wasn't cool ~ and he was right.

The Mexicans had known from past conflicts that black inmates would often try to seek a peaceful resolution before going into battle. In doing so, the black inmates would send their toughest and hardest ghetto warriors out in order to negotiate with the enemy, but today, the game had changed and the enemy was now playing by a completely new set of rules.

The Mexicans were smart, because they didn't make a move until they saw the black inmates who they viewed as being the most dangerous leave the main body of the group. They then strategically stationed their warriors around the rest of the brothers without them even noticing a thing. Now they were surrounded on all sides, and there was nothing for them to do but pull all the bunks together in a semi-circle, like that of a wagon train, thus doing all their fighting from the inside. Rick Rocc and the others were stranded, left on the outside, from the safety of the bunks.

A quiet hush fell over the dorm. The feeling was unlike anything that Michael had ever felt. Fear dominated the air while anticipation flowed through the veins of everyone. Even the white inmates feared what was to come of them because there was no such thing as being neutral in a situation like this. Choosing the wrong side could serve to be fatal for them later on, so they decided to ride along with the Mexicans. Now the stage was set, and there was no turning back.

Like a spider slowly creeping upon its helpless prey, the Mexicans began to slowly converge upon the black inmates. As they did, one of them shouted, *Aqui estamos!" (*Spanish, meaning, here we are*).

"And here we are, too," stated Ricc Rocc.

"Estamos cansados de ustedes' pinches Negros faltandonos el respeto sobre los telefonos y otras cosas," *(*Spanish for: We're tired of you fucking black people disrespecting us over the telephones and other things*).

"A poco se?" *(*Spanish for: is that so?*), stated Ricc Rocc, surprising Michael with his knowledge of Spanish.

"Chinguen su madre entonces pinches mallates," said the Mexican as he lunged forward with his shank catching Ricc Rocc high in the shoulder.

Ricc Rocc let out a low pitch groan as he rolled away from his attacker. Everything was on automatic at that point. Pandemonium broke out everywhere as Mexicans, blacks, and whites clashed together in a rhythmic dance of violence and bloodshed.

Rushing headlong into the chaos, Michael pounded everything within his reach. He was doing well, too. That's until he caught a blow to the back of his head that sent him where no man had gone before.

Soon as Michael hit the ground, he felt himself being snatched up by someone who had thrust him forward back into the battle like a child being thrown into a swimming pool for the first time. Bodies bounced and bobbled as ghetto combatants jockeyed for the best positions to deliver their blows and fatal stabs. Michael immediately fell back into the fight along with a few others who had been knocked down. Each man fought valiantly and relentlessly. Not one man displayed cowardice. Blood was seen everywhere, but that didn't hinder the war. Black inmates showed that they had heart, and so did the Mexicans. The only ones who didn't fare too well were the few white inmates who kept running into the black inmates' deadly rights and lefts. A few even got stumped out into another reality altogether.

The sounds of stomping boots and shouts suddenly permeated and overwhelmed everything in the dorm as dozens of sheriff deputies rushed inside the unit in riot gear and gas masks. The inmates fell to the ground and covered their heads as the deputies unleashed a reign of terror upon them with their battle batons.

Blacks and Mexicans who weren't injured in the war with each other were seriously injured by the sheriff deputies ~ some even beyond recognition. This was the part of the job the deputies loved the most. They knew that the conditions of overcrowding, poverty, and racial disparity between the classes would ignite into a race war, thus giving them the justification for beating the inmates at will. *This practice will continue until someone decides to change the system and the way it operates.*

The clash that occurred between the blacks, Mexicans, and whites would be one of many that would occur within the system for years to come. It was truly by the grace of God that none of the inmates were killed, though many were seriously injured. Those with slight injuries were transferred to other jail facilities within the city to begin the process of war and hate all over again. But for Michael, he was one of many who had to face the process of being sent to segregation for ninety days. Some even received longer sentences, but it didn't matter because the time was all the same. Michael was now doing his in another part of the jail...

15

Choices and Strange Voices

*"In the ghetto the Urban Warrior understands that
revenge is a dish that is best served cold..."*
—Ronald Henry

April 1975-1983

In Los Angeles County Jail time has a funny way of
playing with one's mind. It can be an ally to one
man, and an enemy to another. For Michael, it was
both. At times, it seemed like it took months for just
a day to pass. Then there were days when a whole
week would escape without even noticing it. There
were days when he would lose his sense of space and
time altogether. This phenomenon occurred with most
inmates naturally. Some perceived this as a way to escape the tyranny and despair of incarceration, while
others saw it as one of the first signs of succumbing to
the mental madness of imprisonment.

Michael didn't know if he was living on the edge
of insanity or not, but when he heard his name being
called over the loud speaker for a visit, he thought to
himself that this was too good to be true. Michael had
been incarcerated now for about nine months. During
this time, he hadn't received one single letter or visit.
So quite naturally he felt that someone was playing a
cruel joke on him. So, instead of running to get himself
cleaned up and groomed as others did when they were
called out for visits, he just returned to his lonely game
of solitaire. As he began to deal himself a new hand of
cards, a guard suddenly came up to Michael and asked,

"Are you Inmate Michael Lewis?"
"Yes," he answered, nervously.
"You got a visit."
This had to be a mistake. This couldn't be true. *Who
would come and visit me? Would it be my homeboys?
No, it couldn't be them because most of them had war-
rants. So who could it be? Is it Cherianna? Or is it my
home girls? Or maybe it's my lawyer?* Michael didn't
know who it was, and the anticipation was so great
that he couldn't let the guard leave without first inquir-
ing about the identity of his visitor, so he called out to
the guard who was turning to leave and asked, "Do
you know who it is that's here to visit me?"
"No, I don't, but if you wait a minute I can find out."
Michael waited patiently while the officer went to
find out who it was that had come to visit him. As he
waited, he began to think about all the lonely months
he endured while in the County Jail. Even though
he was surrounded by thousands of inmates, he still
longed for the closeness and love of his family, but he
knew that was not to be. He had done the ultimate
wrong. He had committed a crime against his family, a
crime that merited no second chances or forgiveness.

Looking up, Michael smiled nervously as the officer approached him and said, "It's your father and brother."

"Are you sure?"

"Sure as I know that you're not going out there to be released."

Michael didn't know what to think. It had been nine long months since his arrest. During that period he never made an attempt to contact his family. He felt they didn't care about what happened to him, and to be truthful, he didn't care either.

Stepping into the long corridor with his visiting pass in hand, Michael strolled quietly toward the visiting room. He didn't worry about being harassed or stopped by some officer because in L.A. County Jail an inmate can travel about freely without any worry as long as you displayed the appearance of one who was authorized to be on the move. Plus, there were so many inmates that it was impossible to know where everyone was supposed to be at any given moment. That's why it wasn't an uncommon occurrence to find inmates in cells where they weren't assigned to, or on floors loitering with other inmates who resided in different living units. In fact, the jail was so populated that they had to install flashing neon signs in all the units just so inmates would know their upcoming court dates and times. They used the signs to display attorney visits, regular visits, as well as scheduled releases; and if by chance the inmate count was messed up due to all the free movement, then each unit would be taken up to the roof for a formal inmate head count.

Upon entering the visiting room, Michael was shocked to see a group of inmates handcuffed together like they were part of a southern chain gang, but he later learned that these inmates were the most dangerous ever known to the Los Angeles County Jail. Most of them were hardened gang members, double and triple murderers, serial killers, and serial rapists. Those among them who were gang members were housed in a unit called the Crip module. Their rivals, the Pirus were housed in the Blood module. There was also a high security unit called 'high power' which housed the celebrities and psychopaths ~ people who would kill a person at the drop of a dime and wouldn't think twice about adding a couple more for good measure. Thank God they had units for such people as these, otherwise Michael's stay could have been something else altogether.

Michael finally found the visiting booth that he was assigned to. There behind a thick piece of glass sat his father and brother, who appeared to be sullen.

After a few awkward seconds Michael's father smiled and then motioned for him to pick up the phone.

"How are you doing, Son? He quickly asked.

"I'm okay," Michael responded.

"I'm here because your mother and I have been contacted by the district attorney regarding a recommendation in reference to your case."

"And what is their recommendation?"

"Well, the district attorney feels that you should be sent away for at least seven years, and your lawyer is asking for one year county time, three years' probation and some community service."

"And what do ya'll want?"

Michael's father didn't answer, clearly he was in pain and Michael could see it. So instead of waiting for his response, he said, "You agree with them, don't you?"

Tears slowly filled his father's eyes, and upon seeing that Michael's brother took the phone from him and said, "No one is tryin' to put you away, Michael, but you're not the same person. We don't know who you are anymore. Everyone is afraid of you, and we don't know when you'll snap again. Plus, we don't know why you snapped on Marie the way you did. And mom feels that you might kill us all one day in our sleep."

"So ya'll don't want me at home no more," he said angrily.

"I'm not saying that, but we need some assurance on your behalf that what you did would never happen again."

Hearing his brother speak to him the way he did made Michael feel strange. He was four years younger than him, and they weren't that close. That was Michael's fault because in his heart, he felt his parents had loved his younger brother more than they loved him. So Michael always tried to find ways to pick on him. There were even times when he tried to influence him into doing crime. Sometimes he would succumb to Michael's urgings, and sometimes he would reject them altogether. But all in all, he was Michael's brother, and he loved him.

Staring down at his identification tag that was affixed upon his wrist, Michael asked his brother, "Are you afraid of me, too?"

"Not really," he answered.

"What do you mean by that?"

"Because you act different when you're with homies, plus you disrespect me when they're around."

"How do I do that?"

Michael's brother paused for a moment to look over at his father who said, "Go on, and tell him, boy. Finish what you started to say."

Clearing his throat, he said, "Remember all those times when you would be in our room with your friends talking, and I would come to sit down among you all, then you would start doing annoying things to me so I would leave?"

"I did that because I didn't want you to end up involved in the things I was in. Plus, I didn't want you in gangs and I sure didn't want you involved in selling drugs. If I allowed you to hang around and be exposed to what I was doing, then everything in life that you have accomplished up 'til now would be lost."

"What about your life? Why do you have to be involved in gangs?"

Fighting back the tears, Michael asked, "When you go to school and other places does anyone ever bother you?"

"No," he answered.

Looking his brother directly in his eyes, Michael said, "I'm the one reason why no one bothers you or this family. Plus, I sacrificed myself so you won't have to endure the pain of proving yourself to the 'hood."

"I don't believe that," he said.

"You betta' believe it because if I was a punk you would be getting' picked on in ways you can't begin to imagine, and you know it, too."

"Well, let me deal with it."

"I can't," Michael said slowly. "You don't have any idea as to what's out there in those streets. You can't even begin to imagine the ghetto mentality of some of those niggas, especially the ones who I deal with on an everyday basis. They don't care about life, love, or family because none of them have a real family of their own. Therefore, it means nothing to them when they make up their minds to *smoke (slang for to kill) your ass or anyone else's that's on their list at the time."

Grabbing the phone, Michael father said, "But what's your excuse, Son? You have a family, and we all love you."

"I know that Dad, but…"

"But what, Son?"

Michael pondered for a moment and then answered, "I know you all love me and I love you too, but I can't just call it quits. It's not that simple…plus it's not as bad as you both think."

"Pulling a gun on your sister and beating her up isn't considered bad?"

"I didn't say that, and it didn't happen exactly the way you both think."

"Well, tell us, how did it happen?"

"Dad, you know how Marie runs her mouth."

"So you pulled a gun on her for that?"

"No, it wasn't because of that."

"What was the reason then?"

"She was beatin' the hell outta me," Michael said in his defense.

"But what did you do to her to cause it?"

"I gave her a quick one-piece to the jaw."

"You gave her a what?"

"I hit her, but I wasn't tryin' to hurt her, and the only reason why I pulled the gun on her was to scare her."

Smiling, Michael's father said, "Well, you did a damn good job at that, so good that she's the only one who doesn't want to see you come home, and if your case goes to trial, the district attorney is going to put her on the stand to testify against you."

Running his hand across his forehead, Michael said, "Well, I'm glad, because I'm not taking my case to trial."

"Don't be glad yet."

"What do you mean by that?"

His father slowly turned to his brother who nodded his head in a gesture for him to answer. "Listen Son, we have a problem that concerns you."

"Me?"

"Yes Son, you...that's why we came here."

For a moment Michael was brain boggled. He didn't know what to think or expect. He had done so much dirt to others that he had forgotten to protect his own self from the shovel, and like the adage goes, 'Momma said there would be days like this.'

Looking up at his father, Michael asked, "Is the problem more charges?"

Confused, Michael's father asked, "Is there something else out there that you've done and now are running from?"

Without thinking, he answered, "Daddy, at the moment I'm running from everything."

Concerned, his father said, "Son, I'm not here to preach to you. But you know if you plant bad seeds, you get bad fruit, and if you establish gangster ties among those who you consider your peers, then everyone else would be an enemy, including your family."

"But that's not true," he countered.

"On the contrary, it is."

"How is that?"

"Because God didn't place in the chest of any man, two hearts, nor can a man serve two masters. If he tries, he'll find himself loving one and hating the other."

"But what does that have to do with me and our situation?"

"A hell of a lot, Son," his father answered. "See, as a Crip, the street is your master, and as your master you must follow the ways and means of those who serve the same gods as you. In your case, your gods are alcohol, drugs, whores, pride, and fast cash which will eventually lead you to that place where you'll meet the true God up close and personal."

"But..."

"Let me finish," his father said quickly. "We being your family don't serve it like that. We trust in the true God, therefore, you can't love your homies, your life-style, and think at the same time you can love us, too. It won't work. You're either going to love one, or rebel and love the other. Definite signs of that were already shown by what you did to your sister."

Michael hated his father's wisdom at times. His way of instilling reality hurt badly enough. Now he was faced with another reality ~ the prospect of prison.

Changing the subject back to the original context, Michael asked, "So what is the problem if it ain't any new charges?"

His father cleared his throat and said, "Your sister is the problem."

"How is that?" he asked nervously.

"It's like this, Son; the district attorney in your case has asked your sister to speak against you at your sentence hearing."

"And she's going to do it?"

"She's afraid of you."

"But I wasn't serious! Damn, how could she do me like this?"

"Your sister is asking the same thing 'bout you."

"Daddy, this isn't funny," he quickly said. "You don't know what's it's like in this place, and the penitentiary will be much worse if have to go."

"What do you want me to do, Son?"

"Talk to her for me, please. Let her know I was just trying to scare her."

Without warning, an officer came and informed them that they had to end their visit. So his father looked up at Michael and quickly said, "Son, I'll do my best, but I can't promise you anything. We also left you forty dollars to get whatever you'll need in here."

"Thanks, Dad."

"I love you, Son."

"Me, too," said his brother as they left Michael to rejoin the world of the living and free.

Michael had been incarcerated for a little over eleven months and now the day had finally come for him to be sentenced. He knew his chances for prison were great, despite what his lawyer had said. He knew the score better than anyone, because in jail, information flowed like illegal drugs. No one was left ill-informed or completely in the dark. Inmates knew about the judges, the district attorneys, and the *public pretenders (*slang for court appointed attorneys who performed below standards which often led to 95% of their clients going to jail or prison*)*. They knew that the 'so-called' court appointed lawyers were a part of a system designed to take most of them down. They worked right along with the district attorneys and judges. Their interest was in self-preservation, not in defense of the clients that were assigned to them. That's why many of them hurry to make a deal even if the person in question is seen as being clearly innocent. Court appointed attorneys are nothing but another spoke in the wheel that turns the controls of this legal form of slavery. If possible, it would be better for most minorities to represent themselves rather than to allow a court appointed attorney from the state to sell them out to the highest bidder.

Not only are African Americans victims of this cruel system, but anyone who is poor, uneducated, and unaware falls victim to a miscarriage of injustice. Hopefully, Michael wouldn't be added to the list of the betrayed.

The time had come for Michael's day in court. His case was called and he was escorted into courtroom four, division seven, in the Municipal Court of Compton, California, the judicial district of the county of Los Angeles.

Sweat began to pour profusely down the sides of Michael's face and under his arms as he scanned the courtroom for a familiar face. Surprisingly, to his left sat his whole family, including a few of his homeboys. It felt good to see them; but still, it didn't ease the tension and apprehension he felt.

As the Judge motioned for the hearing to begin, a representative of the State stood up and said, "We're at the sentencing hearing of The State of California vs. Michael Lewis, with the Honorable Judge Hugo Hill presiding."

After that was said, the representative for the state sat down as the district attorney stood up and said. "Your Honor, the defendant, Mr. Michael Lewis has been charged with Reckless Endangerment, Attempted Assault One, Brandishing a Loaded Firearm, Carrying a Concealed Weapon, and Assault in the fourth degree. In a plea bargain that was offered by the State of California, Mr. Lewis had agreed to plead guilty to the crime of Attempted Assault in exchange that the State would drop the other charges."

"And what other agreements were made as a result of Defendant Lewis' guilty plea?" The judge asked.

"The only promise made to the Defendant Lewis was that the State, along with his defense attorney would reserve the right to make certain recommendations in regards to his sentence."

"And what is your recommendation?"

The district attorney cleared his throat, paused in an effort to appear melodramatic, and then said, "Considering the seriousness and the intensity of Defendant Lewis' conduct, I recommend that he serve seven years in the California State Penitentiary, with three years' parole to follow, a fine and/or restitution to the victim which is also his sister in this case."

"Is there anything else?"

"Yes, there is your honor."

"Then proceed."

"I request to reserve the right to call the victim to the stand so she can convey to the court what she feels would be the appropriate sentence for the defendant."

"So granted," said the Judge as he turned to Michael's lawyer and said, "The floor is yours."

"Thank you, your Honor," Michael's lawyer responded as he rose. "The case brought before you today is a case of a young man crying out for help. I don't think we can address his need for help by sending him to the state penitentiary. It would only further the problem. Therefore, I recommend that he be sentenced to a year county time, with five years' probation to follow. I would ask for a period of that to be reduced to two years after completing an adult residency program that offers anger management, social skills development training, conflict resolution classes, and drug prevention classes."

"What is the history of his past criminal conduct?"

"He has only two juvenile priors, one for incorrigibility and the other for malicious mischief."

"Excuse me, your honor, but can I interject?" asked the district attorney.

"Yes, you may," said the judge.

Reading from a computer printout that was given to him by one of his assistants, he began by saying, "Defendant Lewis does have a minimal past criminal history, but that in itself is misleading, and I can establish that by this police contact report which shows that over a period of three years, Defendant Lewis had numerous police contacts."

"And what were these contacts for?" asked the Judge.

"He has several contacts for suspicion of arson, five for suspicion of burglary and theft, two for being a suspect in a murder, plus he's a known documented gang member."

"That's the reason why I made my recommendation for him to be placed in the Adult Residency Program," countered his lawyer.

"Doesn't prison offer such programs?" asked Judge Hill.

"Yes, they do, your Honor, but sending him to prison would make him a hero in the eyes of his peers. He'll never be able to get any real help if he's spending most of his time trying to defend an image brought on by the negative ills of the streets and prison."

"Are you saying that if I decide to send him to prison it would only cause him to further his endeavors in crime?"

"I believe so, your Honor."

"I see," said the Judge as he removed his glasses, rubbed his head and then peered out over the court-room. After a few moments, he said, "Both of you have presented some very valid points, but I would like to hear from the defendant's sister and parents before I make my decision in this case, and I prefer to con-duct these interviews separately within my chambers... Bailiff, would you please bring Ms. Marie Lewis to my chamber?"

"Yes, your Honor," said the bailiff as he led Michael's sister out of the courtroom.

"It's all up to what your sister says and how your parents respond," whispered Michael's lawyer.

Signing heavily, Michael said, "I just wish I could speak, too."

"You may have to do just that before this is all over," said his lawyer wearily.

"Have a seat, Ms. Lewis," said the Judge. "Now I know you're probably wondering why I decided to have you come to my chambers and speak with me privately rather than speak under oath in an open court."

"Yes, I was just wondering that."

"Well, my reason for doing this is because when family members have to testify against each other it has always been a very tense and delicate issue. Most of the time the delicate situation has the tendency to destroy the precious fabric that ties the family together. Therefore, cases that are under my care, I try my best to prevent that from happening. I would like to do that in this case, do you understand?"

"Yes, I do," she answered.

"That's good," said Judge Hugo Hill. "Now I want you to describe your relationship as to you and your brother."

Marie cleared her throat and then said, "Many people may not believe what I'm about to say but I love my brother regardless of what transpired between us. At times he may be insensitive to my feelings, but I know that's due to the negative environment he finds himself in every time he enters the street. But again, that's my little brother and I love him regardless. I feel that if you send him to prison it will only serve in making us both victims in this situation."

"So what does he do that you consider negative?"

"Crazy stuff...like, trying hard to be like the other kids in our neighborhood."

"Where do you live?"

"Right here in Compton, between Central and Alondra."

"Isn't that close to the Compton Airport?"

"Yes, it is."

"I know that neighborhood pretty well. In fact, I know a couple of police officers that used to live in that area. They told me that neighborhood is very dangerous, and drug ridden. I know that's not a good place to raise a family, but when that's all you can afford you have to try, right?"

"It may be that way for some, but it's not that way for everyone," she said.

"Then your brother must be one of those individuals who is like a magnet, constantly drawn to trouble."

"You can say that, but I think he's just trying hard to fit in and belong, but he's doing it with the wrong crowd, and for the wrong reasons."

"Is he a gang member?"

"I don't know really. He tries to dress and wear the same things that they wear, but again, I don't know."

The Judge smiled and then said, "Now tell me what happened between you two that caused you to be here today."

Tears began to form in Marie's eyes as she began to recall the incident in her mind. "Everything happened so fast," she began. "One minute I was telling him that he couldn't have a rag hangin' from his back pocket and the next moment we were fighting."

"Why did you tell him he couldn't have a rag hanging from his back pocket?"

"Because my mother had already told him he couldn't wear the rag around the house because it caused trouble, and she was afraid that the trouble would follow him home."

"What kind of rag can cause trouble?" The Judge asked, appearing slightly confused.

"Those different color head rags that gang members be wearing."

"Oh, you're talking about those bandannas that most people use as head bands to keep the sweat out of their faces."

"Yes, that's what I'm talking about."

"Now, I understand," said the Judge. "Your brother fought you because he felt you were trying to intimidate him, but all you were doing was enforcing the rules set by your parents."

"That's exactly right."

"What made him pull a gun on you?"

"I don't know, but my father went up to visit him last month and he told my father he did it just to scare me."

"Do you believe that?"

"Yeah," Marie answered weakly.

The Judge suddenly picked up the phone and said, "Bailiff, will you send in Defendant Lewis' parents and escort Ms. Lewis back to the court room? Thank you."

"Your honor," Marie called quickly.

"What is it, Ms. Lewis?"

"Please don't be too hard on my brother; he's really a good person."

Judge Hill smiled, and then said, "You'll have my decision shortly."

It took forty-five minutes for Judge Hill to interview Michael's parents and sister. But to him, it seemed like an eternity. He couldn't get his mind off the fact that he may go to prison, and the more he thought about it, the more nervous he became. He knew how to make it in jail, but prison was another thing altogether. He heard many stories of new convicts becoming punks, literally overnight, while other convicts fought it out with each other just so they could be the first to get a new piece of fresh tight ass. If that's what prison was truly about, he definitely didn't want any part of it.

Michael's chain of thoughts was interrupted when everyone stood up as the Judge reentered the courtroom.

"Be seated," said Judge Hill as he rifled through the notes he made during the interviews. After a few moments he looked up and said, "Will the defendant please rise?"

Michael looked over his shoulder as he rose. He wanted to see his family for what he presumed would be his last time for quite a while. He knew the crimes he committed against his family were too great to be overlooked, especially in front of a white judge.

Michael's thoughts were suddenly interrupted when the judge said, "In lieu of everything I gathered, I still haven't heard from you, Mr. Lewis, and I'm a firm believer that there are always two sides to every story. Therefore, do you have anything to add before I render my judgment?"

"Yes, I do your Honor."

"You may proceed then."

Michael didn't know where he got the nerve, but he suspected his incentive came from his fear of going to prison. He couldn't see himself going down without a verbal fight. With that thought in mind, he stepped forward and said, "Your Honor, what occurred between my sister and myself was truly an act of cowardice on my part. I got into a fight with her, and somewhere between the punches and the shouting, I found myself pulling a gun on her. But you have to believe me when I say I done it in order to scare her. I truly never meant her or anyone else any harm. I love my sister. I just responded ignorantly, and for that I'm sorry. I'm sorry for everything. I'm sorry for not being a responsible son to my parents and for all those times I failed to listen to them. I'm even sorry for being here."

"Is that all?' asked Judge Hill.

"I just want another chance. I don't wanna go to prison," he added tearfully.

"Mr. Lewis," said Judge Hill after a long silence. "You really don't have an extensive criminal record, but on the other hand, you have past police contacts that indicate a behavior pattern that's consistent with someone who has been involved in a lot of criminal activity but hasn't been caught yet. After hearing the recommendation of your parents and talking to your sister, I have the feeling that you can be rehabilitated. Therefore, I'm going along with the recommendation of your defense attorney. You will serve one year in the Los Angeles County Jail, with credit for any time served, five years' probation, but that will be reduced after your completion of the Adult Residency program. You will also complete a thousand hours of community service working in a homeless shelter. Another stipulation of your conditions will be that you will not associate with any known gang members or ex-felons. Nor will you carry or possess any firearms. If you violate any of these conditions I will personally sentence you to fifteen years in the California State Penitentiary. Now, do we have a firm understanding?"

"Yes sir, your Honor," he nervously answered.

"For your sake, I truly hope you understand."

"I do, sir," Michael said. "And thank you," he added.

"Next case!" shouted the Judge, as Michael was escorted back to jail.

Michael was elated and there was no other way to put it. The Judge had given him back his family, his life, and his freedom. Plus, he had given him a new chance, a chance that Michael found himself betraying over and over again despite the threat of spending fifteen years in prison. The threat didn't matter to Michael, because what he had to face within the streets of Compton, California was far greater than any threat of prison.

16

Ghetto Fallout

"It was originally said by a famous ghetto warrior that there is nothing in our book, the Qur'an that teaches us to suffer peacefully. Our religion teaches us to be intelligent. To be peaceful, be courteous, obey the law, respect everyone; but if someone puts his hand on you, send him to the cemetery..."

—Malcolm X

June 1975-1983 (Continued)

Pages of Michael's life began to fall in and out of order, like pieces of a jigsaw puzzle during his first two weeks of freedom. Every day negative influences assaulted his conscious and subconscious mind like waves upon the ocean attacking the shores of a deserted beach. He felt like one who was stranded between fact and fiction. Life for him had become chaotic, unbalanced, and unpredictable. He didn't know which way was up, and to tell the truth, he didn't care.

"Is anyone home?" Michael yelled as he knocked upon his parents' front door.

"We're in the back!" his mother answered.

Michael felt sort of strange as he stepped into the living room of his parents' home. He had been away for over a year, but it felt more like a decade. He stood there for a moment, reliving the episodes of the past that occurred between his sister and himself. As he stood there, the feelings of shame over-powered the depths of his conscience, and for a brief second, Michael felt like running out of the house. The feeling dissipated when his sister stepped into the living room and said, "I'm glad you're out of that awful place."

"Me too," he said, hesitantly.

Stepping toward Michael, his sister handed him some money and said, "Here, I know you're gonna need this, and don't tell mom about me giving you this money either."

"Okay," he said as he gave her a big hug.

Letting go of her, Michael said, "Marie, I want to thank you for your forgiveness and helping me out in court with the judge."

"Oh, that was nothing, little brother. I knew you didn't mean to hurt me, plus I'd rather have you here at home than being another statistic of prison violence."

"Damn girl, I didn't know you knew about prison statistics."

"If you would have taken the time to listen to me, you would have learned that I had once belonged to several organizations that represented the betterment of people of color."

"You got to be joking!"

"Nah, I'm serious…I use to be a follower of *Angela Davis* and *Elaine Brown*."

"Who are they?"

"They both were Black Panthers. In fact, Elaine Brown took over the Black Panther Party when Huey P. Newton was forced into exile."

"I never knew about women leading the Black Movement and I should have because when I was little I wanted to be a Panther."

"I remember that," his sister said, excitedly.

"You knew that? How? The only person I told was Daddy."

"That's who told me."

"But why did he tell you?"

"Because he knew I was active in the movement, and I was the only person who could have assisted you in your endeavors."

"But why didn't you help me?" he asked, curiously.

"I didn't help you because I was afraid."

"You were afraid of what?"

"I was afraid of losing you."

"Losing me to what?"

"To a system of violence that was destroying black males and black role models," she answered as she reflected. "During those days young black males were being assassinated on a daily basis. In fact, do you remember when Dr. Martin Luther King was killed? You were out in the streets up to no good, and we had become so upset with you because you had no idea what was really going on at that moment. If you did, the streets would have been the last place you wanted to be."

"How do you know that? *I was not afraid*, plus, I spend most of my time in the streets now, just like back then."

Marie paused for a moment and then said, "Things were much different back then than they are now. During those days, every black male in the city was a potential target of the police. Every black male was considered to be a revolutionary and an enemy of the state. This resulted in a mass hysteria, and black males were being gunned down on sight. I couldn't let that happen to you, especially after what they did to Little Bobby James Hutton."

"Who was he?"

"Bobby Hutton was one of the youngest ghetto soldiers of the Black Panthers, and like you, he had a lot of heart. Unfortunately, he died for the cause on April 6, 1968, just two nights after King's assassination."

"Who killed him?"

"The same people who are out there financing the war between the Crips and Bloods."

Michael couldn't say anything at the moment because all along he thought it was himself who was protecting his family from the violence of the streets, but he was wrong. His sister was the one who was actually sheltering the family from the violence of the oppressor.

"Marie," he began. "Why didn't you tell me all of this in the beginning?"

"Because I didn't think you were ready."

"But why tell me now?"

"Because, what you and your friends are doing is against everything I ever stood for, and you said yourself you wanted to be a Black Panther; but the Panthers weren't about killing one another. They were taught that the nature of the Panther is that he never attacks, but if anything attacks him or backs him into a corner, the Panther then comes up to wipe that aggressor out absolutely, resolutely, wholly, thoroughly, and completely."

"But Marie, like you said before, that was then. Things are now different. Brothers ain't trying to hear about that Afrocentric peace shit. All they care about is having some *snaps (slang for money), bustin' caps, and scoring themselves some black pussy."

"Is that what you're about?"

"To tell you the truth, I don't know what I'm about, nor do I have a specific belief."

Marie let out a heavy sigh and then asked, "What do you mean by that?

"It's not easy to explain, but I feel like a man caught between two worlds. On one hand, I enjoy gang banging. It's like a high without using drugs. You can put your skills to the test when conflict arises and shine like a celebrity at the end. But the down side is when you lose a homie in battle. Plus, you have to be on guard twenty-four hours a day. Therefore, you can't allow yourself to get caught slipping or else you can lose your life along with those who may be slipping along with you."

"Are you're saying we all can be in danger when you're around?"

"Not really, but shit happens."

"Then, why don't you just get out of the gang?"

"It's not that easy. You can't just say, time out; I don't wanna' play anymore. People have been killed on both sides, and the thirst for revenge runs deep. Sometimes you don't even have to be from a gang; just living in the neighborhood of a rival can make you a potential victim of gang violence."

"That's sad," she said. "No, it's mad. You're doing just what the oppressor wants you to do. The senseless killing of each other is a self-fulfilling prophesy that satisfies the ways and means of our oppressors. They have ya'll using their drugs, drinking their alcohol, and they got you pulling others into this massive vacuum of destruction and death ~ and you can't see because either you don't care, or you're afraid."

"What in the hell do you expect me to do? I can't change the world. I'm not the one who started this shit, and I won't be the last one to die from this madness," Michael said angrily.

"You can try by changing what's in yourself."

"I'm sorry," Michael said after a moment.

"Sorry for what?"

"For getting angry when you're just trying to help me understand."

"Don't worry, little brother; I do understand your position."

"Hey! What's taking you so long?" Michael's father shouted from the backyard.

"You better go out there," Marie said. "They call themselves surprising you with home style backyard barbecue, and you ain't heard it from me."

"Don't worry, your secret is safe with me," Michael said as he took off for the backyard.

Reaching the backyard, Michael was instantly greeted by his mother who said, "Look at my baby!"

"That ain't a baby, that's my grown man," countered Michael's father as he pulled him close to give him one of those big fatherly hugs. "Damn, you look good, Son," he said as he stepped back.

"Yes, he does," added his mother.

"We thought you forgot yo' way around the house," said Michael's father.

"I was in there talking to Marie; that's why it took me so long to come out."

"Don't worry 'bout that, Son. What matters is you're home, and you're alive and well."

"You're in time to take advantage of your Dad's bar-becue," added his mother, happily.

Even though Michael enjoyed the fact of being home among his family, he couldn't get over the feeling of being of out of place. He felt the love that was being displayed was more forced than genuine. Everyone moved about as if they were actors playing a role. The only person who seemed to show normalcy was his sister, and that was even stranger.

"What's wrong, sweetheart?" asked his mother.

"I was just thinking."

"Thinking 'bout what?"

"About getting a job and going to night school," he answered, lying.

"I thought the program you're in through your probation would satisfy the requirements for you to finish school."

"It does, but if I go to night school I can finish faster, plus I'll have less time to fall back into my negative ways."

"Now you're thinking like a responsible adult," said his father, proudly.

Michael's sister suddenly came into the backyard and interrupted them saying, "Momma, I can't make the potato salad."

"Why is that?" asked her mother.

"I can't because we're outta' mayonnaise."

"Oh, don't worry. I'll go and get some now."

Turning toward Michael, his mother said, "C'mon, I want you to ride with me."

Michael didn't want to go with his mother because he was already violating one of his conditions of probation by carrying a concealed weapon. But his fear of getting caught in the streets of Compton without an equalizer was greater than his fear of prison.

Pulling into traffic, Michael began to take in the scenery as his mother drove along Central Avenue.

It had been quite a while since he had been out on an errand with his mother. The last time was during Christmas, and he hated it because his mother was the type of individual who just couldn't walk into a store and get what she needed. She had to browse, touch, and examine everything she came in contact with. Just the thought of it made him ask, "We're going in just to get one thing, right?"

"Why you asked"

"Because momma, you're like the Navy, you'll turn a moment of shopping into an adventure."

"Aw boy, I'm just going up here to Thrifty's to grab some miracle whip, and a couple of other items and leave."

"Did you say Thrifty's?"

"Yes."

"Momma, I can't go there."

"Why is that?"

"C'mon, you know why I can't go there."

"I hope you're not talkin' 'bout that gang stuff."

"What other reason would I be talkin' 'bout?"

"I don't know, but you don't have to worry 'bout no gang members as long as you're with me."

"Momma, you must be crazy! Those fools don't care about me being with you or anyone one else."

"Boy, I'm not going anywhere else but Thrifty's, so deal with it."

"Can I stay in the car?"

"No."

It was no use. No matter what Michael said, she was adamant, and he knew from past experiences when his mother makes up her mind, the only thing that could change it would be an act of God, so Michael was praying that God would act now.

Michael and his mother weren't in the store ten minutes when all of a sudden he heard someone say, "What's up, Blood!"

Turning, he spotted six hardcore characters that belonged to the Campanella Park Piru gang. They all knew exactly who he was, which wasn't hard due to the bright blue shirt he was wearing along with the powder blue khakis.

"Look man," Michael quickly said. "I'm here with my mother."

"I don't give a fuck about your mother you *crab-ass (*a derogatory term members of the Blood gang use to disrespect Crips*) nigga!"

"You kids betta find yo' selves someone else to mess with," said his mother, surprising him with her boldness.

"Fuck you, bitch!" said one of the Pirus as he picked up a head of lettuce and threw it in the direction of Michael's mother.

What happened next was so chaotic that Michael couldn't believe his own eyes, but living through it made him a believer. To be perfectly honest, Michael would have been the last person to believe his mother would have stepped to someone the way she stepped to those Pirus.

Doing what came natural, Michael's mother used everything from the combination of cantaloupes to cucumbers and other food products to throw those kids off balance. But what really surprised Michael is when he pulled out his gun and started firing on those cowards. His mother didn't flinch one bit; instead, she worked her way along with Michael down the aisle until they reached the front entrance of the store. Then without saying a word, she disappeared; only to return a moment later, shouting from the car saying, "C'mon, get in!"

Michael quickly turned and fired two more rounds into the store for good measure before jumping into the car.

"Let's go!" she shouted once more.

Wasting no time, Michael jumped in and as he did so, his mother took off like she was a getaway driver in a bank robbery.

Heading down Rosecrans, Michael told her to take a right on Wilmington when all of sudden she said, "I should take your ass straight back to jail!"

"Take me to jail for what? I didn't start that madness!"

"I'm not talkin' 'bout that.'

"Then what are you talkin' 'bout?"

"I'm talkin' 'bout you having that gun. You know that's a violation of your probation."

Michael didn't say another word because he couldn't believe how cool his mother had reacted under fire. Another puzzling thing was how she acted as if nothing happened while threatening him about probation.

Laughing slightly, his mother said, "You ain't ever riding with me again. In fact, we can't even walk the streets together."

"I tried to tell you, but you wouldn't listen to me."

"You ain't gotta worry 'bout that anymore...and give me that damn gun, too!"

"What you gonna do with it?" He asked as they pulled in front of their house.

"I'm going to learn how to use it, especially now with all you crazy-ass kids running the streets."

"Are you gonna tell Dad what happened?"

"First, I'm going to call the police and make a report."

"You can't do that; I'll go back to jail."

"Is this gun clean?"

"What do you mean by that?"

"Is this gun legal, or is it stolen…that's what I'm asking."

"Oh yeah, it's clean."

"Then don't worry 'bout the police and going back to jail."

"But you said the same thing about me being able go to that store."

"Well, believe me; you won't go to jail because I'm going to tell em' I done the shooting when those kids attempted to rob me, and I don't think any of those hoodlums will be coming forward to contest the validity of my story."

"Have you forgotten about the people at the store? They had to see what happened."

"Boy, soon as you started shooting, everyone in the store tried to make themselves invisible. Besides, when was the last time you saw anyone coming forward to be a witness to an incident involving gang members?"

"They don't."

"Then you ain't got anything to worry about."

With that said, Michael just laughed. Then, as an afterthought he said, "We still didn't get the mayonnaise."

"After all we have been through, that damn mayonnaise can stay on the shelf."

"I know you're not afraid to go back, are you?" he asked, smiling.

"Nah, I just don't wanna' be banging under false pretenses."

"You had to go there, huh." Michael said, following her into the house.

This one incident brought Michael and his mother closer. It also sparked her interest in forming a community organization that dealt with children involved with drugs and gang violence, but the organization never got off the ground because there were too many black folks talking loud and doing nothing. The rest were too lazy, too scared, or too tired and poor to even care. Therefore, over the ensuing year's violence among ghetto youth continued to rise, and it was increasing daily until it reached the affluent area of Westwood, a suburb of Los Angeles. It was there, one of their citizens was accidentally gunned down in violent gang crossfire. As a result, the city of Los Angeles vowed to launch an all-out effort to crush the rising threat of neighborhood street gangs. But why did it take such an incident as this to get outsiders involved? Didn't Compton merit the same assistance? Didn't the authorities have accurate figures on the rising threat of violence and gang homicides that were occurring in and around Los Angeles on a daily basis? For more information, see the Homicide Zone chart and read the article on homicides in the Appendix.

The Homicide Zone

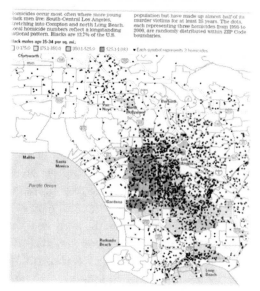

17

The Mark of the Beast

"In the ghetto, everyone seems to be on the run, some running from the evils of drugs and violence; some are running from the responsibilities of life, while others are running for no other reason but to survive..."
—Daishun Neal

August 1979-1984

Between 1979 and 1984, gang violence was slowly beginning to rise, but after 1984 gang violence would become completely out of control. Communities within South Central Los Angeles had become cities baptized by violence and bloodshed. Drive-by shootings were as common as the common cold. Ghetto youths were being eulogized and buried at a rate of one to three a day, some weeks that number would climb as high as three to five a day. The murders that were occurring had become mafia-like in nature, and there was no such thing as sacred ground. A person could be easily gunned down in front of his house or church while his family and friends looked on.

What made things even worse was the war between the Crips and Bloods was no longer a war over disrespect, territory and revenge. It now was a war over drugs. This made every gang an enemy to the other. Even one's own comrade couldn't be trusted, and that caused the streets of Los Angeles to become a literal war zone.

With this deadly increase in violence, the Los Angeles based Crip gang began to suffer the most casualties because they were much larger in number than their rivals... So large that some Crip sets had to travel miles to engage an enemy. But the rules of engagement changed with the advent of such drugs as Phencyclidine (*PCP*) and crack cocaine. Now Crips were killing everything and everyone who threatened the precious flow of drugs; they were even killing one another.

Drugs became the key factor that kept the fire of violence raging within the ghetto streets of Los Angeles, but it wasn't drugs like marijuana or PCP. It was crack cocaine, which became the Sheriff of the Ghetto, and it was as dangerous as any street gang. Everyone was affected in one way or another. It was even reported in the high vice crack areas such as Watts, Compton, Lynwood, and some other sections of Los Angeles, more and more children were taking over as the head of the family. They were selling crack, which led to them being able to earn most of the family income. Even teenage girls were leaving their families to form gangs of their own in order to sell crack cocaine. This alone made the threat of gangs more prevalent.

Street gangs had become a major factor in Michael's life. It was a lifestyle he sought, worshipped, and revered. In this capacity he was often honored, feared, and even preyed upon, but that's what made it so exciting. Michael felt like a pirate traveling upon the waters of the world in pursuit of worldly riches ~ this was his life, and to be anything else was like treason against his soul, which at the moment belonged to none other than the devil, himself.

Michael successfully evaded the police for over a year while conforming to the terms of his probation. Most of the time, he felt like an actor playing the role of two characters, by day, he was the respectable son of Mr. and Mrs. Lewis, but by night, he was Mr. Wheatgerm, the notorious Crip of Compton, California who roamed the ghetto streets in search of the weak, the unlucky, and anyone who wasn't protecting their riches. Michael was the good, the bad, and the ugly all in one package.

"Damn cuz, we been rollin' all night and we still haven't found anyone to fuck wit'," said Michael's homie Ducc, who was a member of the original Palm and Oak Street Crips.

"Yeah, it's like them slobs know we're out on the hunt tonight," added Big Juney.

"It's either that or they're out doing the same thing that we're doing."

"I doubt that," said Ducc.

"Why you say that?" Michael asked.

"Cause you know them suckas ain't got the heart to roll through our 'hood in order to catch us slipping."

"They ain't gotta' roll through the mothafuckin' 'hood to catch us slipping." Michael said. "All they have gotta do is wait for us to carelessly slip into their 'hood and smoke our ass while we're trying to grab a double chili cheese burger or some pussy."

"I ain't never gone to no burger joint in slob territory," said Ducc.

"Yes, you have, cuz," Michael said quickly.

"And when was that?"

"The other day when you were taking me back to my house and we stopped at the Jack-n-Box on Central Avenue, just one block south of Compton Boulevard.

"I didn't know that was Blood territory."

"Well, it is."

"Why didn't you say something?"

"Because I thought you knew. We both were *heated (*slang for packing a concealed weapon*), so there was no cause to worry."

"But, what if we weren't heated?"

"Then, I would have told your ass."

They fell silent for a few moments as they approached a stoplight at the intersection of Century Boulevard and Compton Avenue, which is the territory of Bounty Hunters, one the most notorious Blood gangs in all of Los Angeles. Every Crip within the city made sure they kept a wide berth when it came to the Bounty Hunters.

"Say cuz," Ducc suddenly said. "How much gas we got?"

"Why?"

"Because don't you realize what 'hood we're in?"

"Yeah, I know what 'hood we're in but that still doesn't tell me why you want to know about how much gas we have left."

"I tell you why nigga, if we run out of gas over here, everybody will be hearing 'bout our stupid asses on the Channel Seven news."

"They'll be hearing only 'bout you," Michael countered.

"Why you say that?" Big Juney asked.

"I say that because if we were to run outta gas over here, I'm not gonna be the one standing 'round waiting for them Bounty Hunters to catch my stupid-ass. I'm blastin' them niggas dead on sight, and that goes for anyone else who runs up."

"I'll be doing the same thing too, cuz," Ducc added as they pulled off when the light turned green.

Again they rode in silence until a lime green low riding Chevy pulled alongside of them. Inside were three young gangsters who appeared to be Crips. From their menacing appearance, Michael could see that they were sizing them up, and they were doing the same. After rolling about three blocks in this manner, the guys in the other cars decided to *hit them up (*a gesture that gang members make with their hands and fingers to show what gang they're from, and also a gesture used to formally challenge anyone who is not a Crip or who is not from their particular Crip set*) with a Crip hand gesture. Michael and his crew returned the gesture by hitting them up with Crip signs of their own. After that, they smiled, nodded their heads, turned down a back street, and disappeared into the darkness of the night.

"That was close," said Big Juney.

"Yeah, we're lucky those guys were Crips," Michael added.

"Cuz, I don't care if they were Crips or not, I'm straight up like death, an equal opportunity employer," said Ducc.

"What do you mean by that?" Michael asked curiously.

"It means that he'll kill a Crip just as fast as a Blood."

Michael lowered his head for a moment to hide the displeasure that was clearly visible upon his face. He didn't want his comrades to think he had become weak since leaving jail. In many ways he had changed, but not for the better. He was stronger mind-wise, and he still loved being a Crip. What Michael didn't like was all that Crip on Crip violence, especially after knowing how many of their O.G.'s had died in battle at the hands of their true rivals. It just didn't make sense to him. The Bloods were their true enemies, and that's who he was at war with, not Crips. But who was Michael to convey that fact? He couldn't change this new pattern of violence. Everyone was too deeply involved, too crazy, and too stupid to stop, including him. Michael knew the ignorance among his ghetto comrades ranked supreme, and the perpetrators behind this violence influenced them in the killing of themselves; in most cases, without them even knowing it.

Proof of this is when Michael read an article that stated during the period between 1979 and 1999 certain businesses, clothing designers, and advertisers started producing products and advertising slogans that perpetuated the violence among black youth. Some of this was done in ignorance, but not all of it. For instance, the famous clothing designer, Calvin Klein, had designed shirts, hats, pants, and other apparel bearing the symbol or emblem cK which means Crip Killer. When gang affected youth see these emblems they purchase the apparel just because it represents the gang they're tied to. The same goes for other products such as British Knights, Columbian Knights, K swiss, and Burger King.

Michael felt after all the information that has been compiled on gangs; one would think certain people in governmental positions of power would at least make a plea to these clothing designers, asking them to tone down certain elements of their products that are known for perpetuating violence among youth in gangs.

This shouldn't be hard to do, especially when this government, at the drop of hat, can send troops abroad when they think another country is manufacturing weapons of mass destruction. The same should be considered with street gangs and the variables that influence such a culture.

Now recently, there have been efforts where a few politicians were attempting to get measures passed in regards to rap lyrics. Why? Are they afraid these lyrics will influence their children in becoming society's next generation of gang members and thugs? Have they discovered in some way, shape or form that certain rap lyrics and video games perpetuate violence? Have they discovered the violence that once was confined within the minority community is now being proliferated within the realms of their own affluent communities? Of course they know, that's why the boy can no longer cry wolf.

"Is it true?" Michael suddenly asked as he snapped back into the reality of things.

"Is what true?" asked Ducc.

"Is it true that you'll kill a Crip just as fast as a Blood?"

"Hell yes, without a doubt."

"When did you start feeling like that?"

"The day you Compton niggas started tripping."

"Because of that you'll kill a Crip?"

"Listen cuz, we're cool wit' you because you're like one of our own homies from the hood, along with Tiny Man, Turtle and the rest of you Compton niggas who attend Lynwood High and hang out in the 'hood representing Palm and Oak. In reality, you niggas are from Compton, and a lot of your homeboys be *set tripping (*a term meaning people who start trouble when saying that their organization is better than another*), and to the point where a nigga has no choice but to smoke 'em."

"Then the beef is not about Cripping, it's about disrespect."

"Nah cuz, it's about set tripping."

Michael paused for a moment to let what Ducc said sink into his mind. The term, "set tripping" was a new concept that Michael failed to understand. He guessed that was because he was selective in whom he dealt with on a daily basis. The brothers Michael ran the streets with were notorious Blood killers and currency chasers. Set tripping off of other Crip sets wasn't what they were groomed to do. But it was happening all around them, and sooner or later, Michael knew he would be doing the same thing. That's if he lived that long.

"Say cuz," Michael said after a moment. "Everyone has someone in their 'hood who is a shit starter, but most of the time the shit starts on the account of a female and not behind a brother."

"How do you figure that?" Big Juney asked.

"Well, it's kinda' hard to explain, but let me put it this way. Remember when we all went to that house party over in North Long Beach?"

"The party with all those fine bitches from all those different 'hoods?"

"Yeah, that's the party I'm talking 'bout."

"But cuz, everyone at that party was set tripping," said Juney.

"I know, that's the point I'm trying to make," Michael said, impatiently.

"I don't quite follow you, cuz," said Ducc.

Michael paused for a moment to allow several cars that were traveling close behind them to pass. After seeing them disappear into the darkness of the night, He continued by saying, "How many different sets were at that party?"

"There was whole lot, cuz."

"And how many did we have beef with?"

"None until we came to that party."

"And do you remember how the beef started?"

"Not really."

"Well, I do.'

"Then how did it start?"

"It started behind some stupid-ass bitches."

"What? I don't remember any bitches starting those fights."

Michael smiled, and then said, "Cuz, you don't remember when the song by Parliament was playing and those bitches started saying, it's a party over here, and it's a party over there, and then, niggas tried to impress those ho's by saying, N 'hood is over here, and Kelly Park is over there, and so on…"

"Yeah, I remember that!" said Ducc, excitedly.

"Well, if you remember that, then you should remember how those bitches added heat to the situation by saying that certain 'hoods in the city were harder than others. And with the combination of alcohol, weed, black pride, and the prospect of sweet black pussy, niggas started beefing with each other for no other reason than the word of a bitch."

"Damn, cuz is right," said Big Juney.

"I never looked at it that way until now," added Ducc.

"Now you see, and believe this…any time you find trouble lurking about, you'll find a bitch not too far behind."

Everyone started laughing as Big Juney said, "Nigga, your ass is crazy."

"Yeah cuz, you sound just like a fuckin' ghetto Farrakhan," added Ducc.

"I don't know about being no ghetto Farrakhan… I'm just a nigga who watches things a little closer than most people."

"Then why ain't you watchin' those police who have been following us for the last few blocks?"

"What police?"

"I was just kidding, cuz."

"You shouldn't be fucking 'round like that, especially when you know we're heavily heated."

Their conversation ceased because from out of nowhere appeared three L.A. Sheriff Police cruisers who were trailing closely behind them.

"Cuz, hit a right!" said Ducc nervously.

"Give me the straps!" Big Juney added.

"Give you the strap, for what?" Michael stupidly asked.

"Do you wanna catch a case?"

"Hell nah!"

"Then I'm throwing these mothafucka's!"

With that said, Michael hit a hard right, then another and another until he reached an alleyway. There, he made a quick left with sirens wailing not too far away in the background.

"Did you throw 'em?" Michael asked as they hit Tweedy Boulevard.

"Hell yes, a long time ago, cuz."

"That's cool then," Michael said as they slowly proceeded up the boulevard.

"There they are," shouted Big Juney.

"I see 'em!"

"Just drive slow, cuz."

"Alright," Michael said.

As Michael drove onward, he wondered why the police didn't pull them over immediately, but his question was soon answered when they spotted an additional caravan of police cruisers blocking the intersection ahead of them.

"Pull over!" shouted the police from a bullhorn speaker system that was mounted within the front grille of their car.

Complying with their order, Michael slowly pulled the car over to the far side of the boulevard.

"Say cuz," Michael said quickly. "Unlock your doors, roll down the windows and place your hands in full view. We don't wanna give these trigger happy pecker-woods a reason to blast us."

"I know that's right," said Ducc.

After pulling over, eight policemen converged with weapons drawn and bright spotlights shining on them from all directions. The glare was so irritating that they had to close their eyes in order to prevent them from being temporarily blinded. None of them was about to raise a hand or a finger, because they had enough common sense to know any sudden movement on their part would spark a barrage of bullets, instantly sending them to that big blue paradise in the sky, or in their case ~ straight to hell.

As the police approached the car, another police, quite a distance away, ordered Michael to place his hands on the steering wheel.

Slowly and carefully, he complied, and when he did so a police nearest to Michael said, "Unlock your door."

"It's already unlocked," he said nervously.

Satisfied, the police opened his door and quickly placed his large caliber weapon that looked like a can-non, into Michael's face and said, "I want you to place your hands in the air and then step slowly out the vehicle."

Again he complied.

"Now get on your knees and place both your hands on the back of your head and interlock your fingers."

Once again he complied, and as he did, two policemen raced over to where he was, cuffed him, and quickly carried Michael away to an awaiting police cruiser.

The procedure was quickly repeated with the rest of them until they all were safely restrained and subdued. Now they had to endure the process of waiting for them to search the car, run warrant checks, and run them through their system of street interrogation.

After about thirty minutes, one of the sheriff deputies came over to where they were being held and said, "There was a drive-by shooting that occurred earlier tonight at a hamburger stand called Stops, and ya'll fit the description of the shooters."

"We ain't done no shootin'. We don't even have guns," Michael quickly said.

"We'll find that out soon enough."

"What do you mean by that?"

"We're bringing the witness to the shooting over to I. D. you all."

"Bring 'em on," Michael said, feeling somewhat relieved.

It took about an hour and ten minutes for them to be taken through the system of identification. One by one, they were made to stand before a spotlight as the witness looked them over, and by the grace of God none of them were picked out. They even came out squeaky clean on the warrant checks and that made the police mad as hell.

Without warning, a police sergeant approached them, and one by one, he checked their arms, chest, and neck for tattoos, and upon finding them he said, "So what I see standing before me is a bunch of gay-ass *crab (*the word crab is a derogatory term bloods use in reference to Crips*) niggers, and since you want to be hard, I have something very special planned for you niggers."

He then laughed as he walked away, only to return with his deputy at his side. "Deputy Smith, I want you to take these crab-ass niggers to our special no crab allowed zone, and release their asses' right there."

"What about their car?" he asked.

The sergeant didn't reply. Instead, he walked over to their car, removed a long flashlight from a hook that was attached to his belt, and without provocation, he smashed out one of their headlights and a rear taillight. He then turned toward them and said, "Write 'em a citation for operating a vehicle that's not up to code, and then have the damn thing towed."

"Damn," Michael said under his breath.

Quickly, the officer placed them in the back of his cruiser and drove them for what seemed like miles to a location that was unfamiliar to them.

"Where are we at?" Michael whispered.

"I don't know," answered Ducc.

"I think we'll find out soon enough," added Big Juney.

The Sheriff Deputy suddenly turned left off Avalon onto Eighty-fourth Street where he slowly cruised until he reached the middle of the block. He then stopped, exited his cruiser, and ordered them to get out. As they complied, the Sheriff's Deputy grabbed his bullhorn and said, "Hey you slobs, I just brought you some fresh crab meat!"

Without saying a word, they took off running like soldiers caught behind enemy lines. House by house, yard by yard, and alley by alley they traveled until they reached the safety of Crip territory. There they slowed their pace and spoke for the first time in an hour.

"Are you alright, cuz?"

"Yeah man," answered Ducc.

"What about you, Juney?"

"I won't be alright until we reach the 'hood."

"We don't have too much farther to go," Michael said wearily.

"Let's call someone to come and git' us," Ducc said.

"Hell nah, cuz!" shouted Big Juney.

"Why?"

"Because the police might roll up on us while we're waiting for our ride. Then we'll have to do this shit all over again. And I doubt if we'll be lucky a second time around."

"He's right cuz," Michael said. "Let's just keep walking down these back streets until we reach the 'hood."

"Alright then," said Ducc.

It took them every bit of three hours to reach their neighborhood. When they arrived, daylight was already there, awaiting them. But they survived and they had a story to tell, a story that most ghetto soldiers never live to tell about. As Michael pondered upon this fact, he wondered how many more times would the mighty hand of God reach out and intervene, sparing their lives just so they could have another day to fall deeper and deeper into the realms of ignorance ~ this opportunity wasn't given to everyone.

18

The Struggle for Life

"In the urban ghetto black youth are much like the river salmon, swimming downstream in search of prestige, honor, glory, and worldly riches, then swimming back upstream after realizing what they were searching for was actually chasing them ~ death, an element of reality from which there's no escape..."
—Kevin Lewis

November 1983

Summer had come and gone, and no one seemed to notice, but this was because of the common occurrence of death, which was now happening all around Michael and his crew. It seemed as if gang members were randomly being killed when they least expected, and there was no one to blame but their own selves.

In Michael's eyes, society had distanced itself from them as they rode about like cowboys from a distant past, drinking, shooting, and looting at will. Like serial killers, they stalked and hunted each other for the thrill of it, and they felt no remorse as they extinguished the lives of those close to them.

This was the lifestyle that most black youth found themselves living; some were forced into it by the absence of a father, some by the lack of economics within the community, some by the brutality from the police, and others by the rage of it all. Michael observed this fact every day as he journeyed about aimlessly. He saw it in the accused. He saw it in the eyes of helpless fathers as they stood out on the corners and in alleyways, talking big, while drinking that liquid pride. He even saw it in the faces of those countless mothers as they struggled by any means to take care of children that had been abandoned over the passage of time.

Michael also read about the statistics that had been compiled over the years in reference to the conditions of black youth. The question that was asked over and over again was: *When will people wake up to the fact and realize that what is happening to the American black youth is a crisis?* Not just any crisis, but a serious disease that should concern all of America. In an article written by Leonard Pitts Jr., an author and columnist for the *Miami Herald* on social issues, he posed the following question to society: *"Imagine for a moment that one-third of all caucasian youth were being lost to the criminal justice system. Does anyone pretend that this would not command attention at the highest levels of government? Can anyone believe we would not have our finest minds working hard on the question of why this was happening? We would not be content to simply rope those youths off for even longer periods of time in some dark corner of society encircled by barbwire and guarded posts. We would make it our business to save them. We would understand that in saving them, we save ourselves, but who will make that connection with our black youth? Who speaks with urgency of the need to take them back from the forces that seek to destroy them?"*

No one! Michael said to himself angrily. He believed this because black citizens had become too afraid to rock the boat, too comfortable in their own ignorance, and too tolerant of the conditions by which they live. Like their ancestors, many blacks had been reduced to singing songs of "we shall overcome," while their children rape, maim, and murder one another at will.

Michael also believed that this problem was developed by a system that instructed black people on how to admonish and raise their children. This is the same system that sanctioned and legalized racism. *How can anyone trust such a system? Don't black people know how to raise their own children? Hasn't it been said that if you spare the rod you ruin the child, but if you use the rod, you can instill the proper morals and guidance a child would need in order to survive within an environment that is designed to destroy him?*

Gangs and drugs weren't the only things that threatened Michael and his counterparts. There was peer pressure through the subliminal advertisement of alcohol, cigarettes, and other products that are harmful to black youth. Then there were negative influences in their music, video games, and even on television in the countless acts of violence that are propagated and revered in many of the action packed movies and sitcoms shown twenty-four hours a day to youth nationwide.

Under such brainwashing, Michael felt that he as well as other minority youth lacked a chance at being successful. They witnessed violence within their homes, they saw it in the streets, they heard it in their music, and they also saw it being glorified and condoned on television. But when these same youths committed their own acts of violence, society stepped back and painted a horrendous picture of them, often calling them "animals," "little monsters," "callous," "unfeeling," and "insidious." These labels may be true, but how can those who create the laws, pass measures, govern communities, and hold positions of control, Federal and State, call these youth dreadful things when they are the very people who created the conditions by which these things exist?

When Dr. Frankenstein created his monster, did he not have some idea the acts of violence his monster was capable of committing? Didn't the U.S. government know beforehand the destruction the atom bomb would cause? Then, the founding fathers of this country, and the individuals that came after them, knew the cause and effect that institutional slavery would have on blacks. In fact, Michael read in the Political Debates Between Lincoln and Douglas (1897), in which Abraham Lincoln, himself, stated (Fourth Joint Debate at Charleston, Mr. Lincoln's Speech, September 18, 1858):

"I will say, then, that I am not, nor ever have been, in favor of bringing about in any way the social and political equality of the white and black races—that I am not, nor ever have been, in favor of making voters or jurors of Negroes, nor of qualifying them to hold office, nor to intermarry with white people; and I will say in addition to this that there is a physical difference between the white and black races . . . I, as much as any other man, am in favor of having the superior position assigned to the white race."

Abraham Lincoln even further exerted that blacks and whites should be separated, that they could never be equal, nor hold any position along the side of a white man. These words were proclaimed in the following paragraphs:

"You and we are different races. We have between us a broader physical difference than exists between any other two races. Whether it is right or wrong I need not discuss; but this physical difference is a great disadvantage to us both, as I think. Your race suffers greatly, many of them, by living among us, while ours suffers from your presence. In a word, we suffer on each other. If this were admitted, it affords a reason, at least, why we should be separated."

"Even when you cease to be slaves you are yet far removed from being placed on equality with white people. On this broad continent not a single man of your race is made the equal of a single man of ours.

"Go where you are treated the best, and the ban is still upon you. I cannot alter it if I would. See your present condition, the Country engaged in war, our white men cutting one another's throats – and then consider what we know to be the truth; – But for your race among us there would be no war, although many men engaged on either side do not care for you one way or another. It is better for us both therefore to be separated."

—Abraham Lincoln

After reading this material, Michael believed by design, through a cruel invention, that some of the caretakers of America were able to separate black families, destroy their language, their culture, and even their way of thinking. They instilled in them, with the advent of slavery, a reign of terror that was as common as Hitler had done to the Jews. With the Jews, their violent persecution occurred abroad, at the hands of the Germans. With African Americans, their violent oppression occurred here in America, at the hands of American pioneers who are still in the practice of annihilating as many blacks as they can through a systematic program of violence and displacement. As a result, many African Americans have not recovered from the brutality of American oppression, and some white Americans still view the African American as nothing more than subhuman.

Michael laughed inwardly as he thought about these things. He remembered how he tried to explain these things to his homies and how they would argue with him saying that the Jews had it harder. Michael would counter their argument by saying, as of today, Jewish Americans control a sizeable amount of the wealth in this nation. They have a strong family structure, as well as a strong political voice. Most of their children can afford to attend the finest institutions of learning and very few are confronted with the social ills of poverty, drugs, the absence of a father figure, and gang violence ~ even though in New York there are some conditions of poverty and gang warfare among Jewish citizens. However, it has never risen to the level that blacks have experienced. Also, after suffering German persecution, being murdered in the millions, the Jewish people, once reaching America, were able to break free from the negative conditions of German oppression, (psychological and physical), and function as "accepted" American citizens. On the other hand, the African Americans still remain persecuted, hated, and unaccepted in many ways, especially within the judicial system that governs them.

Michael even asserted that according to the National Criminal Justice Commission, blacks account for 13% of regular drug users, 35% of the drug possession convictions, but 74% of all drug possession prison sentences. A black male defendant pays a higher bail than a comparable white one, is significantly more likely to suffer incarceration before trial, is less likely than his white counterpart to negotiate a lenient plea bargain, and can expect to serve more time for the same crime.

A black defendant is also more likely to be sentenced to death than a white one that commits the same crime. The killer whose victim is white is eleven times more likely to be sentenced to death than a white one whose victim is black. The commission report also points out that, though it is true that African Americans commit proportionately more crimes than whites, it is also true that African American crime rates have remained consistent proportionately since the middle 1970's. In other words, Michael went on to say, blacks are committing about the same proportion of crimes as they did a quarter century ago, but they're being incarcerated more ~ a hell of a lot more, and for crimes that occurred as the result of the past and present conditions purposely created by none other than the American Frankenstein. *So therefore, who is at fault, the one who creates the condition by which they know crime will occur, or the one who commits the crime?*

After making his case, Michael's homies just laughed and said, "That's why we don't trust anyone but us, and if we steal and kill, it ain't our fault, it's theirs."

Now taking all of this into account, one shouldn't be surprised when they see the urban ghetto youth congregating and conspiring to destroy that which threatens to destroy them ~ and many people cry out for help when this violence threatens the borders of their comfort zone. But no one cries out for help when these youth are threatened by drugs, gang violence, police brutality and other social ills that affect the minority community.

Therefore, many people in society are content as long as the minority youth contain the violence of their lives within the boundaries of their social zones.

Michael pondered about another article he read in reference to prisons, which stated that in the past, prisons were for some time utilized as a means for rehabilitation among citizens who commit certain crimes. But today, prisons are erected for profit. They are the panacea for unemployment in different communities across the nation, and they cater to a certain social class as well. After all, you can't keep a prison in operation if the conditions by which one comes to prison cease to exist. Just the thought of this should cause one to seriously think about the forces behind the badge, as well as those who occupy certain positions in government. Politicians have led the nation to believe that there is no other cure for these aforementioned problems, but there is; they just don't want to eradicate the problem. Why? It makes money; after all, if it doesn't make dollars, then it doesn't make sense. (Pelaez, Vicky. 2014. *El Diario-La Prensa*. NY: Global Research. The Prison Industry in the US: Big Business or a New Form of Slavery? and Lee, Suevon. 2012. By the Numbers: The U.S.'s Growing For-Profit Detention Industry. *ProPublica*.)

For weeks, Michael and his homies had been planning to rob the Church's Chicken fast food outlet that was not too far from where they all hung out. They had been without money for months and they needed some in order to score some PCP, which would change their status from being financially insolvent to being financially set.

It seemed as if the entire neighborhood was involved in the sale, manufacture or handling of PCP in one way or another. Overnight, PCP had become the ghettos' most wanted drug. Like the sacred waters of *Zam Zam (*an ancient well of Arabia which flows to this very day*), people travel for miles just to get a *dip (*slang for a taste of a certain drug*). For many this dip would become a trap to which countless black men and women would fall prey. Like zombies, they wander around in a chaotic state of mental aberration while having delusions of the mind and exhibiting wild behavior. Many would kill themselves as they descend into a world of fictitious animation. Others would act upon deep hidden fantasies and inhibitions, while others who were shy and withdrawn would suddenly become vivacious and vociferous.

The ghetto gangster, slash dope dealer, slash hustler, slash ghetto entrepreneur saw this only as a means of profit and entertainment. They didn't care about the consequences or the receiving end of their acts because most of them didn't believe in the element of cause and effect, karma, or God. Living this way allowed them to feel immune to the evil that their hands set forth. Most of them would continue to dwell within this state of mind until they became victims themselves; after all, what comes up also must come down. That's just another part of human nature.

"Say cuz, what's taking that bitch so long?"

"We just got here, cuz...be patient," Michael said, as he looked at his watch. "Besides, it's only 1:45 p.m. and she told us that she'll have someone dumping the trash exactly at two o' clock. So let's use the extra little time we have to make sure we got everything right."

"All right cuz," said Tweedy Bird.

It was a rarity to get gang members from different neighborhoods to work together on a *lick (*slang for robbery, burglary, etc.*), but like the old saying goes: '*money and greed are the route to evil.*' These brothers also added another element to that adage, which is: *money and greed are the motivation by which many will steal, maim, and murder their own homeboys in order to have it all to themselves.*

Shaking his ill feeling, Michael turned to Birdman, who was also from Nutty Blocc, and asked, "Say cuz, what are you gonna do with your share of the take?

"That depends."

"That depends on what?"

"On how much we get."

"According to the bitch, they always stack about eight hundred dollars just before two o' clock every Friday."

"If that true, then there's a whole lotta' chicken eating mothafucka's in this 'hood," said Tweedy Bird.

Laughing, Ducc said, "What are we gonna give the bitch for helping us out?"

"Some of this dick!" said Birdman, grabbing his crotch.

"Say cuz, I know you niggas ain't gonna change up on the game now," Michael quickly interjected.

"Cuz," Ducc began. "If eight hundred dollars is all we're gonna get outta this, then that bitch gotta' wait."

"And what if she snitches?"

"That's not going to happen," said Tweedy Bird.

"I don't see it that way, cuz," Michael said. "That bitch could easily tell the police that we forced her to cooperate, and then what would we do?"

For a moment everyone was lost in thought. Each man intoxicated by the element of greed. No one truly wanted to share their part of the take, yet no one was willing to risk their freedom over a foolish move.

"Let's just stick to the original script," Tweedy Bird suddenly said.

"Yeah, I'm wit that cuz," added Ducc.

"I'm down with it, too," Michael said.

Turning to Birdman, they all asked, damn near simultaneously, "What about you?"

"I told ya'll in the beginning that I'm a full time Crip, not a damn dope dealer!"

"Then how do you expect us to cop, bank, and extend our *ends?" (*Slang for money*). "Cuz, you all will have plenty of scratch to git the *water (*slang for PCP*) you'll need to start business."

"But we agreed that we all would put in on this," said Ducc.

"No, I didn't cuz. I said if we scored more than eight hundred, then I would put in on the water, but we don't know what we're gonna git once we get inside."

"That's why we're gonna make em' open the safe, empty the registers, and their pockets," said Tweedy Bird.

"We didn't discuss that, cuz," Michael said.

"We'll face it, cuz. If we're going inside, we might as well git it all."

"He's right," added Ducc.

"Well, let's go," Michael said, as he opened the door.

As planned, the back door of Church's Chicken opened, and out walked one of the employees carrying a large bag of garbage that never reached its destination.

Like second nature, Birdman swung into action placing a small .32 automatic into the small section of the employee's back, and said, "If you wanna be a hero, then here's yo' chance."

"I don't want any problems," said the employee, barely audibly.

"You won't have any problems as long as you do exactly as I say, understand?'

"Yeah man, I understand."

After securing an understanding, Birdman and the employee eased their way into the back of Church's Chicken. He then motioned for the rest of them to come inside after seeing that everything was cool.

"Look at this place," whispered Tweedy Bird, as he stepped inside.

"Damn," Ducc exclaimed. "This place looks like a fucked up slaughter house."

"I never seen so much nasty shit," Birdman added.

"Fuck all that shit, cuz. We didn't come here for no health inspection, let's handle our business and git the fuck outta here," Michael said.

With those words said, Ducc turned to the employee and asked, "Where's the freezer?"

"Over there," he pointed.

"Go check it out, cuz," Ducc ordered.

Wasting no time, Michael opened the freezer and took a quick look inside finding two large vats containing what appeared to be about two hundred or so whole chickens, along with a machine that looked like a band saw, plus a bunch of loose boxes of frozen chickens, corn, and assorted fruit pies.

"It's cool, cuz," Michael said, after a few moments.

Turning back to the employee, Ducc asked, "How many people working up front?"

"It's just me, Sherry, Teresa, and the manager, Mrs. Robinson."

"That's cool, cuz. There's nothing but a bunch of bitches working here," said Birdman, excitedly.

"But that will change at two-thirty," said the employee.

"What you mean by that?" asked Tweedy Bird.

"We have a security guard that comes in around two-thirty, plus two extra workers come in around that time for the three o' clock to eleven shifts."

"We'll be long gone before that," said Birdman.

"Alright then, let's do this," said Tweedy Bird.

Slowly, they all eased their way into the front section of the chicken place without being noticed. They used the kidnapped employee as bait to snatch up the others. One by one, they led them into the cold meat locker where they were made to strip down to their underwear with the exception of the manager. She was personally taken to her office, where she was forced to open the safe, then like everyone else, she was made to strip-down, but completely naked.

Within seven minutes, Michael and his partners in crime had completed their tasks, and they were ready to make an exit when suddenly, Ducc said, "Wait a minute, cuz!"

"What for?" questioned Tweedy Bird.

"Cuz, I gotta tear out the phone cable first so that manager bitch won't be able to make any quick call, plus I'm gonna git me a couple boxes of that hot-ass fried chicken."

"Go on and handle that, cuz, and we'll meet you back at the car," Michael said.

Ducc quickly snatched the phone out of the wall, and then he went back to where the manager was and disabled the phone there. He then quickly looked toward the manager who was tied up, and said, "Look, I'm gonna untie you, but you betta' wait at least ten minutes before you make an attempt to leave your office, and when you do, you can go to the freezer and let your friends out. You'll also find your clothes inside one of those big vats with the chickens in it."

After saying that, he closed the door to the office and quickly snatched himself two big boxes of chicken. As he turned to leave, he found himself confronted by three customers who were unaware of what was going on.

Acting like he was the manager, he asked, "What can I do for you?"

"Give me a number two, a number three, a family pack, four strawberry sodas, and ten fries."

Ducc quickly did the math in his head, and said, "That will be $15.99."

The customer handed Ducc a twenty-dollar bill that he took and said, "I'll be back in a minute I forgot the key to the cash register."

He then turned, made his way to the rear of the building where he eased his way out the back door, then disappeared into the late afternoon sunshine.

19

Ghetto Players

"Living in the conditions that most are forced to dwell in causes them to retreat deeper into indolence and violence, deeper into rage, deeper into hate, deeper into drugs, thus making it easier to fall deeper into the destruction of self..."

—Kevin Lewis

November 1983 (Continued)

"How much did we get?" Sherry asked as she forced her way into the garage where they were all held up.

"Fuck that shit about how much we got, how did you know we were here?" Birdman retorted.

Displaying a sudden air of arrogance, Sherry said, "Man, I'm no fool. I didn't trust you niggas. I knew from the start that if I didn't keep an eye on my investment, you niggas wouldn't waste any time in putting some shit in the game."

"How did you know where we were at, especially when we left your ass locked up in the freezer?"

Ignoring the question, she said, "That was fucked up...you didn't have to make me strip down like that!"

"If we didn't, your co-workers and everyone else would have been suspicious, don't you think?"

"Still, you didn't have to make me get naked like that."

"Aw bitch, don't act like you ain't been stripped down to your panties before," said Tweedy Bird.

"C'mon cuz, fuck all that shit, let's just count the money," said Ducc, anxiously.

Stepping forward, Birdman grabbed the bag that contained the money, and said, "Let's count this shit then, cuz."

Quickly, everyone crowded the table like some greedy-ass hyenas as the countdown began. Like vultures, they sat patiently while they watched the procession of dead presidents rise and fall. Over and over again, hungry eyes stared upon shifty hands as the count neared its end.

"And twenty makes seventeen fifty," Birdman said, finally ending the count.

"Damn cuz, that's seven hundred more than what we expected."

"Yeah that means each of us will get exactly three hundred and fifty dollars apiece, and if we stick to the plan, we'll have six maybe close to eight hundred to spend on getting the water," Michael said, calculating.

"Shit, six hundred dollars is way more than enough," said Birdman.

"Wait a minute, cuz!" said Tweedy Bird. "There's five of us, and if my calculation is right, that means we should have at least a thousand dollars to put in on this shit...so who's not putting in?"

"Putting in on what?" asked Sherry.

Turning to Sherry, Michael said, "Our main reason for hittin' the lick was…"

"Wait a minute, cuz. We don't know this bitch that good!" shouted Ducc, cutting Michael off in the middle of his sentence.

"You knew me long enough to ask me to set this lick up," Sherry retorted.

"That's different!" shouted Ducc, effortlessly.

"What's different about it?" Michael asked.

Ducc didn't answer the question right away, and Michael learned later the reason for that was at the moment, his mind was overwhelmed with a series of mixed emotions. He told Michael that he hated last minute changes, especially changes involving women. He believed the less they knew the better things would be, but in this case, the damage was already done.

Finally, clearing his mind of its inner turmoil, Ducc said, "Sherry, personally I don't have nuthin' against you, but what we're planning to do involves some big-ass risks, and from my past experiences, bitches have been known to break down under pressure."

"Let's get one thing straight right now," Sherry began. "I ain't a bitch…. you'll find them type of ho's camped out on their knees, swinging from yo' nuts. Secondly, you have some homies who are just as weak as most bitches, so don't trip off me when you got those weak-ass niggas hangin' around you who ain't got enough heart to blast on a fuckin' wanted poster. Lastly, I know you niggas think I would have snitched if you would have beaten me out of my share of the money, but that's the last thing I would have done."

"So, if we had beaten you outta' your part of the money, how would you handle it?' Ducc asked.

Sherry paused, reached into her bra and pulled out a rare .38 automatic, and then answered, "I would have taken my chances with this."

"Damn cuz, this bitch is *loc (*slang for crazy, and it also refers to locked out Crip*), I mean female," Birdman corrected himself.

"I told you niggas in the beginning that this female wasn't about to snitch... and now you know she's not a punk either," said Tweedy Bird, laughing.

"I don't mean any disrespect, but I can use a bitch like you on my team," Michael said.

"Cuz," Ducc began. "Just because a bitch pull out a fuckin' strap doesn't make her a *G (*slang for gangster*), nor does it convince me that she's hard. There's a lot of coward-ass niggas in the streets carrying straps, and those niggas are more dangerous because they play their part so fuckin' well that you can't tell the real from the fake."

"That may be true," Michael said. "But what does that have to do with us?"

"A whole lot, nigga!" screamed Ducc. "We just can't let anyone walk up and think because they put in a little work or kept their mouth shut, they instantly can be a part of the click, understand?"

"What click?" Birdman asked. "Nigga, I already told ya'll fools, I'm from Nutty Blocc, and that makes me a full-time mothafuckin' Crip, seven days a week, 365 days a year. So the rest of the shit ya'll talkin' 'bout doesn't concern me, just break me off my cut, and I'm outta here."

At that moment everyone stood around as if not knowing what to do next. The only thing that truly mattered was the American greenbacks that lay before them. As Michael pondered about this, he began to realize, that their very lives had centered upon inanimate objects such as money, gold, diamonds, cars, and so forth. Subliminally, they worshipped these things like gods. Like in religion, they performed certain rituals in order to be rewarded with absolute power and control over others. The accumulation of wealth, the love of self, and the power to bring death upon those whom they saw as enemies; these were their trophies. This fact was one of the main controlling factors that kept most gang members under the spell of ghetto ignorance. More surprisingly though, there are some who fight hard to maintain that status of ignorance, but then there are those whose ignorance comes by way of fear.

Another element of gang life that Michael failed to see at the moment was the unseen forces of the unknown, the ultimate power by which they were all created. A voice deep inside of Michael told him that one day he was going to sit before the ultimate power of judgment, and on that day, all that his hands brought forth, good and evil, will be put to test. Just knowing that caused most gang members to feel that they had only one option in life, and that was to live and die as they saw fit.

"Give cuz his part of the take," said Ducc, breaking the silence between them.

"Here," Michael said.

Birdman quickly snatched up his part of the take and proceeded to leave when he stopped, looked over his shoulder and said, "Say cuz, ya'll niggas need to give that bitch a chance, after all, you came this far wit' her, you might as well ride with her the rest of the way."

"I don't need you niggas," Sherry said. "I can do just like Birdman, take my share of the money and git my own shit rollin'."

"Look at us, cuz," Michael said. "We're sitting here arguing over this shit like a bunch of funky-ass bitches when we should be on our way to score the water so we can git' our operation started."

"He's right cuz," said Tweedy Bird as he walked over and picked up an empty shoebox and set it upon an old workbench, "Now you niggas who want to make some money, put yo' share of the investment in this box, if not, sayonara mothafucka."

"What does that mean?" Ducc asked.

"It means goodbye in Japanese," Michael answered.

"Excuse me," Sherry interrupted. "When you two niggas finish your lesson on fuckin' foreign languages, let us know. Otherwise, I'll be here making sure the count is right."

"Let's get this shit handled then," Michael said.

One by one, each person was given their share of the money. When Michael received his, he instantly realized that a mere three hundred fifty dollars wasn't worth the prison time he would have received if they were caught. Therefore, Michael made a promise to himself that he would never go and rob an establishment for less than one hundred thousand dollars. In other words, why go to jail for a few measly dollars, when you can take a better chance on millions. At least that's what he thought at the time.

Within minutes, they all received their cut, and they placed what they were going to put on the water inside the shoebox. They then semi-celebrated their good fortunes with a hit of weed that was passed from one person to another. Everyone seemed to be satisfied and content with the exception of Ducc. He seemed somewhat solemn and withdrawn from the rest of the crew. His sudden change in behavior bothered Michael deeply, to the point he went over to where he sat, and asked, "What' up, cuz?"

"Nothing really, I was just trippin.'"

"Tripping off what?"

"Off certain things we say we're gonna do, but don't follow."

"Like what things?"

"Like how you said that bitches was almost in all cases the source of trouble among men."

"Yeah, I said that, but not exactly in those words."

"Then if you believe that, why would you so easily allow a bitch to enter into partnership with us?"

"I did it because of instinct."

"You did it because of instinct, whose instinct?"

"I did it because of the woman's instinct."

"Cuz, what are you talkin' 'bout?"

"It's like this cuz, a woman has a natural instinctual feeling for when something is not right, or when something is about to happen. Most men lack this instinct; therefore, by us allowing a woman within our circle, it gives us two major advantages."

"And what advantages is that?"

"The first advantage is being able to be forewarned of any problem before it happens, and our second advantage is better than the first."

"And what's that?"

"We'll let the bitch take the heat."

Confused, Ducc rubbed his head and then said, "Cuz, I don't quite understand."

Laughing in a sinister way, Michael said, "What I mean by that is we'll give the bitch the power to run things, and all we have to do is collect and protect. She'll do all the work along with selling the supply. And we'll just sit back and get ghetto fat while stacking a grip of hard earned cash."

"But what if she wises up?"

"By that time it would be too late, plus we wouldn't care anyway because we should have made thousands by then."

"Now that sounds like a plan," said Ducc, smiling for the first time.

Patting Ducc on the back, Michael said, "Let's go git ourselves something to celebrate with."

"Cuz, you don't smoke weed, do you?"

"I wasn't talkin' 'bout any weed."

"Then what are you talkin' 'bout?"

"I'm talking 'bout some of that down home tight-ass ghetto pussy."

"And I know just where to git' it, too," said Ducc, excitedly.

"Well, what are we waiting for? Let's go."

May 1984

Six months had passed, and Michael, along with his crew had become known as reputable suppliers of PCP. From as far as the ghetto to the desert of Palm Springs, people had come in search for their inexhaustible supply. In Michael's mind, this not only made them rich by ghetto standards, but it gave them a whole new status among the warriors within his neighborhood. This status didn't come easily though. There were a lot of negative consequences they had to encounter and overcome. It seemed as if everyone who was involved in the underworld of drug dealing was gunning to put them out of business in one way or another.

For months, Michael and his team had to dodge the police, rival dealers, and those whose number one profession was *player hating (*slang for envious and jealous people*). It was like all eyes were on them in the cities of Compton, Watts, Lynwood, and the surrounding areas of South Central Los Angeles. Every move they made was done with precision and caution. Not one of them made a drug deal without the other knowing the complete details of that deal, and for the most part, they all respected each other's input and advice. Even Ducc seemed to be satisfied with their progress, but how could he not be, when they all were making good money and driving nice cars?

Smiling at the thought of it all, Michael turned to Ducc, who was seated next to him in his car, and said, "Look at them, cuz."

"Look at whom?"

"The *Shermheads," (*slang for individuals who were addicted to PCP*) Michael answered.

Ducc laughed for a moment and then said, "I remember a time when there wasn't any Shermheads 'round here, now there's hundreds."

"And who do you think is to blame for that?" Michael asked, smiling.

"Not us."

"C'mon cuz, you know we're the blame for this shit."

"Cuz, I know you don't seriously think we are responsible for them niggas being Shermheads."

"Hell yeah, cuz. If it wasn't for us they wouldn't be strung-out on that shit like they are."

"That's not our problem, cuz. We didn't force them niggas to buy that shit. They themselves chose to get high, so the blame is on them, not us."

"I guess you're right, cuz," Michael responded as he concentrated upon the traffic that was ahead of him.

"Cuz, pull over," Ducc said.

Doing as asked, Michael pulled the car over as Ducc screamed from the window asking, "Hey Lee, is that you?"

Taking a closer look for himself, Michael saw that it was truly Lee Culpepper, a brother from his junior high and high schools days who was known for being highly multi-talented.

"Damn cuz, what happened to you?" Ducc asked, as Lee approached. "Who...who are you?" Lee struggled to say, tripping over his words as he drew near.

"Cuz, you don't remember us?" they asked in unison.

Wiping the visible mucus from his eyes, and snot from his nose, Lee said, "Can...can you help a nigga out with a couple of ends or something.... I'm trying to git' myself one of those *wet daddies (*slang for a cigarette dipped in PCP*), and all I have is two bucks."

Ducc looked at Michael for a moment and then reached into his pocket and removed a folded wrinkled sheet of aluminum foil that contained three loose *Sherm sticks (*a brand of cigarette dipped in PCP*) and gave it to Lee.

"Here, cuz."

Surprised, Lee quickly grabbed the package and shuffled off without even saying thanks.

"Damn, cuz has really lost his mind."

"Yeah, that shit has fucked him up real bad."

"Betta' him than us," Michael said, pulling back into traffic.

They rode in silence for a while as they took in the surrounding sights. It appeared as if everything around them had changed in one way or another. For instance, the females who they knew as kids, and who they saw as being ugly were now shapely and very beautiful, and the ones they saw as being attractive were either now hooked on drugs, caught in abusive relationships, or struggling with the burden of raising a countless number of fatherless children. Those weren't the only changes they saw. There were other changes that affected the minority community economically.

The government, without notice, had suddenly ended certain social programs such as CETA, Manpower, and the Neighborhood Parks and Schools free lunch program. Minority youth depended upon these programs for summer jobs, and when they were finally eradicated, this left a countless number of youth in search of new means for survival ~ and cutting grass, washing cars, and selling candy had played out with the end of the sixties, and early seventies. The new urban ghetto youth had developed a need, a thirst, and a desire to keep up with the changing times. The urban ghetto entrepreneurs fed that thirst by employing them in the only trade that was available ~ the sale of drugs.

"Stop at the store for a moment," said Ducc, interrupting Michael's inner thoughts.

Like an expert, Michael maneuvered from one lane to another until he reached the left hand turning lane; there he swung his car into the parking lot of the store before the light gave him permission to do so."

"Alright cuz, one day yo' ass is gonna git caught."

Michael laughed for a moment, and then said, "Until then, I'll keep driving like a madman."

Ducc smiled, and then asked, "Do you want anything?"

"Yeah cuz, git me one of those six packs of orange Crush in the can."

"Do you want anything else?"

"Nah, I'm good"

As Ducc disappeared into the store, Michael tried to take advantage of the time by popping in a new tape by Parliament, but his groove was not to be, due to a brother who was dressed in a black suit and bow tie stepping up to his driver's side window.

"Say brother, can I trouble you with the words of the Honorable Elijah Muhammad?"

"What?" Michael asked seriously.

"I said would you like to hear the words of the Honorable Elijah Muhammad?"

"Who's that?"

"He's the messenger of Allah who brings a special message of understanding and power to the black man ~ A messenger that will assist you in breaking your psychological and personal chains of oppression which will empower you with the knowledge of self."

"And how much is this message going to cost me?"

"Just an hour or so of your time. That's if you're not afraid of the truth."

"Why would I be afraid?"

"You'll be afraid because sometimes the truth hurts more than the bullet."

Michael didn't know what it was that this man was referring to, but what he was saying caused him to be somewhat fearful. At that very moment, he knew he couldn't allow this man to leave his presence without first acquiring some knowledge of the things he had spoken.

"Say cuz, I mean brother, how can I hear this man speak when I don't know where to find him?"

"Finding him is easy, but the hard part will be on you."

"And what is the hard part?"

"Allowing yourself to be rid of the ignorance that you so desire."

"Well, I can't do that if I don't know where to go.'

The brother smiled for a long moment and then said, "You can find your answer at the Islamic Temple in Compton around one o'clock."

"Okay, I'll be there," Michael said.

Finally Ducc returned carrying two large grocery sacks full of nothing but junk food.

"That shit gonna' kill you," Michael said as Ducc closed the door.

"We all gotta die sometime."

"But that don't mean you have to rush it."

"C'mon cuz, you beginning to sound like my mother."

Michael laughed for a moment, and then asked, "Say cuz, do you have any plans for later on?"

"Why?"

"Because I was thinking about swinging by this place to hear those brothers throw down."

"What brothers?"

"Them brothers they call Black Muslims."

"Cuz, I don't like fuckin' wit' those niggas. They're crazy, they're large in numbers, and they're not to be fucked with either."

"I already know that. I just wanna see what they're about."

"Well, fuck it, I'll go with you."

"What about your food?"

"We can drop it off on the way."

An hour and a half later, they found themselves sitting in a temple that was full of Black Muslims. The sight was unlike any they could imagine. Every brother was well groomed, nicely attired, and physically fit. The women were also just as beautiful. Each was dressed in white with veils over their faces that enhanced their beauty as well as their spirituality.

As Michael and Ducc sat down in the chairs that were provided for them, Michael began to feel out of place. Those feelings soon changed as the words of several strong speakers began to take him from the depths of ignorance into the light of understanding. The feeling he was experiencing was like a massive flow of energy that had been building for over four hundred or so years. Now it was being released through the essence of words ~ words that gave sight to the blind, hearing to the deaf, and empowerment to the unable.

Like prisoners being set free after decades of incarceration, they listened attentively as the words of truth freed them from their psychological bonds and fears. But the message that touched them the most was a message delivered by a young brother that appeared to be no more than twelve years old.

Sporting a small, well-groomed afro, black dress suit and matching bow tie, the young brother stood at the podium and greeted them with words of *Assalaamu' Alaikum (*Arabic for: May peace be upon you*), and when the crowd answered, *Walaikum' salaam, (Arabic return greeting that means: *May peace be upon you also*), he began his speech by saying, *"My beautiful black brothers and sisters, we're gathered here today to hear the truth, and heal ourselves from the massive atrocities that have been inflicted upon us by our oppressors."*

"Each day we're being used, abused, and lied to. Each day we set out to kill ourselves physically, mentally, and spiritually just because our oppressors have us thinking that we're less than them. They have us calling ourselves porch monkeys, liver lips, toads, jungle bunnies, and now niggers ~ a title by which most blacks have grown comfortable. But let me ask you this...Do you know what it really means to be called a nigger?" Let me enlighten you...the word nigger is derived from two words, Necro and Nekro, both Greek, which is short for the word Necrology which means the list of the recently dead. From the word Necrology, five more words are derived which are: Necromancy, Necromancer, Necropolis, Necrosis, and Necrotic. All these words have

meanings that are associated with death and decay. Therefore, when the oppressor refers to us as nigger, he's actually stating that because we lack the knowledge of self, we're spiritually dead, thus constituting the title and condition of being a nigger."

"Now is it true, my brothers and sisters? Are we dead? No, we're not. In fact, we know we come from a long line of mighty Kings and Queens; and it is not in our physical make up to coexist as dope dealers, rapists, thieves, and murderers. These elements are the characteristics of our oppressor. It's a natural element of his nature, and like a leopard that can't change his spots; the oppressor can't change that which is in him. Therefore, he will be what he always been ~ a liar, a thief, a manipulator, and a master of deception."

"For years, the oppressors have been implementing the method of divide and conquer by the power of manipulation, and using the art of deception in order to suppress the truth. He uses the media as his tool to propagate his lies about us, and he has the entire nation thinking we're nothing but a bunch of rapists and murderers."

"But how can the oppressor call us murderers when it was them who murdered over two hundred and fifty unarmed black men, women, and children, and wounded thousands of others in riots that they provoked during the sixties? How can we be called murderers when it was them and their emissaries who murdered Martin Luther King Jr., Emmett Till, Medgar Evers, George Jackson, Nat Turner, James Chaney, and countless others? How could we be murderers when it was them who plotted and murdered Carol Roberson, Denise McNair, Addie Mae Collins, and Cynthia Wesley, the four black adolescent girls who were tragically murdered in the *sixteenth Baptist Church bombing, which occurred in Birmingham, Alabama in September 1963?"*

"How can the oppressor have the audacity to call us anything less than human when it was they who not only murdered, but also kidnapped millions of black people from the continent of Africa? We were robbed of our language, of our culture, of our human dignity, of our labor, and of our very lives. We have been made to believe that we're thieves in the eyes of many, but yet we're not the ones who rip off billions of dollars every year through tax evasions, embezzlement, consumer fraud, bribes, under-the-table government kickbacks, and swindles."

As the young brother paused, Michael took a quick glance at Ducc who seemed to be absorbed by the content of information that was being delivered. Michael too, was overwhelmed, but yet, he couldn't complain. He needed this information, more so now than he ever had in his life. Michael's thoughts were broken up when the young brother cleared his throat and said, *"In continuing, let me quote the words of one of our beautiful black sisters of the struggle, Assata Shakur, who was targeted by the highest level of the United States government. In a letter that was written by her and broadcast over several radio stations in the state of New Jersey as well as across America, she stated: 'The ruling class of America has often classified blacks as murderers, child molesters, thieves, and bandits, but it was not blacks who robbed and murdered millions of Indians by taking their homeland, then turned around after that and called themselves pioneers. They call black people bandits, but is it us who is robbing Africa, Asia, and all of Latin America of their natural resources and freedom while the people who live there are sick and starving? The rulers of this country and their emissaries have committed some of the most brutal, vicious crimes in history, and for no other reason than that of greed and power.'"*

The young brother paused once again in order to let the words of understanding and power sink into the frontal cortexes of his large audience. Michael couldn't believe the power and strength that illuminated behind the presence of knowledge. Possessing such a gift eliminated the need to belong to a gang or anything else that led to the destruction of self, but it would still take years of hard learning before he realized that deep within himself.

Continuing, the young brother concluded his speech by saying. *"Therefore, my brothers and sisters, we're not what they say we are, but on the other hand, they are everything they say they're not. They are the bandits. They are the murderers...and they should be treated as such. Remember these words, and know that every revolution in history has been accomplished by actions. We must rise up as a show of force. We must create shields that protect us and spears that penetrate our enemies. Black people must learn how to struggle by struggling, and we must stand up now or be condemned to live a life of degradation and servitude.... Now in closing, I must greet you as I did in the beginning, Assalaamu' Alaikum'."*

With those words said, the young brother exited the podium, and as he did so, the audience began to applaud, but in a reserved and quiet manner. It was almost like magic, and everywhere Michael looked he could see the effects of what was said in the behavior and mannerisms of those around him. Michael even felt that Ducc was affected in one way or another, but the feeling changed once he spoke.

"I knew it," Ducc whispered.

"Knew what?"

"I knew these niggas were gonna start asking for money."

"Aw cuz, at least it ain't like what they do in church."

"What you mean by that?"

"Cuz, you know how those fools in church be passing 'round those damn offering trays ~ they be asking people to give up everything. Shit, I can even remember when I went to church one day wit' my sister. I started with twenty dollars in my pocket, and by the time I left church, I barely had enough to buy a two-piece combo at Kentucky Fried Chicken.

"It's all a hustle, cuz, just like here...it's all a hustle."

"I don't think so, cuz. Those niggas, I mean brothers, really had their shit together, and if it was just a hustle, then everything we heard today would be fake, and we both know, what we heard today was the truth."

20

Ghetto Metamorphosis

"In the process of life, one finds many obstacles. Some stand as a tool of enlightenment, some as a test of endurance, some for the purpose of learning, but the obstacles which are found within the ghetto are there purposely to hinder and impede the progress of a people for no other reason than that of their color..."
—For Glenna Long

July 1984

Michael stood along the Long Beach Pier for hours watching the waves of the ocean crash against the rocks below. As he watched this event, the process reminded him of a theory by Charles Darwin, which was *The Survival of the Fittest*. Charles Darwin believed that in nature, all living organisms that coexisted within the same niche competed with one another for their existence. The organisms that were able to adapt, struggle, and overcome all others would be the fittest, and the others would perish.

Pondering upon this concept caused Michael to realize that in some ways, black people were the fittest of American society; because they had adapted and survived the social ills of racism, police brutality, discrimination, negative subliminal seduction, and a countless number of other atrocities that had been inflicted upon them by their oppressors. Despite all these things, black people's greatest enemy had become themselves.

As people of color living in America, the position of blacks is now slowly changing from being that of the fittest to one which is endangered. Each day, Michael witnessed a number of lifeless bodies, young and old, outlined in chalk; each day he struggled with the fact that when he left his own home, it may be for the last time. Many black males living in the ghetto felt the same as he did, and they knew that if they gave up on trying, then they would join the long ranks of the dying.

Turning his thoughts and attention from the rocks below, Michael began to walk along the pier, while casually observing the faces of people whom he passed ~ all white, content, rich, and vibrant. But none of those faces saw him, or that which was in him. He was invisible ~ an object lacking a shadow, a phantom. A specter that is apparent to sense, but in the unseeing eyes of those around him, he possessed no substantial existence. He was nothing but a disembodied spirit, a mere show, just an intrusion into a world that refused to see him for no other reason than he was black. This was his epiphany, an understanding to all that was, and all that is.

Michael suddenly cleared his mind of its inner thoughts as he reached within the waistband of his gray khakis and massaged the only thing that brought

him security and peace, which was his over and under
.357 magnum. Michael worshipped his gun like it was
his woman. She never left him lonely, and like Bonnie
and Clyde, she was always at his side, his number one
girlfriend, his one and only true friend, down to the
very end, living together in a world of sin.

Many ghetto youth felt the same as Michael did
about their guns. It was the thing that gave them power
and prestige as well as ghetto honor. Without one you
were nothing, and to get caught slipping without having one within reach meant the instant termination of
one's very life. For most black gang youth, their guns
had become their ghetto visas, and they never left
home without one. In fact, as the years passed, a great
ghetto philosopher, poet, and rapper by the name of
Tupac Shakur, would write a powerful metaphorical
RAP (*Rhythmic American Poetry*), in detail describing
his love and feeling for his gun. In the words of his
song, *Me and My Girlfriend*, he describes his gun as
a girlfriend. [http://www.azlyrics.com/lyrics/2pac/me-
andmygirlfriend.html]

Michael knew this was a sad reality for young black
men as well as an infatuation gone wild. If one was
to ever to ponder upon this, they would find that for
the gang affected youth, their guns had become many
things. For some, they were their allies in a world of
conflict. Others used them as their shields upon a bat-
tlefield of oppression. The rest used them as their mask
while dwelling in the condition of cowardice. But for
the most part, their guns had become their safety factor
in a nation founded by thieves, now run by crooks.

Feeling somewhat troubled, Michael left the pier
and headed back to his car, which was parked nearby.
As he drew close, he was instantly caught off guard by
someone who yelled, "What's up, Blood?"

Michael slowly turned, only to find several young brothers who seemed to have appeared from out of nowhere. They were staring at him menacingly.

Michael wasn't afraid because he had three major things on his side: experience, the knowledge that no Bloods or Blood gangs were in operation in the City of Long Beach, and lastly, he had his girl at his side, in the form of a .357 magnum. So, with that thought, he turned and said, "What's up with you, cuz?"

For a few seconds, the youngsters stood there as if wondering what to do next. Instead of waiting on them, Michael quickly snatched out his gun and fired upon the closest one near him.

"Oh, shit!" screamed one of the youngsters.

Oblivious of the innocent bystanders who were in and around the parking lot, Michael started dumping on the youngsters like crazy. Sparks flew from all directions as bullets kicked up pieces of earth, concrete, and peeled-back metal. He was mad as hell, but not at the youngsters, because they had lacked the understanding of what they were doing. Michael's anger was directed more so toward the caretakers of society.

Actually, Michael believed that it was the caretakers of society who were to blame for most of the negativity that had occurred within the ghetto among the minority youth. They knew about the guns and drugs, and they knew how it came into their community, yet they had done nothing to eradicate the flow, and why?

Because it was all a part of their design, plot, and plan (see Appendix, page 296).

From the CIA to the FBI, blacks and the organizations they represent have been subject to certain schemes, experiments, and cover-ups. For example, in a 1989 Gallop Poll of the United States, citizens found that crime and violence were growing at an alarming

rate. Much of this increase is blamed on crack cocaine, a drug that was purposely placed within the
black community, *and for what reason?* (see Appendix).
Why would society, or the powers that govern this nation, allow such a thing to happen when they knew
first and foremost the effects these drugs would have
on the community ~ especially the effect these drugs
would have on blacks? In fact, according to Dr. David
F. Allen, and Dr. James F. Jekel, who co-authored the
book, *"Crack, the Broken Promise,"* it was well known,
as they state, in part, on page four.

**"In 1903, cocaine was removed from Coca
Cola because of the fears of southern politicians
about cocaine's effect on black persons. One of
the strongest motivations for making cocaine
illegal in the United States was the general perception that cocaine increased the risk of crime
among blacks, especially the crime of rape..."**

Now after reading this script, how could Michael or
anyone else sit silently after knowing this information
~ especially when a larger part of this plan was implemented under the leadership of J. Edgar Hoover who
launched the most terrifying offensive (*COINTELPRO*)
in U.S. history against black Americans ~ and he didn't
stop there; he also targeted any and all people who
supported black Americans and their organizations, especially the Black Panther organization (see Appendix
for more information).

With his mind in turmoil, Michael wrestled with
his conscience. *How could he continue to wage war
against his black brothers and sisters? They weren't his
enemies, and he wasn't theirs. But how could he convey
this fact? And how could he prevent himself from getting*

gunned down every time he attempted to turn a corner? Most of all, how could he heal the wounds of those brothers and sisters that lost loved ones in this senseless street war that's been raging since 1969? He didn't have the answer, but somehow he needed to find it.

As Michael sped away heading eastward along Ocean Boulevard, he couldn't help but think about these problems. The more he pondered, the angrier he became. *Who did those niggas think they were? Didn't they know I could have killed all their ignorant asses? But what would I have gained if I had done so?* Not a damn thing. They would have been just three more black victims added to a long list of statistics, Michael finally thought.

Upon reaching his neighborhood, Michael began to feel better. He didn't know why, but his neighborhood was always a source of refuge for him, and it was the only place in which he felt safe.

As he stepped out of his ride, Ducc and Tweedy Bird pulled up on him in a tan sixty-four Chevy, hit the switch, rolled down the window, and quickly said, "C'mon cuz, and git in."

"What's up?"

"We'll tell ya on the way."

As Michael jumped into the back seat, Ducc said, "Cuz, them slob nigga's just rolled thru the 'hood lettin' everyone have it."

"Did anyone get hit?"

"Just a couple of cars and a few houses," answered Ducc.

"Yeah cuz, those nigga's is always shootin' up someone's house," said Tweedy Bird.

"Maybe we should call them nigga's house killers," Ducc finally said.

Laughing slightly, Michael added, "It's either a full moon, or them slob nigga's are really mad today."

"Why you say that?"

"Because earlier today, I went up to the Long Beach Pier to think, and when I got there I was challenged by three slob nigga's who were trying their best to be hard by punking me without realizing the consequences they had to deal with."

"Cuz, you got to be joking, there ain't no slobs sets in Long Beach," said Tweedy Bird.

"I thought that, too," Michael added.

"Cuz, there ain't no slobs in Long Beach. Those nigga's just be out there sometime visiting their relatives, and if they catch a Crip slipping while they're out here visiting, they'll smoke his ass quick. It's just another a part of the game," Ducc added.

"Well, them nigga's didn't get the chance to prove themselves hard because they spent too much time talkin' shit. I ended the conversation with' some hot-ass .357 slob killers."

"I hope you have some left," said Tweedy Bird.

"Cuz, I always keep a grip of these mothafuckas on hand. After all, this bitch only holds four at a time."

"That's right. You have that funny looking over and under .357 magnum, " said Ducc.

"Yeah nigga, she may be funny looking, but ain't no nigga gonna tell her that to her face."

Suddenly, they fell silent as five police cruisers sped past them doing at least fifty miles an hour, with flashing lights and no sirens.

"Cuz, you thinkin' what I'm thinkin'?" asked Tweedy Bird.

"Yeah cuz, let's go!"

Fifteen minutes later Michael and his crew had learned the Bloods had come back through their neighborhood, but this time they caught their comrades with their pants down. Eight people were wounded in sporadic gunfire that was sprayed from at least five cars, and two of the wounded were innocent bystanders who were in serious condition, one being a five year old boy.

"Let's go hit them nigga's," whispered Ducc, angrily.

"Nah cuz, that's what they're expecting us to do, plus it's too hot, and it's already been enough shootin' for one day," Michael said.

"Fuck that shit, cuz!" said Tweedy Bird. "I'm gonna blast on them nigga's. I don't care where it happens... those nigga's can be in church and I will still blast them, right there before God and the Devil."

Two detectives who were wearing suits that looked like they came out of K-Mart general store suddenly interrupted their conversation. "Did anyone of you see what happened here?"

"Are you talkin' to us?" Michael asked, angrily.

"Yes, we are."

Michael paused for a moment and then said, "We ain't got shit to say to you people, plus ya'll are the perpetrators behind this shit anyway."

"I think you betta' watch yo' mouth, boy!" said the detective, angrily.

"What you gonna do? Beat my ass and kill me like ya'll done Emmett Till."

"It looks like ya'll niggers are doing a good job of that all by yourselves, and yes, I said niggers..."

"What!" Michael shouted

"C'mon cuz, fuck those peckerwoods," said Ducc as he pulled Michael away.

"Yeah, you better git him before he bites off more than he can handle."

"And what is that 'pose to mean?" asked Tweedy Bird, talking loud enough that a small crowd began to gather.

"Let's go, Bill, before things get outta of hand here."

As they walked off, Ducc said, "Damn cuz, why you trip on the police like that?"

"I'm trippin' because the police are just as much to blame for this shit as those slob niggas."

"What you mean by that, cuz? And who in the fuck is Emmett Till?"

Michael didn't say anything for a moment because it just dawned on him that his comrades didn't have any knowledge when it came to the political struggle of their people. If they did, it probably wouldn't matter anyway.

Clearing his thoughts, Michael turned toward his comrades, and finally said, "Cuz, this shit we're in is deeper than you can even imagine, and you both may think I'm crazy when I say this, but every time a slob kills someone close to us, it makes me so mad that I wanna go out and smoke the first police I see."

"But cuz, the police ain't done nuthin' to us," said Tweedy Bird.

"Cuz, that's where you're wrong. Since the fuckin' 60s, the police and the FBI have been working hard to keep us divided so we can continue to kill ourselves. And what you both don't know is they been using some of our own homies to ensure that the killing between Crips and Bloods continues. These same homies are also undercover snitches as well."

"Cuz," Ducc began, "The shit you talkin' 'bout is way over my head."

"Mine's too," Tweedy Bird added.

"All you have to do is see the proof for yourselves."

"And where are we supposed to find this proof?"

"My father gave me the proof a long time ago when he was trying to stop me from gangbanging."

"Your father?"

"Yeah cuz, my father always stated that gangbanging was a useless war that fools fought. So he tried to get me out of it by teaching about things that happened while he was growing up. Plus, he gave me all these special papers and newspaper articles that were titled, "Government Plots Uncovered." (See Appendix, for government plots.)

"Do you still have that stuff?" asked Tweedy Bird.

"Yeah cuz, I have it, but we don't have time to look at that shit now."

"I think we betta make the time."

"Why?"

"Because if there are homies around us that are snitches, then we can't do nuthin to them slob niggas until we get rid of the snitches."

"That's what I been trying to tell you in the first place."

"I'm still confused," said Ducc.

"Everything will be clear once you read the shit I have."

"Go git it then, cuz."

"Alright, let me use your car and I'll be back in twenty minutes."

"Cuz, fuck that...I'll take you myself," said Tweedy Bird.

"What's wrong, cuz? You don't trust me with your wheels?"

"Cuz, I don't trust my own mother when it comes to my ride."

"Alright then, let's go."

An hour later, Michael and his comrades found themselves sitting quietly inside of Chico's Pizza restaurant.

They had been going through hundreds of pages of material that contained information on Jim Crow, the civil rights movement, the police and the FBI involvement to destroy minority political organization by any and all means possible.

"Damn cuz, you see all these pages of this shit?" said Tweedy Bird. "And look at this," he said excitedly, as he handed Ducc a memo that said in part:

"April 1968 the FBI's counterintelligence program (COINTELPRO) identified the party as one of the most dangerous threats presented by black America. So dangerous that, J. Edgar Hoover would deem the party as the greatest threat to the internal security of the country. Soon after the party was infiltrated with informants..."

"What does this have to do with' us?" Ducc asked as he paused from what he was reading.

"A whole lot, cuz, just keep reading," stated Michael.

"But this is a whole lot of shit to read, cuz."

"You said you wanted to know, right?"

"But damn..."

"Keep on reading," said Tweedy Bird.

With that said Ducc picked up the material and continued to read until he couldn't read any more. After ten minutes, he rubbed his eyes, laid the paperwork aside and then said, "Dam cuz, this shit is deeper than what I thought."

"Shit, if you think that is something, then read this," Michael said, handing Ducc another large volume of papers.

"What is this about?"

"It's about Dr. Martin Luther King, Jr., and what they were doing to him."

"Let me read it then," asked Tweedy Bird, reaching for the documents.

"And can you read it out loud so we all can hear?" asked Ducc.

"Shit, we gonna have to take turns reading this shit because it's way too many pages for me by myself," said Tweedy Bird.

"Okay cuz, you start off and we'll each take a turn until it's finished."

"Alright, cuz."

With that, Tweedy Bird picked up the documents and started reading, which began:

"DR. MARTIN LUTHER KING, JR., CASE STUDY"

I. INTRODUCTION

From December 1963 until his death in 1968, Martin Luther King, Jr. was the target of an intensive campaign by the Federal Bureau of Investigation to "neutralize" him as an effective civil rights leader. In the words of the man in charge of the FBI's "war" against Dr. King:

No holds were barred. We have used [similar] techniques against Soviet agents. [The same methods were] brought home against any organization against which we were targeted. We did not differentiate. This is a rough, tough business.

1 The FBI collected information about Dr. King's plans and activities through an extensive surveillance program, employing nearly every intelligence-gathering technique at the Bureau's disposal. Wiretaps, which were initially approved by Attorney General Robert F. Kennedy, were maintained on Dr. King's home telephone from October 1963 until mid-1965; the SCLC headquarters' telephones were covered by wiretaps for an even longer period. Phones in the homes and offices of some of Dr. King's close advisers were also wiretapped. The FBI has acknowledged 16 occasions on which microphones were hidden in Dr. King's hotel and motel rooms in an

"attempt" to obtain information about the "private activities of King and his advisers" for use to "completely discredit" them.

2 FBI informants in the civil rights movement and reports from field offices kept the Bureau's headquarters informed of developments in the civil rights field. The FBI's presence was so intrusive that one major figure in the civil rights movement testified that his colleagues referred to themselves as members of "the FBI's golden record club."

3 The FBI's formal program to discredit Dr. King with Government officials began with the distribution of a "monograph" which the FBI realized could "be regarded as a personal attack on Martin Luther King,"

4 and which was subsequently described by a Justice Department official as "a personal diatribe ... a personal attack without evidentiary support."

5 Congressional leaders were warned "off the record" about alleged dangers posed by Reverend King. The FBI responded to Dr. King's receipt of the Nobel Peace Prize by attempting to undermine his reception by foreign heads of state and American ambassadors in the countries that he planned to visit. When Dr. King returned to the United States, steps were taken to reduce support for a huge banquet and a special "day" that were being planned in his honor.

The FBI's program to destroy Dr. King as the leader of the civil rights movement entailed attempts to discredit him with churches, universities, and the press. Steps were taken to attempt to convince the National Council of Churches, the Baptist World Alliance, and leading Protestant ministers to halt financial support of the Southern Christian Leadership Conference (SCLC), and to persuade them that "Negro leaders should completely isolate King and remove him from the role he is now occupying in civil rights activities."

6 When the FBI learned that Dr. King intended to visit the Pope, an agent was dispatched to persuade Francis Cardinal Spellman to warn the Pope about "the likely embarrassment that may result to the Pope should he grant King an audience."

7 The FBI sought to influence universities to withhold honorary degrees from Dr. King. Attempts were made to prevent the publication of articles favorable to Dr. King and to find "friendly" news sources that would print unfavorable articles. The FBI offered to play for reporters tape recordings allegedly made from microphone surveillance of Dr. King's hotel rooms. The FBI mailed Dr. King a tape recording made from its microphone coverage. According to the Chief of the FBI's Domestic Intelligence Division, the tape was intended to precipitate a separation between Dr. King and his wife in the belief that the separation would reduce Dr. King's stature.

(7a) The tape recording was accompanied by a note, which Dr. King and his advisers interpreted as a threat to release the tape recording unless Dr. King committed suicide. The FBI also made preparations to promote someone "to assume the role of leadership of the Negro people when King has been completely discredited."

8 The campaign against Dr. King included attempts to destroy the Southern Christian Leadership Conference by cutting off its sources of funds. The FBI considered, and on some occasions executed, plans to cut off the support of some of the SCLC's major contributors, including religious organizations, a labor union, and donors of grants such as the Ford Foundation. One FBI field office recommended that the FBI send letters to the SCLC's donors over Dr. King's forged signature warning them that the SCLC was under investigation by the Internal Revenue Service. The IRS files on Dr. King and the SCLC were carefully scrutinized for financial irregularities. For over a year, the FBI unsuccessfully attempted to establish that Dr. King had a secret foreign bank account in which he was sequestering funds. The FBI campaign to discredit and destroy Dr. King was marked by extreme personal vindictiveness. As early as 1962, Director Hoover penned on an FBI memorandum, "King is no good."

9 At the August 1963 March on Washington, Dr. King told the country of his dream that "all of God's children, black men and white men, Jews and Gentiles, Protestants and Catholics, will be

able to join hands and sing in the words of the old Negro spiritual, 'Free at last, free at last. Thank God almighty, I'm free at last.'"'

10 The FBI's Domestic Intelligence Division described this "demagogic speech" as yet more evidence that Dr. King was "the most dangerous and effective Negro leader in the country."

11 Shortly afterward, Time magazine chose Dr. King as the "Man of the Year," an honor which elicited Director Hoover's comment that "they had to dig deep in the garbage to come up with this one."

12 Hoover wrote "astounding" across the memorandum informing him that Dr. King had been granted an audience with the Pope despite the FBI's efforts to prevent such a meeting. The depth of Director Hoover's bitterness toward Dr. King, a bitterness that he had effectively communicated to his subordinates in the FBI, was apparent from the FBI's attempts to sully Dr. King's reputation long after his death. Plans were made to "brief" congressional leaders in 1969 to prevent the passage of a "Martin Luther King Day." In 1970, Director Hoover told reporters that Dr. King was the 'last one in the world who should ever have received' the Nobel Peace Prize.

"Damn cuz, can you believe this shit? Them peck-erwood mothafuckas were actually setting niggas up, and in the worse way," exclaimed Tweedy Bird.

"That's what I was trying to tell you. In fact, if they'll go to all these lengths to frame and discredit King, what do you think they will do to us?"

Everyone fell quiet for a moment. None of them could believe that the government would go so far, especially in America. This was something they often saw on television, not in real life. But real it was, and it was happening all around them.

"So you believe they still are doing these things?" asked Ducc.

"Read what they say in the conclusion," Michael responded.

Ducc grabbed the paper that Michael shoved his way and read out loud:

"CONCLUSION"

"Although it is impossible to gauge the full extent to which the FBI's discrediting programs affected the civil rights movement, the fact that there was impact is unquestionable.

449. Rumors circulated by the FBI had a profound impact on the SCLC's ability to raise funds. According to Congressman Andrew Young, a personal friend and associate of Dr. King, the FBI's effort against Dr. King and the SCLC 'chilled contributions. There were direct attempts at some of our larger contributors who told us that agents had told them that Martin had a Swiss bank account, or that Martin had confiscated some of the monies from the March on Washington for his personal use. None of that was true.'

450. Harry Wachtel, one of Dr. King's legal counsels who handled many of the financial and fund raising activities of the SCLC, emphasized that the SCLC was always in need of funds. 'Getting a grant or getting a contribution is a very fragile thing. A grant delayed has a very serious impact on an organization, whose financial condition was pretty rough.'

451. Wachtel testified that the SCLC continually had to overcome rumors of poor financial management and communist connections. The material '... stayed in the political bloodstream all the way through to the time of Dr. King's death, and even after. In our efforts to build a King Center, it was around. It was like a contamination.'

The SCLC leadership assumed that anything said in meetings or over the telephone would be intercepted by wiretaps, bugs, or informants. Ironically, the FBI memorandum reporting that a wiretap of the SCLC's Atlanta office was feasible stated:

452. 'In the past when interviews have been conducted in the office of Southern Christian Leadership Conference certain employees when asked a question, in a half joking manner and a half serious manner replied, "You should know that already, don't you

have our wires tapped?" It is noted in the past, the State of Georgia has conducted investigations regarding subject and Southern Christian Leadership Conference.'

453. Harry Wachtel commented on the impact constant surveillance on members of the SCLC: 'when you live in a fishbowl, you act like you're in a fishbowl, whether you do it consciously or unconsciously.... I can't put specifies before you, except to say that it beggars the imagination not to believe that the SCLC, Dr. King, and all its leaders were not chilled or inhibited from all kinds of activities, political and even social.'

Wachtel also pointed out the ramifications stemming from the Government's advance knowledge of what civil rights leaders were thinking:

454. 'It is like political intelligence. It did not chill us from saying it, but it affected the strategies and tactics because the people you were having strategies and tactics about were privy to what you were about. They knew your doubts ...Take events like strategies in Atlantic City.... Decision-making concerning which way to go, joining one challenge or not, supporting a particular situation, or not, had to be limited very strongly by the fact that information which was expressed by telephone, or which could even possibly be picked up by bugging, would be in the hands of the President.'

Perhaps most difficult to gauge is the personal impact of the Bureau's programs. Congressman Young told the Committee that while Dr. King was not deterred by the attacks, which are now known to have been instigated in part by the FBI, there is "no question" but that he was personally affected:

455. "It was a great burden to be attacked by people he respected, particularly when the attacks engendered by the FBI came from people like Ralph McGill. He sat down and cried at the New York Times editorial about his statement on Vietnam, but this just made him more determined. It was a great personal suffering, but since we don't really know all that they did, we have no way of knowing the ways that they affected us."

"I can't read no mo' of this shit, cuz," said Ducc, placing the documents on the table.

"Yeah, this shit is too much for me, too," said Tweedy Bird, "Plus, they were talkin' 'bout communists, Black P. Stone Rangers, a whole lotta' white people that I don't even care about, nor will I ever see."

"But you have to care about it, because if they target some of their own people, then there's nothing in the world that would stop them from doing us."

"If that is so, what can we do to stop all of this?" asked Ducc.

"Nothing," Michael said solemnly.

"What do you mean nuthin'?" asked Tweedy Bird.

Wearily, Michael turned and said, "Cuz, we been killing each other for so long that it will take an act of God to stop what has already started. Plus, there are some niggas who are addicted to gangbanging like an addict addicted to crack cocaine. They can't get enough of it. It's the only thing that they know, and without bangin' they're nothing. They'd rather die in a state of ignorance than to dwell in a state of peace."

"But there must be something we can do, can't we?" asked Tweedy Bird.

"I'm not so sure, cuz, and I say this because things is already way outta' hand."

"What about telling the homies what we know? We can show them this stuff and git a crew together and start a war on the fuckin' police," said Ducc.

"The homies ain't going to listen, cuz. They're too comfortable with selling dope to each other, hating on each other, and fuckin' each other's women. They're in too deep, and the bloodshed between us Crips and Bloods runs even deeper."

"Then why did you show us this shit if we weren't going to try to change things?"

"I did it because I felt that if you both knew the truth, then you would at least think twice about taking the life of someone who is less informed."

Tweedy Bird slowly shook his head and said, "You're right, cuz."

"He's right about what?" Ducc asked.

"He's right about this shit being deeper than we could ever imagine."

"I know how you feel cuz, but there are maybe a few things we can do."

"And what's that?"

"Either die in ignorance, or let this shit go and become something we all can be proud of."

"Fuck that proud shit, cuz. I'm gonna keep Cripping until I can find something better," said Ducc.

"What about you?" Michael asked, turning to Tweedy Bird.

"I don't know, cuz, this shit is too deep for me right now...I guess I'll just slang for a while until I make enough money to leave this place. Yeah, that's what I'm going to do."

Turning toward Michael, Ducc asked, "And what about you?"

"I going home and try to be a son to my parents and if that doesn't work then I guess it will be back to Cripping, but for now, I'm through with it."

"Once a Crip, always a Crip...and both you niggas know that, so stop bullshittin yourselves and let's go git those slob niggas for what they done today."

Michael slowly turned to Ducc and then said, "Let's do this just one more time."

"Alright, cuz, just one more time..."

Slowly, they headed for their cars to embark upon a task that many youths across the nation take part in every day ~ retaliation and revenge, a task that will claim the lives of thousands of youth nationwide. Hopefully through God's intervention, America's urban at risk youth will come to an understanding and stop the killing among one another.

1984-1989 the Conclusion

By the end of 1984, Michael found himself in a big tug of war over his love for his gang, his home boys, and his thirst for power through the sale of illegal drugs, which now had become crack cocaine — a new enemy to the gangs, the community, and to all who sought its possession. It seemed as if overnight Michael had moved up in status from being ghetto poor to ghetto rich, and the war between the Crips and Bloods had now became a war over drug profit and territory. Things had gotten so bad that the Crips and Bloods had begun killing some of their own members just to have a bigger take on the prize. Bloodshed between homeboys was rising so fast that many neighborhood gang sects began to venture to other areas of the city to form new territory to proliferate their drugs. Some gang members even left the state of California altogether in order to forge new territories abroad which was the case with Michael.

Michael left Compton, and ventured to Portland, Oregon with a few other Crips from various Crip sects within Los Angeles. There they quickly established new neighborhoods and recruited Portland's newest young males and females who were infatuated with the glamour and glory of this new lifestyle. Children who were once family oriented, and shared a common interest in positive things of life were now lured into a life of death and destruction, and within five years Northeast Portland, Oregon would find its community being turned upside down by gunfire, gang warfare, and death. But for Michael, his time was up; his illegal endeavors led him to become once again standing in front of the halls of justice, facing over 30 years for crimes he committed, and for some he didn't. He knew his train was coming to an end—finally—and on or about June 1987 Michael was taken off the streets, and sentenced for more years than he could count. As he was handcuffed and led away to prison, he looked up toward the sky and whispered, "Lord, if I would have only listened to my parents…"

EPILOGUE

*"Like an unchecked cancer, hate corrodes the per-
sonality and eats away its vital unity. Hate destroys
a man's sense of values and his objectivity. It causes
him to describe the beautiful as ugly and the ugly as
beautiful, and to confuse the true with the false and
the false with the true."*

—Dr. Martin Luther King, Jr.

Through the ensuing years many youth will fall
victim to the "smoking gun" by way of gang violence, drugs, and other social ills found within their
environment. Within this time, many families will be
left wondering, while their children continue dying.
Statistics will be compiled, studied, and then placed in
such a way that these statistics barely gain the attention
of those who could make a difference. Therefore, I, the
author of this book, have taken it upon myself to com-
pile a list of black men, women, and children who have
died in the ghetto streets as a result of gang violence
and drugs. I also included those men and women who
were murdered in cold blood while trying to establish
the civil rights of an oppressed people. I've included
tables, charts, maps, and illustrations in an effort to
illustrate the importance and need for new strategies

in reference to the social ills that are killing minority people nationwide, at an alarming rate. Look at this information, digest this information, and then act upon this information. Please do it now before it's too late.

NATIONAL DEATH LIST

The following is a list of many Civil Rights Activists, Revolutionaries, and young innocent children who were tragically murdered during the struggle for Civil Rights during the 1960s and 1970s nationwide.

Jonathan Jackson, August 7, 1970, murdered in action, defending the cause

George Jackson, August 21, 1971, murdered in San Quentin by prison guards

Bobby James Hutton, April 6, 1968, murdered by Oakland police

Martin Luther King, April 4, 1968, murderer unknown to date

Fred Billingslea, murdered, date unknown

Ron Black, Black Panther, murdered, April 5, 1969

W. L. Nolen, killed by prison guards in Soledad

Cleveland Edward, killed by prison guards in Soledad

Alvin Miller, killed by prison guards in Soledad

Cynthia Wesley, murdered, September 1963, Birmingham Church Bombing

Carol Robertson, murdered September 1963, Birmingham Church Bombing

Addie Mae Collins, murdered September 1963, Birmingham Church Bombing

Denise McNair, murdered September 1963, Birmingham Church Bombing

James Chaney

Fred Hampton

Apprentice "Bunchy" Carter, murdered, January 17, 1969

John Huggins, murdered, January 17, 1969

Alex Rackley

Robert Webb Samuel Napier

299

Ronald Carter
William Christmas
Mark Essex
Frank "Heavy" Field
Mark Clark
Woodie
Changa
Ougbala Green
James McCain
Zayd Malik Shakur
Anthony Kuma
Olugbola White
Harold Russell
Rita Lloyd
Rickie Bodden
Clifford Glover
Herbert Lee
Malcolm X, murdered, February 21, 1965
Jim Lee Jackson
Jim Reed
Sammy Younge, Jr.
Huey P. Newton, leader and founder of the Black Panther
Party
Lewis Allen
Natasha Harlans, murdered in L.A. by Korean store owner
Sammy Younger, Jr.
Jimmy Lee Jackson
Denzil Dowell
Kathleen Smith
Wilfred Lu Tour
Louis T. Johnson
Sandra Pratt, Black Panther member and the wife of
Geronimo Pratt
   Megar Evers, Born: July 2, 1925 Decatur,
Mississippi – Died: June 12, 1963, Jackson,
Mississippi

Emmitt Till (July 25, 1941 – August 28, 1955) Emmitt was killed by two white men who kidnapped him in the middle of the night. Then they drove him to the Hallatachie River. First, they beat him up with a bat and then they got 75 lbs bag of cotton gin, tied it around his ankle with barb wire, and threw him in the river. Those two men were found innocent in a court of law. Emmit's family  had two other trials and the men were still found innocent. The reason why those two men were found innocent was because it was the 1950's and it was segregated and the trial had an all-white jury.

Young black males murdered because of color

Denise McNair, **Carole Robertson**, **Addie May Collin**, and **Cynthia Wesley** were tragically murdered by a system of violence – Sixteenth Baptist Church Bombing

Deaths of Active Gang Members
Los Angeles deceased Eight Tray Gangster Crips

Chili Red
Big Opie,
Baby Evil
Big Moe
Tiny Squowly
Baby Wilbone
G-Roc
Bernadette
Lil Casper
Tiny Ducc
Baby Sidewinder
Big Schoolboy
Baby Moehead, 1996
Lil Sidetracc
Baby Junior, 1997
Baby Evil, 1995
Gangsta Tre, 1997
Gangsta Rocc, 1992

Long Beach Crips that were killed in gang and drug violence

Big Cool Aid
Big Slept Rocc
Big Fruity
Big Meach Dog
Big E
Big Chuco
Robert Earl Love
Lil Loc
Lil Tray Fingers
Lil J. Capone
Lil Man
Lil Boo Dog
P-Love
Gangster Nutty
Q-Dog
Young Meach Dog
Suspect C-dog Lil Bandit

Lil Dirty Bird
E. V.
Baby Laid
Jacoby
Big T. Dog
Big Stan
Lunatic
Horace
Bully
Big Tag
Sadiki
Big 5-0
Big Frog Dog
Capone
Catman
Dezman
Big Ernest
Boo Merkandale
Cripto
Big Half Dead (L.B. 20's)
Scarface (L.B. 20's)
Silver
Sin Badd
BeBe
Baby Scrap
Nasty Nugget
Big Poppa
Big Tag Along
Shy Dog Small
Durocc
Deaf Toney
Boxer
Lil Dave
Stupid
Itchy Rat
Cartoon Big Jay
Vern Dog
Sky Blue
Lil Roc

The following are the deaths of gang members, innocent bystanders who were caught in the middle of gang crossfire and some who died as a result of gang drug deals gone bad:

Minelva Tippie, 48, was standing near the corner of 116th Street and Avalon Boulevard about 3:30 p.m. when she was struck in the head and killed by a stray bullet in Los Angeles, 2001

Rosa Garcia, killed in Harbor City, CA, 2002

Samuel Mendez Ramirez, killed in Harbor City, CA, 2002

Abraham Olazabal Jr., 19, of South Gate, killed in Harbor City, CA, 2002

Jose Perez, 25, killed in Harbor City, CA, 2002

Carlos Florina, 22 killed in Los Angeles, 2002

Manuolevao Stibbie, 23, killed August 18, 2002, in Harbor City, CA

Eliseo Rodriguez, 27, killed in Los Angeles, 2002

Samuel Mendez Ramirez, 17, killed in Los Angeles, 2002

Manuel Edgardo Palacios, 41, killed by gang member in Los Angeles

Eliseo Rodriguez Moreno, 28, innocent bystander killed by bullets in Los Angeles

Carl Smith: Murdered on March 28, 2003, in Inglewood, CA

Andre Morgan, murdered November 26, 2006, in Inglewood, CA

Genesis Regalado, 11, New York, killed July 19, 2006

Dreshawna Monique Washington Davis, 8, killed in Jacksonville, FL, July 27, 2006

Tracy Rose Lambert, murdered August 1998 as a part of a Crip initiation (not gang members)

Susan Raye Moore, killed August 1998 as a part of a Crip initiation (were not gang members)

Michael "Salty" Leblanc; October 9, 1972, Compton, CA

Kim "Bullet" Tate, 1979, Santana Blocc, Compton, CA

Turtle, Santana Blocc, 1989, Compton, CA

Angelo, Santana Blocc, Compton,, CA

Terry Tarzan, Compton, CA

Bartender, Compton, CA

Raymond Washington, Los Angeles, Born 8-14-53, Died 8-9-79

Robert Ballou: March 1972

Mauricio Ibarra, 20, murdered August 2, 2002, Los Angeles

Helen Coronado killed in a drive-by shooting, Chicago, IL, October 8, 2006

Ethan Esparza, 3, killed in drive-by shooting, Pomona, CA, November 21, 2006

Daniel Chantha, killed in Long Beach, CA, 2003

Woodtee Bunthong, killed in Long Beach, CA, December 31, 2003

Sakorn Phan, killed, 2004, Long Beach, CA

DeAndre M. Parker, 20, killed on September 2, 2006, in Kansas City

Jamee Finney, 13, killed in 1988 by gang member in Los Angeles

Latonjyia Stover, 18, killed in 1988 by gang member in Los Angeles

Lee Westley Horne, 20, July 8, 1985, killed by gang member in Los Angeles

Jason Demyers killed in drive-by shooting, Los Angeles, 1988

Enrico Bonner, 20, killed in 1998 by gang members in Los Angeles

Jose Platero, killed in drive-by shooting in 1988, Los Angeles

Fernando Gutierrez, 22, killed in drive-by shooting in Santa Anna, CA

Willie Bogan, killed in 1993, in Los Angeles by LA gang members

Gloria Lyons and **Georgia Jones** were killed by LA gang member for being witnesses 1994

Albert Sutton killed in 1992 after testifying against LA gang members for shooting his brother

Darryl Modisett, 19, killed in 1992 in North Hollywood, CA, mistaken for a gang rival

Marco Melgar killed in Hollywood, CA, in 1995, for testifying in court

"Crazy" Ray Nichols killed August 1994 in Los Angeles

Clarence Gaston Jr. found beaten to death in Los Angeles by a known gang member

Donald Ray Loggins and **Payton Beroit** were killed in 1991 by LA gang members

Selwyn Leflore Jr. killed in gang crossfire, October 1997, Compton, CA

Omar Sevilla, 22, of Culver City was killed in Santa Monica, CA, in 1998

Lori Rene Gonzalez *(granddaughter of LAPD Chief Bernard Parks)* murdered in Los Angeles, 2000

Adriahana Prothro victim of a drive-by shooting in 1993, Los Angeles

Nicole Williamson, 19, killed on November 29, 2003, Los Angeles

Ramiro Tamez, 20, killed in North Hollywood, CA, 2001 Los Angeles Police Officer **Brian Brown** and **Gerardo Cernas** killed during a drive-by shooting, November 29, 1998 **Elvira Ramirez**, 15, killed by gang members, Compton, CA, 2001 **Ricardo Reynoza**, 28, killed by gang members, Los Angeles, 2001 **Kylah Witrago** (*a baby*), killed by 21 year old gang member; Kylah was the only child younger than 5 to die in a drive by shooting in Los Angeles County in the year 2001 LAPD Officer, **Filbert Cuesta Jr.**, killed by gang member, Los Angeles, 1998 **Martin Hernandez**, of South Gate was shot in South Los Angeles, 2002 **Manuel Edgardo Palacios**, 41, was hit by a stray bullet in Los Angeles, 2002 **Ernie Williams**, was gunned down by gang members on his way to a neighborhood store in Los Angeles **Clyve Jackson**, 14, was killed on November 21, 2002, Los Angeles **Ernest D. Williams**, 17, died of multiple gunshots to the head in Los Angeles **Baby Lane**, SSCC, 1999, Compton, CA **Tupuc Shakur**, murdered in Las Vegas, September 6, 1996

Blue, Grape St. Crip, murdered in Tacoma, WA **Lil Blue**, Grape St. Crip, murdered in Tacoma, WA **Tray**, Shotgun, Crips, murdered, Tacoma, WA **Lil Nucc**, Westcoast Rollin' 80's Crips, murdered, Los Angeles **Big O**, Rollin' 60's Crips, murdered, Seattle, WA **Stevie Boy**, Fruit Town Piru, murdered in Seattle, WA **Keith Stone**, Rollin' 60's Crip, murdered, place unknown (Los Angeles) **J. Capone**, Ten-Four Crip murdered, Los Angeles **Ken Dog**, Four Deuce Gangster Crip, murdered, Los Angeles **Big Monk**, Main Street Mafia, murdered, Los Angeles **Baby Main**, 98 Mafia Crip, murdered, Los Angeles **Big Chimp**: Underground Crip, murdered, Los Angeles **Magic**, NBCC, murdered, Compton, CA **Christopher Lynch**, murdered by Ralph Flores, Los Angeles, May 14, 1999 **Claudia Chenet**, murdered in Los Angeles, Nov 19, 2003 **Miguel Reyes**, murdered, Los Angeles, December 2004 **Fenise Luna**, murdered, Los Angeles, December 28, 2004 **Sweet Pea**, killed in accident, Compton, CA **J. Blacc**: Seven-Four Hoover, murdered, Seattle, WA, 1993

Wolf Loc, Eight-Tray Gangster, murdered in Seattle, WA, 1993
Jun-Jun: Seven-Four Hoover, murdered in Seattle, WA, 1993
Biggie Smalls (*Notorious B.I.G.*) murdered March 9, Los Angeles, 1997
Mac Thomas: Original Compton Crip, murdered in Compton, CA
Michael Stone: Front hood Crip, murdered, Compton, CA, 1997
Tamika McFadden-Harris, murdered in Chicago November 16, 2001
Nakeda Stroud, 23, murdered in Chicago, November 18, 2001
Mike Boyd, killed at 15, murdered in Chicago, 2001
Severo Enriquez, killed at 14 in Chicago, 2001

Sok Khak Ung, killed October 19, 2003, Los Angeles
Vouthy Tho, killed, October 13, 2003, Los Angeles
Francis Joel Rivers, 26, was killed on October 18, 2003, Los Angeles
Patricia Anne Miller, killed, June 2003, Los Angeles
Tony Lopez, 18, 2005, murdered in Los Angeles
Anthony Lopez, 14, 2005, murdered in Los Angeles
Timothy Soto, 17, murdered in 2003, Los Angeles
Jamiel Shaw Jr., 17, killed on March 7, 2008, Los Angeles
Marquel Smith, 32, murdered, December 17, 2006 Baltimore
Carl Lackl Jr., 38, murdered, July 2, 2006, Baltimore

Police say **Shauntay Henderson** lead the 12th Street Gang and could have possibly been involved in at least four other murders, in addition to Parker's death.

Alleged gang leader Shauntay Henderson sentenced to three years in prison for killing a man at a south Kansas City convenience store in 2006.Circuit Judge Robert M. Schieber convicted Henderson, 26, at a bench trial in November of voluntary manslaughter and armed criminal action. Prosecutors originally had sought a second-degree murder conviction. Schieber sentenced her to three years on the armed criminal action count. He gave her 10 years for manslaughter, but suspended the imposition of the sentence and put her on probation for five years. Henderson briefly made the FBI's Ten Most Wanted Fugitives list before her capture in 2007.The trial did not address allegations by police and federal officials that Henderson was a violent street gang member.

Ernest Williams, 17, innocent bystander killed in a gang shooting, Los Angeles, 2002
Daniel Lopez, 19, innocent bystander killed in a gang shooting, Los Angeles 2002
Abraham Olazabal, 19, innocent bystander killed in a gang shooting, Los Angeles 2002
Juan Gabriel Valenzuela, innocent bystander killed in a gang shooting, Los Angeles 2002
Willie Yee Alfonso, 27, innocent bystander killed in a gang shooting, Los Angeles 2002
Lorenzo Romero, 29, innocent bystander killed in a gang shooting, Los Angeles 2002
Isiah Samuel Moore Jr., 41, innocent bystander killed in a gang shooting, Los Angeles 2002
Jose S. Perez, 25, innocent bystander killed in a gang shooting, Los Angeles 2002
John Henry Smith Jr., 33, innocent bystander killed in a gang shooting, Los Angeles 2002
Silverio Luna, 22, a Pacoima gang member was killed in drive by shooting, Pacoima, CA, 2002
Akida Clay, 25, and Daniel Sykes, 34, were killed in an ambush shooting, Pacoima, CA, 2002
Ryan Gonzalez, 16, killed June 3, 2000, by gang member

Alton McDonald, 37, gunned down at a gas station, 2002, Compton, CA
Byron Benito, 19, repeatedly beaten and stabbed in retaliation for a killing, Los Angeles, 2002
Edmund Oreefe Brown, 28, innocent victim killed by gunfire, Los Angeles 2003
Bryan Du'wan Brown, 23, innocent bystander killed by gunfire, Los Angeles, 2003
Javier Martinez, 18, of Anaheim was shot in Los Angles, 2003
Byron Benito, 19, killed by gang members in Santa Clarita, CA, 2003
Victor Flores, 19, killed by gang members in Santa Clarita, CA, 2003
Jonathan Townsend, 18, of Windsor, CA, was killed by gang members in 2003
Lawrence Andrew Middleton, 26, killed on June 26, 2003, by a gang member, Los Angeles
Londell Murdock Jr., 33, innocent bystander gunned down by gang members in Los Angeles, 2003
Frankie Miramontez, 17, murdered December 22, 1999, Ventura, CA
Marcos Arellano, 19, killed in Santa Clarita, California, 2003
Ronald Martin, killed on October 14, 1997, by gang member

Margie Mendoza, 26, killed November 9, 2001, by gang member

Brian Byrd, 23, shot, April, 2003, Los Angeles

Ty Elliott Wilson, 22, shot, April 2003 in Los Angeles

Damon Burris, 32, shot, April, 2003, Los Angeles, CA

Denzell Martin-Sanders, 3-year-old shot, Compton, CA, June 2003

Yetunde Price, 31, (*the sister of Serena and Venus Williams*) was shot on September 14, 2003, as she drove a sport utility vehicle, Compton, CA

Burbank Police Officer **Matthew Pavelka**, was killed in shoot out with Los Angeles gang members, 2003

Monica Agustin Noriega, 35, mother of three, shot in front of her husband and children, Los Angeles, 2003

Anthony Brown, 16, a Crenshaw High School student was gunned down by an apparent gang member

Luciano Ramirez, 18, was killed by a gang member, May 31, 2002, Lakewood, CA

Paul Griego Jr., 17, was killed by a gang member, July 6, 2002, Long Beach, CA

Darryl Dewayne "Kactus" White, 19, shot, Compton, CA, November 27, 2003

Damar White, 18, shot, Compton, CA, January 2, 2003

Horace Ray-Ray Ferguson, Jr., 9, shot six times, Compton, CA, January 2003

Lewis Wright Jr., 16, murdered in the streets of Los Angeles, 2003

Tyronn Bickham, 22, innocent victim of gang violence, Los Angles, 2003

Jamaal Nelson, 18, innocent victim of gang violence, killed February 16, 2003, Los Angeles

Peter Drake Jr., innocent victim of gang violence killed in Los Angeles, 2003

Roshod Hamilton, 16, murdered at Jefferson Park in Los Angeles, 1996

Brian Wofford, 21, an innocent victim who was fatally shot in Los Angeles, June 3, 2002

Darrik Cobb, James Williams, Victor Nunez, Alfred Vicuna, Derrick Young, and **Robert Parker**, all died in 1988 near the same intersection in Los Angeles

Jhana Leah Wilson, 20, an innocent victim who was fatally shot on July 16, 2001, Los Angeles

Donte Briggs, 22 years-old, shot and killed October 13, 2003, Los Angeles

Lewis Wrights Jr., 17 years-old, shot and killed October 13, 2003, Los Angeles

Paul Mitchell, shot, November 22, 2000, Los Angeles

Astrid "Sandy" Zelada, 24, was shot while in her vehicle, on February 25, 2001, Los Angeles

Tamile Cooper, 19, shot and killed in Los Angeles on July 7, 2001

Frederick "Red Boy" Pettaway, 42, killed in Los Angeles on July 9, 2001

Willie Henry Williams Jr., 42, shot and killed in Los Angeles on July 9, 2001

Darrin Blackmon, 22, killed in Los Angeles, 2003

Marquese Prude, 13, shot, Los Angeles, November 2001

Donald Deshon Bonds, 21, shot, April 4, 2003, Los Angeles

Pearlina Laporte, 21, was killed January 1st in a drive-by shooting in Watts, Los Angeles

Terrell Porter McNeil, 19, of Tacoma, WA, shot, December 31, 2003, Los Angeles

Manuel Suarez, 21, from Van Nuys, CA, shot in Los Angeles, 2004

Rasheed Agee, 21, died January 21, 2004, when at least two gang members shot him at his Los Angeles home

Donald Watkins, 39, an innocent homeless man was beaten to death by gang members in Los Angeles, 2004

Jorge Lua, 24, and **Eric Daniel Arzola**, 23, both suspected Los Angeles gang members were killed 10 hours apart outside a bar, 2004, Los Angeles

Edward Mauricio Rendon, III, shot, March, 2004, Los Angeles

Yasmin Toledo, 18, an innocent bystander killed in front of home in drive-by, Los Angeles, 2004

Laudelina Salazar Garcia, a mother decorating her Christmas tree was killed by a stray bullet, Los Angeles, 2004

Demario Moore, 15, and **Quinesha Dunford**, 13, students at Manual Arts High School in Los Angeles were killed September 10, 2003, when gang members pulled up to a crowd of students and opened fire on them.

Daniel Alizar Hernandez, 28, of Oxnard was shot several times in a gang-related attack, Los Angeles, 2004

Allen Davis, 27, of Lancaster, killed outside his home on October 20, 2003, Los Angeles

Julio Villegas, 16, while walking with a friend in Los Angeles, was struck in the head and died at Antelope Valley Hospital three days later, October, 2003

Trevon Coleman, 27, was shot during an argument at 9:15 a.m. October 16, 2003, Los Angeles

Venus Hyun, 21, shot by gang members, Los Angeles 2004

LOS ANGELES — A Los Angeles man and gang member was sentenced today to life in prison without parole for carjacking, kidnapping, raping and murdering a 23-year-old Glendale woman whose body was dumped in a Culver City park.

Jason Thompson, now 26, pleaded guilty January 13 to the February 22, 2001, slaying of **Roberta Happe** sparing him a possible death sentence if the case had gone to trial. In a courtroom brimming with emotion, the young woman's father said he had intended to help his daughter plan her upcoming wedding. To help identify her assailant, police used surveillance camera footage from a bank ATM where Happe was taken to withdraw money. Her body was found in Culver City Park less than two hours after she was abducted, authorities said. She had been raped, beaten, strangled and stabbed.

Raul Aguirre, 17, was hit in the head with a tire iron after trying to break up a gang fight, Los Angeles, 2004

Kelley Browner, was killed on November 12, 2002, as he walked down a sidewalk in Los Angeles

Ishmail Durden, 9, shot inside his Los Angeles home, February 2003

Quorne Warren, 21, shot over a greeting that was taken as disrespect, Los Angeles 2004

Jose Corona was shot at about 1:30 a.m. as he walked out of a house with a group of friends, Los Angeles, 2004

Byron Lee Jr., 14, was first wounded by two men as he rode his bike (in broad daylight) near his home in South Los Angeles, and then pleaded for his life before the suspects shot him dead

Gustavo Ceballos, 17, of Palmdale, was killed in what detectives believe was a gunfight between rival gangs in front of an east Palmdale home, Los Angeles 2004

On March 10, 2004, a stray bullet from a drive-by shooting hit 19-year-old **Jesus Hernandez** in the head as he drove home from work. In a sad coincidence, Hernandez's 10-year-old cousin, **Stephanie Raygoza**, was killed four years earlier on the same street after a stray bullet hit her in the chest as she was riding a scooter on the sidewalk.

Keiyontate Bailey, 19, West Los Angeles college student from Ladera Heights, was shot in mid-morning along South Budlong Avenue and taken to a hospital where he died 2003

Dave Cortez, 21, was shot and killed in North Hollywood, Los Angeles, 2004.

Officer Steiner, 35, was shot multiple times including a gunshot to the head outside the Los Angeles County Superior Courthouse in Pomona, April 21, 2004, by a 16 year old, who was trying to impress a gang.

Devontay Oats, 18, a student at Lancaster High School, was shot to death May 8, 2004, during a party at a Los Angeles home

Jimmy Drisdom, 35, shot on a sidewalk outside a Los Angeles home, 2004

Calvin Edwards, 33, shot November 2004, Los Angeles

Keyante Reed, 22, wrongfully killed in Long Beach by a police officer who was later fired as a result of the shooting

Frankie Lopez, 17, shot on December 25, 2004, Los Angeles

Carlos Pinon, 16, shot by gang members, Los Angeles, 2004

Deliesh Allen, 15, shot in the head outside of Locke High School, Los Angeles, 2005

Lamoun Thames, 15, stabbed by gang members in Los Angeles, August 5, 1992

Michael A. Arrellano, 15, stabbed by a 14-year-old gang member in Los Angeles, September 25, 1992

Sheila Lorta, 16, Paramount California High School student was killed in a gang-related shooting crossfire, Los Angeles, September 30, 1992

Michael Johnson, 15, stabbed with a screwdriver and knife as a casualty of school violence by watching a gang fight, January 22, 1993

Michael Shean Ensley, 17, shot at Reseda High School, Los Angeles, February 22, 1993

David Marceleno, 23, killed by gang member, Oxnard, CA, 2005

Joey Swift, 13, killed in a drive-by shooting just after he left church, March 23, 2003, Los Angeles

Michael Livingston, 20, shot in the head by a gang member while driving on the freeway in Los Angeles, March 29, 2005

Lindsey Hasan, 20, shot on Super Bowl Sunday in Los Angeles

Erika Izquierdo, 11, shot at home by gang members while sitting in a hammock with her father on an unlighted porch, Huntington Park, CA, October, 1995

Mario Millan Jr., 13 and **Bobby Millan**, 12, were both shot and killed when their parents' car was sprayed with gunfire on the way home from a Halloween party in Compton, CA, October 2005

Marco Delgado Jr., 13, was killed in Los Angeles, October 2005 by former classmate

Sheriff's Deputy **Stephen Blair**, 35, was shot and killed as he stepped out of his patrol car while attempting to contact two known gang members

Officer **Brian Brown**, 27, was the victim of a gang shooting on, November 29, 1998, as he and his partner, Francisco Dominguez, chased two gunmen ~

The gunmen who had just committed a fatal drive-by shooting in Culver City peppered the squad car with assault-weapon fire. Brown, who didn't have time to get out of his car or draw his weapon, was struck in the head.

Zatarain, 23, of Rancho Cucamonga, who was one of the gang members involved in the killing of Officer Brian Brown was shot and killed at a nearby shopping mall by officers in pursuit of him for the killing of their fellow officer

Daryle Black, 33, shot when he and his partner were ambushed in Long Beach by Compton, CA, gang members

Jason Bandel, 19, of Victorville, was killed while attending a wake in Long Beach, CA, 1992

Ralph Preciado, 19, shot in Long Beach by a 16-year-old gang member, 1992

Chad MacDonald, 17, was strangled to death in March 1998 by trio of gang members

Joe Hawkins, 21, mistaken for a rival gang member was shot by gang members the night before Thanksgiving in Los Angeles, 1988

Gerald Hawkins, 22, was shot in Compton, CA, by two drug addicts (one of whom was on probation) who tried to take his car

Victor Centeno, 32, and **Rodney Lee**, 14, were fatally shot on August 14, 1999, in Los Angeles, both were gang members

Moises Martinez, 20, was the victim of a drive-by shooting in the circle area of Norwalk, CA, 1999

Kayla Witrago (10 months old), shot as she sat in her stroller, Compton, CA, 2000 ~ Her killer has not been caught but the driver, Jesse Sosa, 21, of Long Beach, was sentenced to life in prison without parole for his role in a drive-by shooting.

Tiana English (2 months old), shot once in the head; her father, Brandon English, was hit by six bullets in the legs and chest, Compton 2002

Denzel Sanderson, 3, was killed as he rode his bicycle in his Compton, CA, driveway, June 2003

Patricia Miller, 52, an elementary school teacher at Gompers Middle School in Los Angeles was gunned down when her car was sprayed with gunfire on June 22, 2003.

Javier Gutierrez, 17, a Jordan High School student was shot in the back and one of his friends was shot in the face a block from their campus in Los Angeles, 2004

Tara Correa-McMullen, 16, an actress was hanging out with friends in front of an apartment complex in Inglewood, CA, when she was fatally shot ~ Police described her as the innocent victim of a gang-related shooting.

Labrina Pullard, 17, shot while sitting in a car with her boyfriend who was wounded in the attack, Compton, CA, December 11, 2005

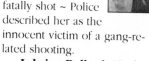

Richard Lopez, 38, a Santa Ana, CA, man was fatally shot on Civic Center Drive on Wednesday evening in what police say was a gang-related shooting 2006

Fernando Magana, 17, was killed in an apparent gang-related shooting, according to Santa Ana police, 2006

Larry Marcial, 22, was killed in Los Angeles, 2006, when two gunmen opened fire upon him

David Marcial, 10, killed when two gunmen opened fire upon him, Los Angeles, 2006

Luis Cervantes, 17, was killed in Los Angeles, 2006, when two gunmen opened fire upon him

Kenneth Wilson, 38, killed in Los Angeles in 1999 by a gang

Anthony Prudhomme, 21, was murdered November 3, 2000, in his Highland Park, CA, apartment by two armed members of a gang; he was wearing a T-shirt that said, "Keep the Peace"

Stephanie Kuhen, 3, killed on September 17, 1995, by gang members in Los Angeles ~ The family had turned down the wrong street and when they open fire upon their car killing the child and wounding others.

Cynthia Portillo, 19, and pregnant, was shot to death in February 2005 as she walked down the street with an 18-year-old alleged member of a gang

Christopher Bauser, 28, was killed by gang members, November 11, 2000

Kaitlyn Avila, 3, Police searched a Los Angeles suburb for a gunman who killed a 3-year-old girl and critically wounded her father in an apparently gang-related shooting in Baldwin Hills, 2006

Cheryl Green, 14, was shot by a gang member while walking with a group of friends in Harbor City, CA, December 15, 2006

Christopher Ash, 25, killed because he was a witness to the above killing in Harbor City, 2006

Jonathan Hurtado, 18, killed in Los Angeles, 2007, as he returned to his old gang neighborhood

Marquis Wilbert, 11, was killed on his bike in Los Angeles, 1997

Robert Hightower, 19, Pasadena High School Senior, was shot to death after hugging his sister, whom he had been visiting ~ A 204th Street gang member shot him, according to court testimony, because

he was upset that a black boxer had beaten a Latino in a prizefight.

Eric Butler, 39, shot while trying to protect his daughter from being harassed by gang members, Los Angeles, 2003

Michael Richardson, 22, African American, shot by gang member on a bicycle, who was convicted of murder and a hate crime, April 1999

Dino Downs, 41, African American, shot while standing outside his house, April 2000, by two possible Latino gang members

Kent Lopez, 20, African American, shot while walking to a bus stop ~ Witnesses testified that gang members yelled a racial epithet and death threats at Lopez. Two gang members were convicted of murder.

Arturo Ponce, 34, Latino was a Mexican immigrant and cook was shot on December 6, 2006, in front of his apartment as he talked with friends ~ Witnesses say the shooter, masked and hooded, yelled an anti-Mexican epithet.

Miguel Fernandez, 19, shot after being approached by occupants of another car while driving down the street, Los Angeles

Francisco Lopez-Reynaga, 19, of Palmdale was shot to death by a rival gang member in Lancaster, CA, 2003

Jose Cano, 13, was stabbed to death in Long Beach, CA, in a gang dispute retaliation
Shulma, 17, and **Jason Ramos**, 16, were killed January 31, 2004, by Leon McDonald Brown III who was sentenced to life
Reginald "Reggie" Hays, 16, a known gang member, was fatally shot in the chest while listening to an iPod in his parked car, Carson, CA, 2007
Edwin Catalan, 22, was shot multiple times in an apparent gang-related shooting in East Hollywood, CA, 2007
Maria Hicks, 57, was on her way home when she was killed after confronting taggers in her neighborhood, Los Angeles, 2007
Seutatia Tausili, 65, of Hesperia was shot after she and family members confronted taggers spray-painting graffiti on their apartment wall and trash cans
Oscar Manuel Martinez, 24, of Garden Grove, and **Michelle Nicole Miller**, 19, of Rialto was shot in Garden Grove, CA, by rival gang members in 2007
Kejuan Edward Bullard, 23, shot on March 18, 2008 ~ Authorities said witnesses saw two black men running from the scene after the shooting; one man was carrying a handgun

Luis Garcia, (*23 days old*), killed by a stray bullet and a 37-year-old man was wounded near an intersection in Los Angeles, 2007 ~ The mother was pushing the baby in his stroller as she shopped for clothes spread out on the sidewalk at a vending location. The suspects walked up to the vendor and shot him in the chest. One stray bullet hit the baby.
Rene Vargas, 14, was gunned down in Los Angeles in 2007, because he was affiliated with a tagging crew
Jason Grey, 29, was fatally shot at the Glendale-based Forest Lawn cemetery in Los Angeles on January 1, 2008
Brandon "B.L." Bullard, 25, was shot in the face at a party in a rented hall in South-Central Los Angeles, January 2008
Maurio Proctor, 22, was fatally shot in a drive-by shooting in South Los Angeles on January 27, 2008
Devon Perry, 17, shot execution style in the back of the head, South Los Angeles, 2008
Van Knott, 19, an innocent bystander was shot multiple times in the chest while outside talking with a friend, Watts area, January 28, 2008

Marcos Salas, 36, an ex-gang member was killed when a car full of youths approached him as he walked in front of Aragon Avenue Elementary School to pick up his daughter. Without a word, they shot him 17 times as he carried his 2-year-old granddaughter, February 2008, Los Angeles

Daniel Leon, 20, a gang member was killed by police after shooting an ex-gang member in Los Angeles, 2008

Anthony E. Escobar, 13, was fatally gunned down by suspected gang members after he crossed the street to get lemons from a neighbor's tree, Los Angeles, 2008

On March 2, 2008, **Jamiel Shaw Jr.**, 17, was gunned down by a 19-year-old gang member ~ The gunman had spent nearly four months in a Los Angeles County jail for exhibiting a firearm and resisting arrest before he was released on March 1, 2008, just 28 hours before he murdered Jamiel.

Abraham Manuel Guerrero, 22, shot by a gang-related drive-by in Pacoima, Los Angeles, December 2008

Jose Luis Garcia Bailey, 11, of Long Beach was shot in the upper body by two suspects who approached him while he was standing with a group of kids, Los Angeles, 2008

Roberto Ramirez, 14, was killed in Stockton, CA, by gang member in 2008

Rigoberto Vega, 23, and **David Gallegos**, 32, who was in his wheelchair, were shot and killed by a Compton, CA, gang member, Los Angeles 2008

Marco Corona, 31, was walking down a street when an alleged gang member approached on foot, pulled out a handgun, and fired, wounding Corona once in the upper body, he died later, Los Angeles, 2008

Arcadio Guillen, 18, was shot in the head by one or more young men who approached him outside a taco wagon, March 2008

Troy Green's, 23, a black mentally ill man was shot and found dead in a gang populated area of Los Angeles in May 2008

Thomas Grimes, 27, was fatally stabbed by 6 to 10 suspected Latino gang members, June 2008, Los Angeles

Michael Byoune, 19, an African American, was unarmed when shot and killed on May 11, 2008, by an Inglewood Police officer ~ Allegedly, Byoune and two friends parked their car in the parking lot of the Rally's Burger Restaurant located on the corner of Manchester Ave. and Crenshaw Blvd. They reportedly got out of the car to purchase their late-night meal at the fast food eatery. Gunshots erupted behind the restaurant and Byoune allegedly attempted to flee the immediate danger by running to get into his vehicle. Inglewood Police who heard the gunfire witnessed Byoune running to a waiting vehicle. Inglewood Police issued a statement saying: "As the subject entered the vehicle, he turned toward the officers. The vehicle proceeded in the direction of the officers and almost simultaneously the officers heard additional shots fired. The officers felt their police vehicle being struck and believed they were being shot at by the occupants of the vehicle. Fearing for their safety both officers fired multiple shots at the vehicle and it stopped directly across from them" Byoune died at the scene. The driver, Larry White, 19, was hit in the leg and a third, unidentified friend in the back seat, was not hit by the police officers gun fire.

Christopher Taylor, 19, an African American was shot and killed outside his home in the Jefferson Park (CA) area on June 13, 2008 ~ According to a neighbor; Taylor and a friend were leaning against a car, text-messaging on their cell phones, when a vehicle drove up next to them. A person from inside the car said "*what's up homie*," then began shooting, hitting Taylor at least once in the head. The neighbor said she ran out and saw Taylor's mother holding him. "*She kept screaming, 'My son, my son.'*"

Ashley Lunsford, 19, and Shannon Fortune, 19, suffered multiple gunshot wounds in a Pomona, CA, shooting incident; both victims were found on the sidewalk

Cynthia Perez, a 14-year-old Latina girl, was caught in gang crossfire as she sat in the back seat of her family's car on May 26, 2008, Los Angeles ~ Los Angeles Police Department officials said while stopped at a light, the car next to them got into an argument with a gang member who was on the sidewalk. The gang member pulled out a gun and fired several shots: one struck Perez, another her 7-year-old brother (survived), and the driver of another vehicle (survived). Two hours after the shooting, authorities arrested the 16-year-old alleged gang member on suspicion of attempted murder.

Rosalio De La Rosa, 22, died after arguing with a man in North Hills, June 2008, Los Angeles ~ De La Rosa claimed to be a gang member, and then pointed a gun at the man, who allegedly used his own weapon to shoot De La Rosa.

Robert Howard Carrion, 19, was pronounced dead in June 2008, after being found late Saturday in Riverside's Nichols Park with a gunshot wound to the torso, Los Angeles

Derek Chambers, 21, shot by suspected gang members

Edward Jones Jr., 20, shot, Los Angeles, 2008

Jose Villalobos, 37, of Bell was shot dead by gang members after a fight at a bar in Los Angeles, 2008

Donald Robert Walker III, 22, found dead on the floor of an upstairs apartment suffering from a gunshot wound, 2008.

Jonathan M. died as a result of the blunt force trauma to his head, June 6, 2008

Ezequiel Gonzalez, 22, was killed in July 2006, when rival gang members exchanged gunfire while riding in a car that collided head-on with another car and caught fire

Miguel Reyes, 21, of Anaheim, CA, was found dead when five suspected gang members started shooting at a graduation party, 2008

Martha Puebla, 16, was shot in the face as she sat outside her San Fernando Valley home on May 12, 2003 ~ Days earlier she had testified at a preliminary hearing for Jose Ledesma, a Vineland Boyz member who was on trial for a 2002 shooting death that occurred outside her house. Puebla testified that she did not see the shooter.

Zuri Williams drove to a local liquor store in an unincorporated area of Los Angeles County with her 5-year-old son and as she entered the store, a vehicle drove by and fired volley of gunshots, striking her in the stomach, July 20, 2006

Jahaira Keys was attending a party in Carson, CA, when she was shot and killed in the parking lot after the party ended, May 3, 2007

Kyutza Joan Herrera was shot and killed while seated in her vehicle, which was parked in front of a store in Lynwood, CA, August 4, 2007 ~ The male black suspects were shooting at two male blacks, who were injured, while they were standing near the doorway of the store.

Adrian Garcia-Diaz, 16, was killed July 2008, when a fight broke out at Los Angeles High School and escalated until the suspect pulled a handgun and fired a shot into the crowd, striking Garcia-Diaz in the chest.

Veronica Gonzales was shot while standing in a doorway when the suspects drove up and starting shooting, April 30, 2004, Los Angeles

Diamond Baysinger, 19, shot and killed December 12, 2004, in Los Angeles, he had no known gang affiliation

Herman Rosales was shot and killed on the stairwell of a pedestrian bridge, Los Angeles, on March 6, 2009

John Leonard, 20, was found dead on July 2008, of a single gunshot wound in Palo Alto, CA

Jasmine Sanders, 8, was playing with her brother outside a South Los Angeles apartment building when she was struck by a stray bullet that was fired by her 13-year-old cousin who was aiming at another ~ The cousin was sentenced to 50 years plus two life sentences for the first-degree murder of Sanders.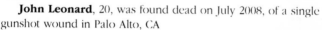

Dazohn Roberts, 16, was killed on September 13, 2006, by an 18-year-old rival gang member in Los Angeles

Raymond Franklin, 23, was shot and killed in the driveway of his home on May 2, 2008 ~ Franklin was an African American father of three with another child on the way. He grew up in gang territory, however, was not a gang member. Rather, he became a mentor who discouraged neighborhood youth from joining gangs and encouraged them to become model citizens. Franklin himself completed school to become a correctional officer.

Marshawn "Derrick" Hampton, 18, of San Bernardino, CA, was killed in a drive-by shooting near his home, September 2008

Jose Alfredo Farias, 24, his brother **Victor Manuel Farias**, 25, and **Vidal Hernandez Rebolledo**, 23, were fatally shot in September 2008, Los Angeles, CA

Henry Watts, 28, was shot multiple times in September 2008, Los Angeles, CA

Kimberly Bonds, 19, on July 13, while visiting with friends in front of her apartment complex, two black men walked out of an alley and began shooting at rival gang members standing near her; Bonds, attempting to take cover, was struck by gunfire

Charles Corey, 31, was in front of his apartment building when a suspect in a car drove by and fired multiple gunshots, April 23, 2008, Los Angeles

Emitt Love Jr., 25, was found shot to death at a bus stop in Athens, June 2008, Los Angeles

Jemal Trotter, 39, was shot and killed, November 8, 2008

Alvaro Ely Calderon, 31, had no apparent gang ties was fatally wounded in a drive-by shooting two blocks away from his home, January 2008, Los Angeles

Stephanice Latrice Smith, 37, was driving back from the store when another car pulled up and fired shots into her car, Los Angeles

Damon Lamont Jones, 38, was fatally shot by two men who walked up and yelled out a gang reference before opening fire upon Jones and another victim (survived) who stood with another man in front of a residence, Los Angeles, October 20, 2008

Jayquan Johnson, 16, a Hamilton High School Student was fatally shot on Octtober 20, 2008

Filberto Ramos, 22, was shot to death in Arleta, October 21, 2008

Isai Jimenez, 30, was killed inside a restaurant on October 18, 2008

Ladislao Chavez, 52, a Latino who died when he was shot in the head while riding a bicycle in Los Angeles, September 15 ~ Police said the gunman was a black man who fled the scene.

Carlos Pulido, 28, was shot outside a party in unincorporated Los Angeles County near Watts, October 18, 2008

Christopher Dajan Avery, 29, shot in South Los Angeles, September 6, 2008

John Schula, 30, a Latino male from Montebello, and a 17-year-old boy were fatally wounded in what sheriff's deputies described as a gang-related shooting, October 18, 2008

Manuel Angel Torres, 17, a Latino male from La Puente, was fatally wounded in a double shooting, October 18, 2008

Juan Duarte, 21, was shot and killed

Christoper Don Woods, 23, died of a gunshot wound to his back, October 4, 2008

William Stanford Workman III, 24, died after being shot in the back, September 30, 2008, Los Angeles

Kevin Dion Baldwin, 33, was fatally shot while standing with four friends in the driveway of a residence, October 6, 2008, Los Angeles

Kevin Harding, 23, shot multiple times in a drive-by shooting while standing outside a store, October 2, 2008, Los Angeles

Columbus Lanard Campbell, 39, (*at right*) and **Kavette Hashani Watson**, 16, died in a an apparant gang-related shooting on October 6, 2008

Eric Sims, 17, was shot and killed in South Los Angeles while riding his bicycle, August 11, 2008

Steven Munoz, 11, and **Luis Rodriguez**, 18, of Long Beach were sitting with a group of people when someone in a passing car fired at them several times killing them both, October 2008, Los Angeles

Damion Cook, 39, was shot and killed in the Vermont Knolls area, Los Angeles, November 2008

Carrington Henderson, 25, shot while standing in the street by a drive-by shooting, Los Angeles ~ The killing is believed to be gang-related, police said.

Rodney Smith, 22, died of a gunshot wound to the back, March 23, 2009, Los Angeles

Frederick Piggee, 55, died of gunshot wounds to the head and left hand, April 8, 2009, Los Angeles

Dennis Brown Jr., 21, was shot and killed as he was walking to a store in Watts, November 1, 2008

Eric Perez, 26, died from a wound to his upper torso, November 2008, Los Angeles

George Ramirez, 20, of Pico Rivera, was fatally shot multiple times in his garage when a car drove by, November 2008, Los Angeles

Ulysses Real, 19, shot, Los Angeles, November 2008 ~ The police stated that they believe the shooting was gang-related

David Flores, 23, of La Puente, was stabbed several times, November 2008

Teresa Ortiz, 17, of North Hollywood, a female passenger in a car was killed when a car drove by and someone inside fired several shots at her, November 2008

Gilberto Ramos, 33, of South Gate, was shot, November 2008

Monique Palmer, 17, and **Michael Taylor**, 15, among others were leaving a party when two young men confronted the group and began shooting

Jabari Benton, 15, was gunned down on a street corner in Long Beach, CA

Juan Abel Escalante, 27, a Latino man, also an off-duty Los Angeles County Sheriff's Deputy, was killed in a drive-by shooting near Thorpe and Aragon avenues in Cypress Park on August 2, 2008

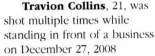

Vannaly Tim, 24, a mother and an Iraq war veteran and her boyfriend **Sarith Em**, 25, were shot and killed outside their apartment, Long Beach, CA

Roberto Lopez Jr., 4, was killed on January 13, 2009, when gang members exchanged gunfire near his Los Angeles home

Melvin Almendares, 41, a man who is believed to be a gang member was found dead with a gunshot wound to the head, Los Angeles, January 2008

Miguel Espino, 23, was shot and killed in Baldwin Park, January 2008, Los Angeles

James Shamp, 48, father of two was killed by two Mexican gang members in Los Angeles because he was black

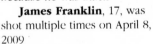

James Franklin, 17, was shot multiple times on April 8, 2009

Angela Willis, 21, was shot multiple times on December 26, 2008

Travion Collins, 21, was shot multiple times while standing in front of a business on December 27, 2008

Jonathan Miranda, 27, was shot multiple times while driving his car in Los Angeles, December 26, 2008

Juan Correa, 24, was shot multiple times on December 26, 2008, Los Angeles

George Glass, 40, was shot in the torso on December 14, 2008, Compton, CA

Rodolfo Castaneda Alvarado, 23, died of a gunshot wound to the head on December 10, 2008

Malik Guiden, 18, was shot multiple times while walking in South Los Angeles on November 29, 2008

Jabari Benton, 15, was fatally shot while walking in Long Beach, CA, November 29, 2008

Leopoldo Ramirez, 2, was shot and killed on November 25, 2008

Tashell Rader, 15, was shot while standing on the sidewalk on November 25, 2008, Los Angeles

Eric Thompson, 27, died from gunshot wounds to the arm and abdomen on April 24, 2009, Los Angeles

Alberto Dionicio-Ramirez, 22, was shot multiple times in the chest, left arm and left hip on November 24, 2008, while standing in a driveway

Gabriel De Lira Carlo,
25, died of a gunshot wound to the neck on November 24, 2008, in Canoga Park, CA
E. Nelson Montanez, 26, was found with multiple gunshot wounds, lying on the sidewalk, January 2009 ~ The shooting was gang related.
Gregory Thomas, 37, was shot and killed on Budlong Avenue in Los Angles, February 2009

Keith Orange, 45, and **Joe Carl Caver,** 26, known gang members were shot and killed as friends and family gathered at the site of another slain man
Damien Cordell White, 19, an alleged gang member of Los Angeles was fatally shot in his car in South Los Angeles, April 2009
Iseman was murdered on June 13, 2003 in Los Angeles, California.

Deaths of gang members, innocent victims, and other senseless killings among Black youth in Wichita, Kansas:

Keo Intavong, 66, January 25, 2009
Jeffrey Chitanavong, 22, January 25, 2009
Tisha Jones, murdered February 3, 1998
Keith James, murdered on February 3, 1998
Umanah Smith, murdered on August 5, 2004
David Barney, murdered July 2, 2006
Tyron Squires, 21, killed November 2008
Chanh Chanthavong, 20, 2008
Tony Gajvan, 8, 1998
Robert Ridge, 19, January 5, 2008
Jennie Heltsley, 42, February 12, 2008
Terrence E. Phillips, 17, May 2008

Laquishia Starr, 21, was six and a half months pregnant and feeding her 2-year-old son noodles when a bullet apparently meant for her boyfriend struck her on April 25, 2007
~ Laquishia's baby had to be delivered prematurely by emergency C-section. He died later.
John C. Reed, 35, May 2008
Antonio Judice, 37, February 22, 2008
John Reed, 35, May 30, 2008
Brandon Moore, 22, July 27, 2008
Marilyn Arreola, 54, August 23, 2008

Juan Martinzez, 22, August 23, 2008

Larry Barnett, 21, August 24, 2008

Satin Huffman, 28, September 15, 2008

Damion Thomas, 2, September 19, 2008

Antonio Ridge, 21, killed September 20, 2008, Wichita

David Tabor, 30, killed September 30, 2008, Wichita

Teresa Hastings, 42, killed July 2007, Wichita

Dylan Cole Schaffer, 17, was shot and killed in Wichita, March 2009

Arturo Moreno, 28, killed in Wichita, 2009

Keith "Fritter" Peters Jr., 18, graduate of East High was killed August 26, 2007, Wichita

Quincy Williams, 17, shot and killed in Wichita, December 8, 2008

Iesha Donaby, 17, from West Helena, Arkansas, was shot several times and killed by a teen for blowing her horn at their car which was stopped in the road, June 30, 2008, Wichita

Deshonda Walker, 23, was gunned down over an argument. She was sitting in a car when her long-time friend Albert Thomas shot and killed her. They call each other life-long friends. But now, they're on different sides of the same tragedy. A member of one family is dead and a member of the other family is accused of killing her.

Jeff Johnson, 22, died after suffering multiple gunshot wounds in a gang-related shooting, Wichita, 2006

Raeshaunda Wheaton, 18, shot and killed in Wichita, December 8, 2008

Odessa Ford, 17, shot and killed in Wichita, December 8, 2008

Jermaine Levy, 19, shot and killed in Wichita, December 8, 2008

Juan Martinez, 22, ran over by gang members, March 2009

Marilyn Arreola, 54, ran over by gang members, March 2009

Below are Wichita Kansas Attempted gang murders.

February 16, 2005, attempted murder of **Samuel Tolliver**

August 5, 2004, attempted murder of **Joshua Walker**

February 8, 1997, attempted murder of **Adrian Blanchard**

May 15, 1995, attempted murder of **Nathan King**

January 11, 1995, attempted murder of **Carlos Beasley**

April 3, 1994, attempted murder of **Tyree Straughter**

March 20, 1993, attempted murder of **Quincy Blue**

February 19, 1992, attempted murder of **Damon Vontress**

February 7, 1992, attempted murder of **Grail Dates**

February 7, 1992, attempted murder of **Dennis McGaugh**

Lemmie Alford, 25, was shot to death on the night of July 24, 20013

James Gary, 27, was shot to death July 14, 2013.

Gang Deaths and deaths of innocent victims in Portland, Oregon:

Lashane Lawson, May 10, 1994

Joseph Ray-Ray Winston, 1988

John Sweets, 1994

Stanley Winston, *(brother above)* 1997

Rose C. Henry, 1998

Anthony "Smirf" Branch

Henry Jay Johnson, murdered March 2, 2000

Jamone Andre Griffin, 23, murdered, August 30, 2000

Amone Rogers murdered 2002

Darious Mendal Martin, 28, murdered September 28, 2000

Sharveil Laroy Moerer, 26, murdered, October 19, 2000

Laraye Donyell Lewis, 25, murdered, October 19, 2000

Tyrone D Abraham, 25, November 7, 2000

Bertrell Coleman, 26, murdered December 19, 2000

Anthony "Cheese" Branch, *(nephew above)*

Big Spider, *("author")* 1989

Tyrone M. Hayes, 21, *("Cowboy")*, killed May 11, 1994

Toyereia (Toya) Martin killed in Northeast Portland

Erik Deiter Jordan killed June 14, 1995, Southeast Portland

Willie Banks Jr., 19, killed November 15, 1996

Michael Anthony Yeggins, 22, killed July 11, 1996

Adrian Bible, 29, killed on August 8, 2005
Darshawn Cross, 31, December 12, 2008
Willy Butler, 18, December 24, 2008, Gresham, OR
Darius Perry, 18, December 24, 2008,
Davonte Garland Lightfoot, 14, killed January 7, 2007
Christopher Adam Monette, 25, killed in December 2007, Northeast Portland
Jason Manuel Adams, 28, killed in 2008
Christopher Darrell Richardson, 22, killed in 2007
Harry James Villa III, 24, killed in prison, Pendleton, OR
Tyree (Harris) murdered in Portland
Aaron Michael Prasad-King, 16, killed December 31, 2003, Portland
Jamaal Wells, 23, killed January 31, 2004, Portland
Winston Morris Moton II, 29, killed January 31, 2004, Portland
TyNiece "Mia" Corvey, 14, killed in gang crossfire, February 1, 2004
Lavelle Anthony Mathews, 35, killed March 24, 2004, Portland
Marcus Mill, 16, killed April 9, 2004, Portland
Robert Orlando Holliday, 24, killed April 11, 2004, Portland

Enrique Rodriguez Borja, 23, killed April 29, 2004, Portland
Alex Alexander, 16, killed 2004, Portland
Andre Andaur, 14, killed in 2004, Portland
Marcus Moultrie, killed in 2004, Portland
Michael West, 28, killed in July 1996, Portland
Lonnie Gaston, 27, killed in Portland
Asia Bell, 24, shot eight times outside her home, November 2002, Portland
Isaiah Strickland, 17, murdered Nov 2, 2003, Portland
Richard Minnifield Jr., 17, was killed Sept. 25, 2003, Portland
Wilbert Menefee Jr., 27, was killed on November 29, 1986, Portland
Kern McClure, 34, beaten to death on January 19, 1996, Portland
Wilando Bell, 20, was shot and killed, February 7, 2005, Portland
Stefan Baptist Daebney, killed December 2002, Portland
Ronald Anthony Johnson, killed in 1999, Portland
Terry Lee Spencer, 44: murdered in Portland
Tracy Green, 17, killed in a drive-by-shooting, Portland
Thomas Henry Graham, 24, killed in 1997, Portland

Kenny Ray Wells was shot to death, May 19, 1992, Portland

Lachelle Renee Banks, murdered June 6, 1998, Portland

Andrew Mikes, 23, killed July 7, 2003, Portland

Jerry Lewis Harrison killed Portland

Cameron Ware, 22, killed October 12, 2003, Portland

Jerome Winston Piggee was shot to death March 6, 1993, Portland

Dwayne Hampton, 29 killed in Portland

Joseph Ray-Ray Winston, 17, murdered August, 1988, Portland

Big Devious

James "Mookie" Davis, 18, was shot and killed on October 7, 2010, by officers from Los Angeles Police Department

Unknown black male, 20's, November 20, 2011, in Pico-Robertson, Los Angeles

Richard Rodriguez, 17 Richard Rodriguez, a 17-year-old Latino male, died Sunday, Nov. 20, 2011

Edward Gaines, 21, Edward Gaines, died November 19, 2011, after being shot in Compton, CA

Jose Villa, 22, died November 18, 2011, after being stabbed in Westlake, CA

Nathan Vickers, 32, died November 17, 2011, after being shot in Hollywood

Michael Douver, 21, died November 16, 2011, after being shot in Vermont Knolls, CA

Dannie Farber, Jr., murdered on Memorial Day 2009, while eating dinner at a restaurant in Compton, CA

Roy Shephard, 40, was shot on June 9, 2012, Willowbrook, CA

Steven John Simmons, 33, died June 9, 2012

Emmanuel Vargas, 29, died June 7, 2012, Los Angeles ~ Officials said the killing appears to be gang-related.

Oscar Duncan, 23, died June 4, 2012, Venice, CA ~ The assailants shouted a gang name as one of them fired a single shot that struck Duncan in the upper body.

Angel Cortez, 1, died June 4, 2012, in Watts, CA

Laderrick Rogers, 20, died June 2, 2012, Pomona, CA

Shanerra Jones, 20, died June 2, 2012, Compton, CA

Terrill Thomas, 20, died June 2, 2012, in Pomona, CA

Jaime Polino, 26, died June 2, 2012, in Panorama City, CA

Emanuel Gutierrez, 21, died June 2, 2012, after being stabbed in Lennox, CA

David Eutsey, 30, died June 2, 2012, was shot and killed in Compton, CA
Hernan Rubalcaba, 35, was shot and killed by police June 1, died June 1, 2012

Taalib Pecantte, 7, died December 3, Los Angeles
Jarret Marque Crump, 21, was shot and killed, November 25, Los Angeles

Following are the newest victims of Los Angeles gang and drug violence (listed in no particular order). Each person has been murdered/killed as a direct result of a gang attack, drug deals gone bad, and innocent bystanders caught in the middle of the crossfire:

Marcela Franco, 26

Elroy Anderson Schenck, 41

Michael Espana, 22

Kenneth Flanders, 55

Jose Alberto Damian Valdez, 45

Ezequiel Jacobo, 33

John Westley Matthews, 36

Leonard Joseph Pina, 28

Richard Tyson, 20

Pervis Patterson, 33

Brandon Wright, 27

Cesar Ramirez, 25

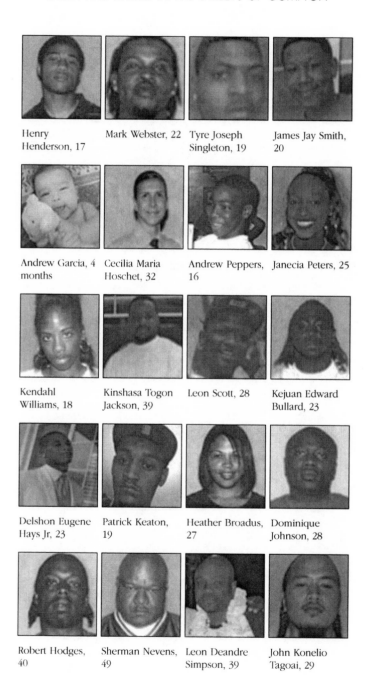

Henry Henderson, 17   Mark Webster, 22   Tyre Joseph Singleton, 19   James Jay Smith, 20

Andrew Garcia, 4 months   Cecilia Maria Hoschet, 32   Andrew Peppers, 16   Janecia Peters, 25

Kendahl Williams, 18   Kinshasa Togon Jackson, 39   Leon Scott, 28   Kejuan Edward Bullard, 23

Delshon Eugene Hays Jr, 23   Patrick Keaton, 19   Heather Broadus, 27   Dominique Johnson, 28

Robert Hodges, 40   Sherman Nevens, 49   Leon Deandre Simpson, 39   John Konelio Tagoai, 29

Angel Cortez, 1   Ebrahim Torbati, 71   Vanessa Rankins, 21   Antwan Cole, 19

Samuel Earl Burge, 21   Jamil Lyles, 17   Ellis Lewis, 24   David Galegos, 30

Lynsie Ekelund, 20   Olatage Filemoni, Jr., 25   Diego Cruz, 15   Deon Mitchell, 21

Ronald Barron, 40   Melvin Bright Jr., 39   April Denise Jace, 40   Joe Alvarado, 22

Samuel Om, 21   Dirk Jackson, 26   Alfonso Nava, 26   Damon Lamont Jones, 39

Nicole Harvey, 21   Andre Maurice   Robert Martin, 24   Diana Tomas, 14
               Jones, 37

Edwin Rivera, 20   Ervin Brown, 52   Ashley Lunsford,   Atilio S. Amaya,
                             19   39

Arnell Smith, 20   Herbert Stevens   David Garcia   Tyreace Ross, 19
                III, 47   Keys, 59

Alfred Flores   Kaitlyn Avila, 3   Bili Bradley, 20   Eligah Rhaburn,
Jr, 18   25

Tynisa Lagail   Kristine Carman,   Gerald Atlas, 43   Orlando Iles, 24
Hicks, 37   17

Okpara Wright, 35

Che Grady, 39

Lanell Barsock, 29

Roberto Herrera, 44

James Monroe Daniels III, 36

Darryl Leon Ross, 53

Tamela Lynea Hemphill, 24

Harry Risley Major, 82

Marie Lorraine Smith, 32

Luis Javier Garcia, 25

Kathy Holland, 53

Christina Salazar, 17

Robert Jalomo, 35

Paul James, 40

Michael McGuire, 21

Deric Wesley, 40

Tyrone Green, 68

Bryan Frost, 23

Reginald Paris, 56

Joseph Edward Beaman, 36

Michael Lee Roberts, 50

John Doe #14

Hutch Jackson, 30

Elizabeth Ann Yanez, 43

Alan Turcios, 20

Samuel Leonard, 22

Sheila Montelongo, 39

Jesus Guevara, 24

Xinran Ji, 24

Noel Velasco, 26

Carlos Diaz, 26

Tedmund Hall, 47

Steven Alaniz, 50

Riko Robinson, 22

Brian Ramos, 20

Jose Gonzalez, 51

Salvador Murillo, 24

Richard Gonzales, 25

Gerson Rodriguez, 33

Leonard Pina, 28

Jaime Abu Awad, 27

Kody Ryan Cook, 18

Billy Alfaro, 27

Jascent-Jamal Lee Warren, 26

Christopher Moreland, 19

Gwendolyn Taylor, 61

Daniel Lotaki, 20

Daniel C Yealu, 29

Dante Willis, 24

Jonathan Val, 17

Clark Quinton Hubbard, 31

William Perez, 35

Frederic Lombardo, 45

Albert Valencia, 32

Luis Palomera, 25

Adrian Soto, 22

Lee Kinikini, 25

Ivison Washington, 27

Jason Grey, 29

Anthony Javen Holmes, 28

Jonathan McCarroll, 23

Andrew Vicente, 24

Deborah Ann Treptor, 35

Alex Contreras-Rodriguez, 17

Michael Byoune, 19

Pedro Antonio Rodriguez, 36

Julio Olivares, 34

Anne Ward, 77

Ruben Garcia Castillo,16

Ricardo Contreras, 45

Oscar Reyes, 33

Michael Huguez, 23

Brenda Aguilera, 21

Timothy Monroe, 72

Miguel Pasaye, 26

Richard Broussard, 20

Enrique Rincon, 44

Miguel Antonio Romero, 46

Terence Ray Mayeaux, 46

Dannie Farber, 18

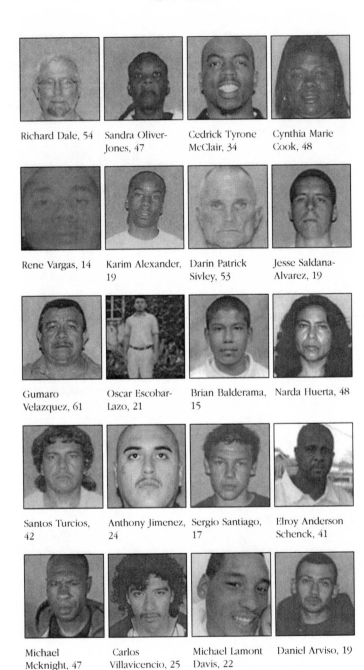

Richard Dale, 54

Sandra Oliver-Jones, 47

Cedrick Tyrone McClair, 34

Cynthia Marie Cook, 48

Rene Vargas, 14

Karim Alexander, 19

Darin Patrick Sivley, 53

Jesse Saldana-Alvarez, 19

Gumaro Velazquez, 61

Oscar Escobar-Lazo, 21

Brian Balderama, 15

Narda Huerta, 48

Santos Turcios, 42

Anthony Jimenez, 24

Sergio Santiago, 17

Elroy Anderson Schenck, 41

Michael Mcknight, 47

Carlos Villavicencio, 25

Michael Lamont Davis, 22

Daniel Arviso, 19

Robert Burrus, 67   Marcos Salas, 36   Wanda Mittie
Threadgill, 45   Adam Pacheco,
31

Brittney Gene
Barnett, 25   Priscilla Jimenez,
31   Jose Orellana, 52   Wilbert
Robertson, 22

Carmel Joshua,
27   Jason Valdez-
Perez, 17   Shuichi
Sugimoto, 40   Leamon Turnage,
69

Walter Vega, 30   Dean Ybarra, 48   Miguel Gonzalez,
33   Wayne McKinney,
24

Kenneth Glass,
39   Sharon Carter, 31   Katrina Rene
Harris, 28   Eddie Green
Jr., 31

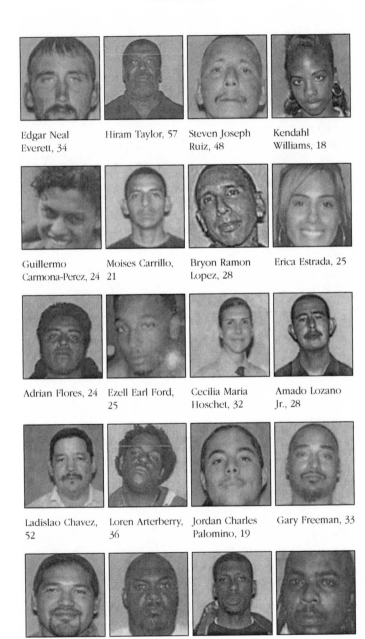

Edgar Neal Everett, 34

Hiram Taylor, 57

Steven Joseph Ruiz, 48

Kendahl Williams, 18

Guillermo Carmona-Perez, 24

Moises Carrillo, 21

Bryon Ramon Lopez, 28

Erica Estrada, 25

Adrian Flores, 24

Ezell Earl Ford, 25

Cecilia Maria Hoschet, 32

Amado Lozano Jr., 28

Ladislao Chavez, 52

Loren Arterberry, 36

Jordan Charles Palomino, 19

Gary Freeman, 33

Tito Vargas, 35

Thomas Miles Ingram, 43

Carlton Turner, 31

Eric Redd, 36

Albert Love, 23   Rene Pichardo, 26   Robert Brown, 84   Ruben Breedlove, 28

Manuela Padilla, 52   Anthony Harris, 24   Joseph Marcello Rafael, 31   Robin Ridgeway, 49

Cynthia Parker, 24   Carlos Clavel, 29   Juan Valenzuela, 38   Vincent Ramos, 31

Keonta Karnell Daniels, 17   Christopher Rice, 22   Detrick Ford, 20   Overland Campbell, 20

Qristyonn Augustine, 1   Alexis Guzman, 18   Stephanie Elyse Moseley, 30   Joey Romo, 19

Karina Michel, 31 Craig Moore, 18 Dominique Lee Austin, 25 Paul Martinez, 22

Beatrice Santiago, 21 Herbert Seymour Jr., 31 Daniel Leon, 22 Landry L. Calhoun, 43

Roxanne Paul, 28 Norman Stauffer, 47 Jae Oh, 38 Manuel Saucedo, 29

Jorge Duarte, 22 Maurice Hill, 41 Dwight Caldwell, 25 Johnny Robinson, 34

Diane Newlander, 73 Mireya Mccall, 5 Rogelio Delgado,18 Giuliana Perrotta, 47

Calvin Eugene Gray, 33

Princess Berthomieux, 15

Tanaya Shanette Goins, 32

Robert Washington, 38

Jeffrey Nicola, 22

Allen Alexander, 48

Corey Raymon Norflin, 42

Jermaine Watson, 34

Glenn Carr, 45

Lamar Rambo, 31

Darius Truly, 26

Clayton Montgomery, 15

Ernesto Castaneda, 22

Kevin Cohen, 49

Jonathan Pinto, 28

Antwan Cole, 19

Arnaldo Quinones, 34

Charlie Howell, 47

Carl Sebastian Betts, 51

Domingo Reyes, 33

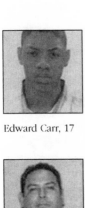

Edward Carr, 17   Juliana Redding, 21   Nelli Rodriguez, 16   Lucy Preciado, 26

Charles Santisteban, 43   Marisol Aguayo, 22   Antonio Bland, 25   Lusine Safaryan, 8

Randy Almanza, 17   Dean Hyde, 44   Scott Grant, 40   Timothy Johnson, 37

Rudy Hendley, 35   David Delacruz, 25   Dovon Harris, 16   Klaudia Y Alas, 32

Martell Reed, 18   Ikime Sims, 20   Chris Purnell Stephens, 27   Vicente Castillo, 19

Frank Castro Jr., 19   Jamiel Shaw, 17   Lamont Crayon, 27   Dexter Luckett, 23

Joseph Edward Galvan, 22   Autumn Johnson, 1   Diego Rey Garcia, 20   Edwinta Hereford, 19

Shawn Eleby, 24   Byron Weston III, 20   Markeith Wilson, 25   Asbel Melara, 1

Daniel Marrero, 20   Daniel Correa, 28   Walter McGowan, 64   Herbert White, 49

Terry Ray Maiden, 35   Joe Lobos, 24   Mya Renee Migneault, 4   Cesar Ramirez, 25

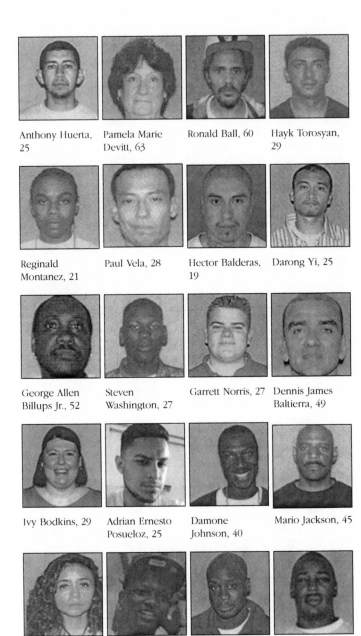

Anthony Huerta, 25

Pamela Marie Devitt, 63

Ronald Ball, 60

Hayk Torosyan, 29

Reginald Montanez, 21

Paul Vela, 28

Hector Balderas, 19

Darong Yi, 25

George Allen Billups Jr., 52

Steven Washington, 27

Garrett Norris, 27

Dennis James Baltierra, 49

Ivy Bodkins, 29

Adrian Ernesto Posueloz, 25

Damone Johnson, 40

Mario Jackson, 45

Genny Herrera, 39

Leon Antwan Scott, 28

William Hansbrough, 36

Clyde Paschal, 35

Andre Johnson, 19

Augusto Zapata, 26

Jose David Flores, 28

Carol Jean Crabtree, 80

Lance Ennis, 41

Norman Schureman, 50

Terry Carter, 55

Paula Torres 44

Adolfo Medina, 61

Destiny Monique Aguirre, 18

Sidney Duane Wallace Jr., 19

Juan Aguiar, 29 gunshot

Ian Valway Hoyt, 45

Kelly Hales, 56

Maria Inasaret Perez, 55

Rocky Lopez, 46

Draysean Earl, 13

Willie Sykes, 47

Damon Barney, 32

Melody Ross, 16

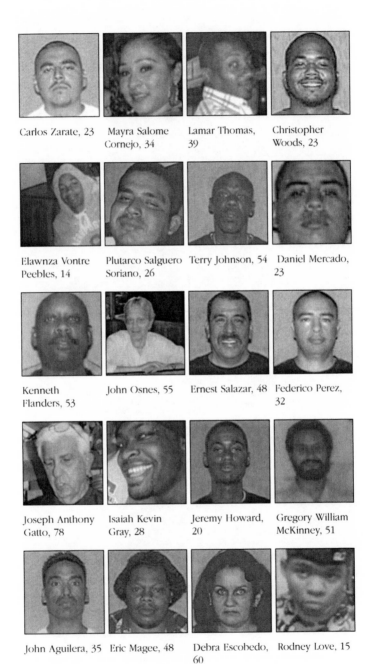

Carlos Zarate, 23 Mayra Salome Cornejo, 34 Lamar Thomas, 39 Christopher Woods, 23

Elawnza Vontre Peebles, 14 Plutarco Salguero Soriano, 26 Terry Johnson, 54 Daniel Mercado, 23

Kenneth Flanders, 53 John Osnes, 55 Ernest Salazar, 48 Federico Perez, 32

Joseph Anthony Gatto, 78 Isaiah Kevin Gray, 28 Jeremy Howard, 20 Gregory William McKinney, 51

John Aguilera, 35 Eric Magee, 48 Debra Escobedo, 60 Rodney Love, 15

Rita Morales, 87   Carlos Jimenez Jr., 20   Francisco Revolorio, 46   Johnny Berry Cox, 31

Norman Strawder, 56   James Hall, 40   Tecia Yolanda Robinson, 41   Fernando Sedano, 22

Aric Lexing, 26   Venus Jamaal Hardin, 25   Rafael Rivera, 33   Jason Wei, 42

Hugo Hidalgo, 24   Michael Anthony De La Torre, 19   Vicki Yildirim, 45   Fred Godbolt, 21

Christopher Payne, 24   Luis Flores, 66   Patrick Addo Odoi-Kyene, 47   Jana Collins, 26

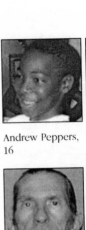

Andrew Peppers, 16   Donald McTier Jr., 29   Ira Tyrone Koger, 21   Herbert Theodore, 51

Earnest Dewitt Brannon, 67   Andrew Ruben Fierro, 31   Aaron George Sneed, 33   Jose Valdez, 45

Robyn Turnage, 57   James Marcus Howe, 42   Ramon Requena, 20   Dwain Charles, 47

Richard Alan Wurtz, 37   Hernan Cardona, 60   Calvin Williams, 38   Herman Johnson, 74 gunshot

Jamal Tims, 28   Erik Diaz, 19   Shantell Martinez, 18   Ruben Whittington, 61

Justin Keishaun
Logie, 19

Jonah Alexander,
24

Gonzalo Garcia-
Garcia, 31

Lucille Wills, 74

Darrel Stanley, 32   Joshua Pipho, 20   Michelle Ann
Kane, 43

Rita Wiley, 70

Gavin Smith, 57   Aaron Shannon
Jr., 5

Jayvon Brister, 18   Karine
Hakobyan, 38

Anthony
Lombardi, 55

Anthony
Hawkins, 46

Alma Cornish, 71   Reynaldo Barnes,
51

Mariah Howard,
2

Alberto Rojas, 46   Conrad Phillip,
41

Antoine Levelle
Earley, 36

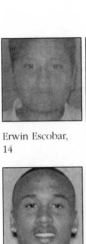 

Erwin Escobar, 14 | Tierney Yates, 37 | Ardis Brown Jr., 36 | Michael Maurice Hess, 47

Treavor Robinson, 22 | Mario Gutierrez, 37 | Luther Magee, 48 | Luis Leon, 19

James Conwall Daniels Jr., 51 | Alisha Johnson, 21 | Trayvon Jeffers, 28 | Lashaun Menifee, 28

Edwin Perla, 19 | Thomas Leroy Dunbar Sr., 84 | Raul Escobedo, 67 | Esquivel Castillo, 51

Neal Williams, 27 | Tavin Terrel Price, 19 | Clay Allen Casey Sr., 49 | Mitchell Maya, 20

Joshua Mario Martinez, 25

Avery Crenshaw, 21

Joseph Cosina, 19

Bree'Anna Guzman , 22

Crystal Coronel, 19

Isaac Gaston Jr., 31

Carlos Valencia, 30

Dwayne Kenneth McKesson, 47

Jose Suarez, 40

Gabriela Melara, 2

Gerald Jones, 33

Jerell Green, 26

Anthony Alonzo Cudger, 47

Joseph Jones, 35

Sebastian Caldera Jr., 18

Shavonna Jones, 30

Anthony Bryant, 33

Donglei Shi, 31

Alfonso Gonzalez, 36

Pedro Renteria Jr., 21

Mark Leonard, 43   Oscar Pelayo, 39   Jamel Kelly, 25   Eric Lorenzo, 20

Willie Myles Jr., 23   Nabil Tawab, 37   Rafael Acosta Jr., 30   Jacob Lipson, 51

Rita Ann Delehanty, 62   Marquise Ortiz, 19   Jose Espinosa, 31   Joel Leach, 28

Carl Young, 23   Daniel Alejandre, 26   Gil DeLeon, 53   Kevin Glen Polinskey, 29

Frederick Blackshire, 19   Osiel Hipolito, 20   Steven Farrell, 23   Morris Moran, 27

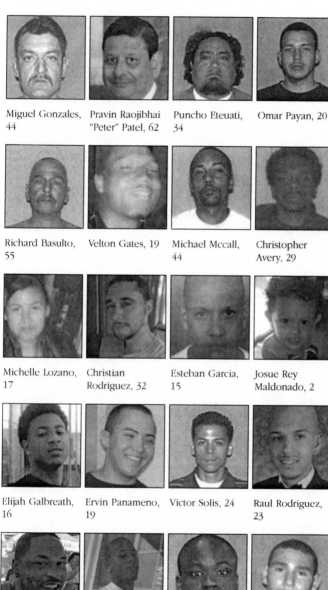

Miguel Gonzales, 44

Pravin Raojibhai "Peter" Patel, 62

Puncho Eteuati, 34

Omar Payan, 20

Richard Basulto, 55

Velton Gates, 19

Michael Mccall, 44

Christopher Avery, 29

Michelle Lozano, 17

Christian Rodriguez, 32

Esteban Garcia, 15

Josue Rey Maldonado, 2

Elijah Galbreath, 16

Ervin Panameno, 19

Victor Solis, 24

Raul Rodriguez, 23

Kellen Mahone, 31

Delshon Eugene Hayes Jr., 23

Paul Henry Franklin, 48

Miguel Angel Sanchez, 20

Joseph Watson, 17   Roberto Santiago Jr., 22   Salvador Avila Jr., 19   Heather Broadus, 27

Mario Jaramillo, 43   Damien White, 19   Julio Garcia, 46   Donald Lee Heard, 54

Brian Herrera, 22   John Wayne Whitmore, 65   Rodrigo Ponce, 17   Larick Matheson, 58

Donzell Ghoston, 18   Lajoya Kamiel McCoy, 31   Charles Gonzalez, 51   Gregory Alexis, 47

Martha Starr, 59   Mylus Mondy, 48   Marvin Tobar, 21   Sergio Moises Wilms, 19

Jason Marquez, 19

England Curtis Russell, 53

Kisha Shelly Michael, 31

Tony Walker, 37

Juan Catalan, 21

Alfred Tarin, 19

Mark Salisbury, 39

Pedro Fernandez, 24

Andre Flores, 21

Lorena Mercado, 27

Ella Suggs, 53

Richard Trujillo Vidaurry, 55

Laterian Tasby, 17

Dannell Willis, 21

William Pious, 23

Christopher Fridd, 28

Keith Hardy, 36

Craig Wright, 50

Naquia Danielle Catching, 22

Pamela Fayed, 44

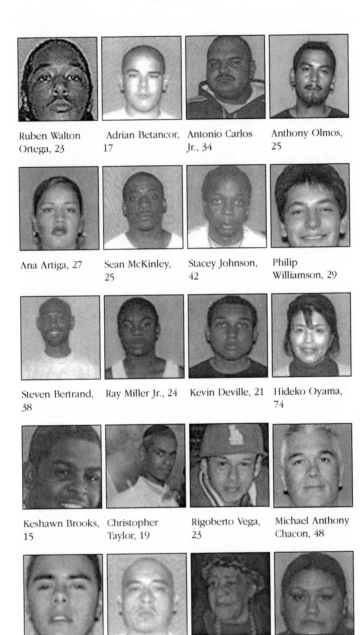

Ruben Walton Ortega, 23

Adrian Betancor, 17

Antonio Carlos Jr., 34

Anthony Olmos, 25

Ana Artiga, 27

Sean McKinley, 25

Stacey Johnson, 42

Philip Williamson, 29

Steven Bertrand, 38

Ray Miller Jr., 24

Kevin Deville, 21

Hideko Oyama, 74

Keshawn Brooks, 15

Christopher Taylor, 19

Rigoberto Vega, 23

Michael Anthony Chacon, 48

Renny Contreras-Mendez, 24

Ricardo Chavez, 24

Annie Margaret Bell, 86

Lina Romero, 31

Jose Navarro, 18   Tyce William Riddle, 19   Monica Reynoso, 29   Darlene Lamb, 38

Charles Leonard Smith, 66   Waymon Weston, 20   Eron Mull, 18   Johnny Espinosa, 30

Daniel Crespo, 42   Joshua Gaither, 30   Reynaldo Tiria Yandan , 60   Bryan Barraza, 17

Reginald Doucet Jr., 25   Monique Campbell, 21   Jarret Marque Crump, 21   Manfred Karger, 71

James Green Jr., 35   Rodolfo Martinez, 28   Janecia Peters, 25   Jovani Quintero, 26

Ricardo Lizarraga, 31　Jason Hernandez, 23　Brian Macias, 17　Shontae Blanche, 22

Roberto Lopez Jr., 4　Charles Edward Bell II, 33　Valerie McCorvey, 35　Gemora Knoxs, 33

Kirk Winter, 53　Howard Gross, 57　Oscar Curiel, 38　Hector Carrillo-Garcia, 35

Jacquelyn Fields, 46　Gerardo Pizarro, 29　Mary Matsumoto, 72　Marie Jimenez-Aldana, 22

Lejoy Grissom, 27　Patrick Fowler, 40　Julie Kates, 46　Steven Guzman, 21

Joshua Montes, 1   Laura Sanchez, 34   Omar Rascon, 18   Hector Leonardo Morejon, 19

Ryan Gonzalez, 26   Khary Kidd, 32   Ortavin Hill, 28   Daniel Anthony Diaz, 33

Tony Argon, 18   Kendrec McDade, 19   Maria Torres, 65   Victor Nunez, 24

Jeremy Solomon, 20   Sean Sylvester, 38   Jimmy Tran, 18   Roshdi Abuawad, 27

Kayon Keith Dafney, 23   Dorian George Hernandez, 42   Kate Yi, 20   John Winkler, 30

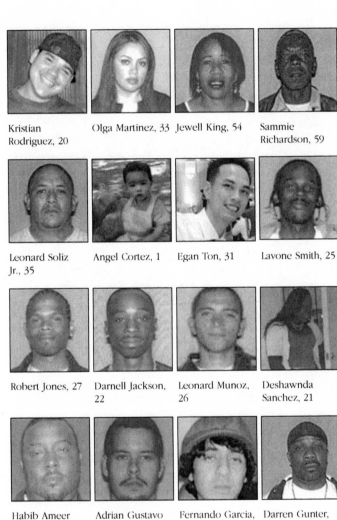

Kristian Rodriguez, 20

Olga Martinez, 33

Jewell King, 54

Sammie Richardson, 59

Leonard Soliz Jr., 35

Angel Cortez, 1

Egan Ton, 31

Lavone Smith, 25

Robert Jones, 27

Darnell Jackson, 22

Leonard Munoz, 26

Deshawnda Sanchez, 21

Habib Ameer Zekajj, 38

Adrian Gustavo Solis, 35

Fernando Garcia, 21

Darren Gunter, 39

Carl Martin Pickering Jr., 26

Frederick Piggee, 55

Jesus Peralta, 29

Heriberto Corpus, 20

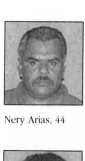

Nery Arias, 44   Luis Hernandez,   Diamond   James Tuggle, 29
                 68   Johnson, 27

Rachelle   Guillermo   Israel Munoz, 26   Natalie Marie
Washington, 27   Saucedo, 23   Rashkov, 32

Ricardo Mendoza, Timmy Moore, 17 Eddie Guerra, 23   William
27   Workman, 24

Dora Lee   Jose Briseno, 20 Jason Alvarez, 29 Fabian Garcia, 24
Dawson, 64

Rodney Nelson,   Francisco Garcia, Severa Madrona,   Armando
34   21   76   Castaneda, 51

Robert Jetter, 45   Hector Jara, 31   Robert Leonard Brewer, 21   Randal Simmons, 51

Francisco Esparza, 25   Matthew Sims, 42   Damar Daniel Rigsby, 24   Walter Hernandez, 23

Kapre Maurice Brown, 31   Robert James Ringer, 61   Antonio Lee Riley, 18   David Cota, 23

William Anthony Treas, 30   Candice L. Barcenas, 26   Flor Medrano, 30   Marco Herrera, 18

Eileen Orta, 22   Aneesah Akbar, 28   Valente Casas, 23   Maurice Leroy Cox, 38

Dre'sean Harris, 22   Eric Acosta, 36   Mike Coffey, 34   Alejandro Hernandez, 20

Hugo Bustamante, 46   Ricardo Cabrales, 14   Danielle Hagbery, 22   Melvin James, 54

Dion Franklin, 35   Michael Rodriguez, 20   Alonzo Ester, 67   Joe Hinojos, 23

Jarrod Atkins, 29   Larise L. Smith, 56   Jameion Benton, 21   Lily Burk, 17

Wenwa Chao, 53   Sergio Alexander Navas, 36   Porche Ledae Charles, 30   Theodore Melvin White, 46

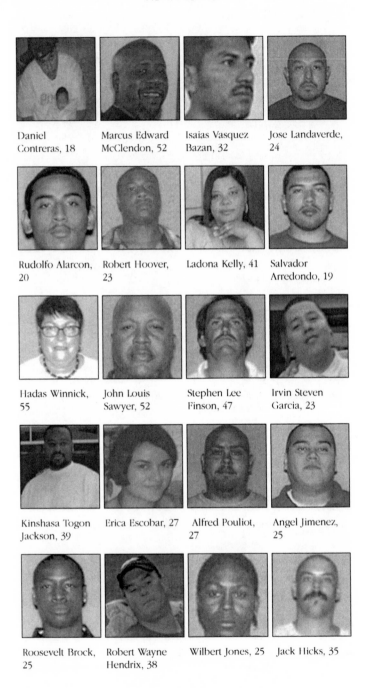

Daniel Contreras, 18

Marcus Edward McClendon, 52

Isaias Vasquez Bazan, 32

Jose Landaverde, 24

Rudolfo Alarcon, 20

Robert Hoover, 23

Ladona Kelly, 41

Salvador Arredondo, 19

Hadas Winnick, 55

John Louis Sawyer, 52

Stephen Lee Finson, 47

Irvin Steven Garcia, 23

Kinshasa Togon Jackson, 39

Erica Escobar, 27

Alfred Pouliot, 27

Angel Jimenez, 25

Roosevelt Brock, 25

Robert Wayne Hendrix, 38

Wilbert Jones, 25

Jack Hicks, 35

Eusebia Rojas, 85   Steve Ontiveros, 34   Erik Peter Ungerman, 34   Marcus Peters, 19

Ronni Chasen, 64   John Ortiz, 46   Salvador Ramirez Sr., 46   Miguel Macias, 22

Matthew Perez, 24   Selene Patricia Mayoral, 24   Robert Gipson, 23   Eugene Robinson, 34

Christopher Nelson Waters, 42   Joshua Davis, 18   Deonte Freeman, 19   Robert Richard Jr., 34

Esteban Caraveo, 36   Paul Ray Kemp Jr., 40   Jesus Castro, 33   Melissa Paul, 16

Marco Parra, 36   Benjamin Clemmons, 36   Reginald Hendrix Jr., 28   Anel Juarez, 37

Kahari Wimberly, 31   Jennifer Darling-Wade, 33   Francisco Velazquez, 33   Eddie Carroll, 40

Quincy Tillett, 18   Ruben Campos, 21   Ricardo Hernandez, 20   Bahati Dunbar, 40

Gabriela Calzada, 19   Jesus Antonio Avalos, 33   Christopher Chorpening, 51   Lemuel Andres Goode, 54

Michelle Lu, 55   Roketi Mosesue, 46   Roosevelt Murray, 71   Francisco Aguirre Jr., 31

Frank Burnell Taylor, 35

Lester Lear, 47

Miguel Guzman, 16

Francisco Licon, 27

Fabian Cooper, 21

Latorria Westbrook, 26

Angel Caldera, 34

Donovan Morris, 34

Kevis Gray, 20

Suzie Marie Pena, 1

Akop Aduryan, 46

Jeffrey Sinclair, 17 gunshot

Aniya Knee Parker, 47

Nelva D. Hernandez, 45

Armie "Troy" Isom, 89

Isabel Rodriguez, 59

Ruben Gomez, 51

Alfred Henderson, 47

Endi Rivera, 25

Juan Alviso, 23

Aykui Agdaian, 65

Eric Mandivelle, 20

Andy Ung, 29

Delray Yarbrough, 38

Willie Flores Jr., 22

Travione Rashad Mason, 26

Ryan Joseph Greenberg, 32

Guillermo Jacobo, 41

Bryan Wooden, 38

Joey Gutierrez, 23

Stephanie Almanzan, 21

Martha Carmona, 21

Jesus Alonzo, 27   Shirley Isom, 74   Charles Logan, 36 Manuel Reyes, 85

Rolando Rodriguez, 44

Oscar Orlando Torres, 64

Florence Anderson, 71

John McGraham, 55

Javier Sanchez, 15

Samuel Trujillo, 19

Alejandro Gutierrez, 19

Adam Blount, 28

Raymond Gage, 41

Andrew Maree, 24

Todd James Britt, 51

Lidia Castillo, 45

Aurora Reynosa, 62

Jorge Aguilar, 33

Seth Grinspan, 46

Christopher Arviso, 27

Alberto Delpino, 62

Roderick Poole, 45

Rayshawn Boyce, 31

Raymond Veloz, 48

Daniel Svoboda, 43

Justo Morales, 25

Kaelyn Michael Tarin, 19

Wilbert Mahone, 18

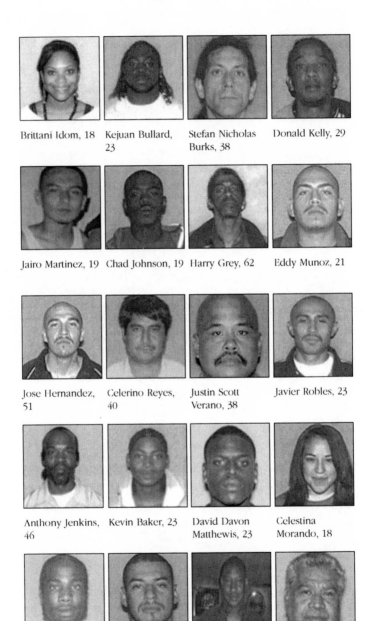

Brittani Idom, 18   Kejuan Bullard, 23   Stefan Nicholas Burks, 38   Donald Kelly, 29

Jairo Martinez, 19   Chad Johnson, 19   Harry Grey, 62   Eddy Munoz, 21

Jose Hernandez, 51   Celerino Reyes, 40   Justin Scott Verano, 38   Javier Robles, 23

Anthony Jenkins, 46   Kevin Baker, 23   David Davon Matthewis, 23   Celestina Morando, 18

Marques McNeil, 28   Ismael Garcia, 28   James Shamp, 48   Mario Tovar, 59

Vartan Avatyan, 18

Adrian Simental, 24

Gerardo Rivera, 54

Gary Lacey II, 19

Omar Duran Saunders, 39

Noelia Vasquez, 30

Ocie May, 26

Albert Barajas, 37

James Cody, 44

Betty Sugiyama, 84

Lorri Anderson, 51

Sarai Lopez, 18

Ricardo Galvez, 29

Andrew Ramirez, 16

Amparo Karina Velarde, 38

Cesar Lopez , 19

Dominique Johnson, 28

Cristela Campos, 23

Ladell Edward Rowles, 50

Jermail Gillis, 26

Luis Gomez, 39

Steve Duwayne
Lawson, 50

George
McCafferty, 53

Lenard Jackson,
17

Rudolph Barnes,
42

Timothy James
Teopaco, 19

Shaun Diamond,
45

Kevin Johnson,
40

Matthew Charles
Held, 47

Brandon Deandre
Myers, 21

Kellye Lynnette
Taylor, 53

Alexandro
Montoya, 35

Douglas Zerby,
35

Ruben Herrera,
26

Alfredo Tarin, 54

Albert Munoz, 45

Humberto Varon,
51

Bernardo
Mendoza, 44

Larisa Sarkisyan,
50

Elsy Molina, 36

Philip Chau, 21   Julie Ann Souza, 53   Santos Castro, 76   Diego Garcia, 25

John Benjamin Alvarado, 35   Gombert Yepremyan, 19   Tina Sanchez, 41   Rudolph Smith, 40

Savoy Ewell, 20   Crystallyn May Nguyen, 18   Willie Singleton, 43   Evelyn Reynoso, 24

Tramel Laqune Kerl, 39   Michael Miller, 25   Antwine Brown, 36   Edward Ochoa, 38

Michael Presley, 19   Francisco Javier Ayala-Mejia, 25   John Konelio Tagoai, 29   Spurgeon McClendon, 19

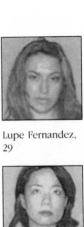

Lupe Fernandez, 29 Alfred Prowell, 44 Eduardo Rodriguez, 14 Stinson Brown, 21

Eun Kang, 38 Edgar Moreira, 22 Luis Jimenez, 26 Otis Williams, 32

Kristie Michelle Perez, 43 Aldale Woodard Jr., 27 Christian Delgadillo, 19 Ryan Mitchell Anderson, 29

Brian Newt Beaird, 51 William Perez, 48 Yazmeen Hassan, 18 Crystal Adams, 34

Lakeisha Glendoral, 32 Desiree Veronica Ramirez, 31 Roy Anthony Sutherland, 48 Ronson Edgerly, 20

Rodrick Brumfield, 44

Kenneth Frison, 18

Tory Alexander Lawton, 36

Miguel Sanchez Jr, 21

Manuel Holguin, 33

Dion Holloway, 17

Devian Luevanos, 20

Harvey Sumpter, 80

David Silva, 21

Juan Manuel Ibarra, 17

Joshua Thierry, 17

Antonio Wooten, 20

Carolina Urrutia, 29

Emilio Moncayo, 34

Jim John Rudometkin, 59

Alejandro Montalvo, 18

James Withers Jr., 20

Tyrone Dewayne Golden, 47

Raven Joy Campbell, 37

Dontae Cotton, 28

Marcel Dupre Johns, 28

Raul Cano, 25

Victor Garza Jr., 23

Christine Darlene Calderon, 23

Jeffrey Tidus, 53

Michael Jefferson Jr., 20

Marquise Alexander, 22

Ivonne Rodriguez, 26

Donnell Taylor, 47

Sigmund Thomas Chornes, 37

Edward Simental, 41

Danny Horn, 20

Robert Jackson, 20

Susan Molina, 44

Eric Thompson, 27

Anthony Adame, 20

Teresa Gale Briseno, 55

Donald Hoskins, 31

Jaime Raul Saldana, 37

Daniel Garcia, 32

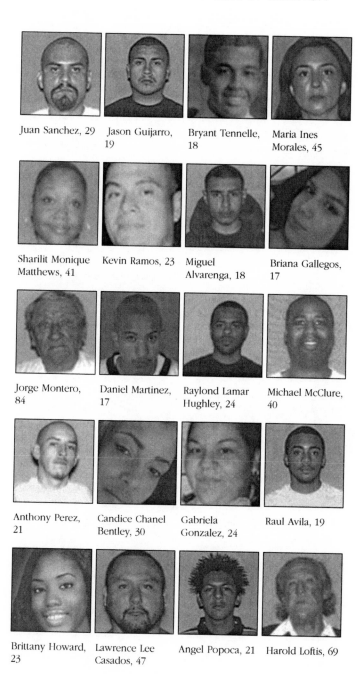

Juan Sanchez, 29 Jason Guijarro, 19 Bryant Tennelle, 18 Maria Ines Morales, 45

Sharilit Monique Matthews, 41 Kevin Ramos, 23 Miguel Alvarenga, 18 Briana Gallegos, 17

Jorge Montero, 84 Daniel Martinez, 17 Raylond Lamar Hughley, 24 Michael McClure, 40

Anthony Perez, 21 Candice Chanel Bentley, 30 Gabriela Gonzalez, 24 Raul Avila, 19

Brittany Howard, 23 Lawrence Lee Casados, 47 Angel Popoca, 21 Harold Loftis, 69

Derrick Morris, 49   Connie Williams, 15   Lavon Ellison, 27   Michael Randolph, 46

Larry McKay, 16   Oran Douglas III, 37   Francisco Sanchez, 21   Kadeemi Forman, 19

Viengkham Hansaya, 48   Efrain Olmos, 39   Marlon Usher, 30   Gerardo Corral Jr., 27

Willie Adams, 31   Jermaine Tryon, 25   Jerasmo Pena, 26   Jose Ramos Jr., 18

Renee Spata, 18   Lloyd Stallings III, 22   Michael Kelly, 27   Jorge Hernandez, 30

Robert Lee Hollie, 33

Susan Kim, 52

Eric Douglas, 50

Jenny Vanny Sor, 40

Denise Figueroa, 22

Herman Owens, 34

Angel Cazares, 25

Osmar Israel Orellana, 18

Lisa La Pierre, 42

Salvador Escalante, 20

Yusuf Latice Davis, 39

Andrew Caprio, 42

Donald Reed, 27

Paul Salazar, 31

Blanca Valdez, 38

Jose Carabantes, 36

Anthony Roland Buckner, 42

Steven Robinson, 48

Orlando Ortega, 31

Lovell May III, 19

Santiago Morales, 23   Eduardo Gonzalez, 25   Jason Gentile, 22   Monty Wayne Barker, 74

Gabriel Ben-Meir, 30   David Medina, 45   Carrie Jean Melvin, 30   Jose Guadalupe Rodriguez, 50

Kyree McCray, 28   Charlzette Bryant, 30   Arturo Alvarez, 34   Agnes Bratton, 79

Ricardo Rivera Jr., 18   Earl Rhodes, 48   Tommie Hayes, 27   Armando Mariscal, 33

Nathan Alexander Sanchez, 6   Maria Hicks, 57   Rogelio Parra, 23   Samuel Beckner, 60

Robert McGhee, 22   Robert Hollis, 75   Joe Encinas, 38   Roger Williams, 41

Michael Baker, 54   Larry Duran Jr., 29   Betty McClellan, 62   Katsutoshi Takazato, 21

Kenneth Cabrera, 45   Jose Merino, 58   Nestor Torres, 37   Woodrow Player III, 22

Hector Ulises Robles, 43   Norman Earl Edwards, 46   Desirae L. Jenkins, 28   Lynette Lucero, 47

Raul Rivera, 49   Wayne Patrick Cooper, 36   Matthew Butcher, 27   Avery Cody Jr., 16

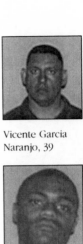
Vicente Garcia
Naranjo, 39

Boo Lee, 20

Tommy Jackson,
58

Moises Arias, 22

Daniel Smith, 20

Dion Miles Jr., 19

juan Escalante, 27

Timothy Ervin
White Jr., 32

Ching Tseng, 35

Marc Darrel
Spinner, 27

Bobby Williams,
30

Yeprem
Khotsuryan, 62

Duncan Battiest,
34

Tyrone Taylor, 18

Lawana Clary, 50

Thomas Pearson
Jr., 29

Harold Joseph
Yeager, 58

Andrew Phillip
Scott, 20

Ezequiel Jacobo,
33

Nicholas
Robertson, 28

Jorge Baez, 41 Ramond Allen, 36 Cyjai Nicole Bell, 16 Walter Vicente, 49

Mark Gregg, 25 Ricardo Molina, 28 Francisco Saray Jr., 29 Denise Berry, 44

Christopher Davenport, 36 Enrique Beltran, 21 Reginald Ross, 42 Keyonta Ansari, 22

Rene Balbuena, 41 Mohammad Chaudhry, 21 Ian Burkett, 31 Edwin Bell, 46

R.C. Jenkins Jr., 29 Columbus Campbell, 39 Brian Caufield, 31 Troy Green Jr., 23

Pedro Hernandez, 19

Taalib Pecantte, 7

Duke Herrera, 24

Alton Mixon, 51

Celeste Jimenez, 31

Serena Tarin, 23

Susan Jane Berman, 55

Jhovanny Ramirez, 26

Ramon Preciado Jr., 19

John Steen, 58

Adrian Steele, 25

William Vasquez, 43

Jaime Aguallo Sr., 50

Gene Valdez, 18

Lamont Thomas Jones, 30

Kenny Ray Harris, 36

Pedro Xochipa, 21

Joseph Lewis, 22

Marcos Casas, 18,

Edgar Rivera, 21

Kenneth Johnson, Manuel Aguilar,
48   19

CLOSING REMARKS

The United States has seen rapid proliferation of gangs since 1980. During this period, the number of cities with gang problems increased from an estimated 286 jurisdictions with more than 2,000 gangs and nearly 100,000 gang members in 1980 to about 4,800 jurisdictions with more than 31,000 gangs and over 1 million gang members in 1998.

An eleven city survey of eighth graders conducted by the *LA Times* found that 9 percent were currently gang members, and 17 percent said they had belonged to a gang at some point in their short lives.

For years, gangs have been a problem in Los Angeles where they account for about half of the city's murders. But gangs are now responsible for 41 percent of the homicides in Omaha, Nebraska; drive-by shootings rose 3,000 percent in Wichita, Kansas from 1991 to 1993; and Oklahoma City is home to 80 separate gangs.

In Wichita, Kansas, there were eight drive-by shootings in 1991 and 267 in 1993, and over 500 reported in 1998. Gang violence is on the rise and the crimes committed vary from drug offenses to property crimes. Certain offenses are related to different racial/ethnic gangs. African-American gangs are relatively more involved in drug offenses; Hispanic gangs, in turf-related violence; Asian and white gangs, in property crimes. Numerous ethnographic studies have provided excellent descriptions of Hispanic gangs in Los Angeles.

They tend to be structured around age-based cohorts, based in a specific territory (*barrio*), and characterized by fighting. The gang provides family-like relationships for adolescents who feel isolated, drifting between their native and adopted cultures and feeling alienated from both. Hispanic gangs have links to the neighborhood, or barrio, which tie them to the larger culture; much of their violence is related to defense of neighborhood turf. In contrast, African-American gangs in large cities tend to replace traditional social networks that linked young adults with legitimate work opportunities. Thus, these gangs tend to be involved in entrepreneurial activities more than other ethnic/racial gangs and may evolve from scavenger groups to turf gangs and drug-trafficking gangs.

Nevertheless, gangs will continue to thrive and the list of deaths I have compiled will continue to grow until communities all over America come together and develop programs that will enable youth to make better choices in their lives. This can be done in many ways and forms, but it will take the whole community, religious and secular.

In closing, I pray that the list I have compiled shows how important it is to render a panacea to the problem of gang violence. We have to act now before it's too late.

REFERENCES

Bibliography and Recommended Readings

The Los Angeles Times archives

http://www.streetgangs.com

FBI files from the Leonard Peltier case * First Nations
Site * FBI Targets Leonard Peltier * Akicita's rebuttal
to FBI media claims * The Covert War against Native
Americans by Ward Churchill * Free Peltier! Campaign
in Czech Republic. Las Carpetas Centro Para la
Investgación y Promoción de Derechos Civiles. The FBI
Probe of CISPES * Interview with Frank Varelli. Albion
Monitor Judi Bari Resource Page & Legal Documents *
Judi Bari Suit Reveals COINTELPRO Against Earth First!
* America's Secret Police

"Political Prisoners and POW's in the US" by the Prison
Activist Resource Center, "Index to FBI Agents and
Snitches" by Drew Hendricks

"Overcoming Repression against Activists" by The Public
Eye. "Secret No More" FBI file numbers of famous
people, including many COINTELPRO targets. Index of
FBI Records Released to National Archives (very few
have been released). The FBI: Past, Present and Future.
"What Really Happened?" Mike Rivero's COINTELPRO
web page CIA on Campus "Nothing Vague About FBI
Abuse: Here Are the Dossiers" by Norman Solomon
and Jeff Cohen "Review of FBI Secrets: An Agent's
Expose" and excerpt: "The Logistics of a Black Bag

Job." Real Audio interview with Wes Swearingen on
Democracy Now
"Some Call it Murder" by Shelly Waxman
"Wages of COINTELPRO Still Evident in Omaha Black
Panther Case"
by Ward Churchill 3/10/99
WBAI Interview with Ward Churchill on *Mumia Abu-
Jamal*
Michael Stec's Collection of Secret Documents
Nation of Islam COINTELPRO Documents
CIA OPERATION CHAOS
CIA OPERATION MOCKINGBIRD

"Confounding Carnivore: How to Protect Your Online
Privacy" by Omar J. Pahati, 11/29/01
Whistleblower Protection for FBI Employees
Executive Order 12958: Classified National Security
Information.
Executive Order: 13142, automatic declassification of
25-year-old records, effective October 2001.

Anderson, Elijah. May 1994. "The Code of the Streets." *The
Atlantic Monthly*.

Alonzo, Alejandro A. 1998. *Urban Graffiti on the City
Landscape*, Paper Presentation. Western Graduate
Geography Conference, San Diego, CA. Available
online.

Bakeer, Donald. 1987. *Crips: The Story of the L.A. Street
Gangs from 1972-1985*. Los Angeles: Precocious.

Bing, Leon. 1991. *Do or Die*. Harper Perennial: New York.

Bjerregaard, Beth, and Carolyn Smith. 1993. "Gender
Differences in Gang Participation, Delinquency, and
Substance Abuse." *Journal of Quantitative Criminology*,
9: 329-55.

Bogardus, Emory. 1926. *The City Boy and His Problems*.
House of Ralston, Rotary Club of Los Angeles.

California District Attorney. 1992. *Gangs, Crime and
Violence in Los Angeles: Findings and Proposals*.Office
of the District Attorney, County of Los Angeles.

Cesareti, Gusmano. 1975. *Street Writers: A Guided Tour of Chicano Graffiti.*

Chin, Ko-Lin. 1986. *Chinese Triad Societies, Tongs, Organized Crime, and Street Gangs in Asia and the United States.* Unpublished doctoral dissertation, University of Pennsylvania.

Cohen, Albert K. 1955. *Delinquent Boys: The Culture of the Gang.* Free Press.

Davis, Mike. 1990. *City of Quartz: Excavating the Future in Los Angeles.* Vintage.

Decker, Schott, and Barrik Van Winkle. 1994. "Slinging Dope: The Role of Gangs and Gang Member in Drug Sales." *Justice Quarterly, 11*(4).

Espinoza, Federico Garcia, Jr. 1984. *A Historical Look on the Growth of Hispanic Gangs in Los Angeles County.* Unpublished Master's Thesis, University of Southern California.

Evans, Williams, et al. 1999. "Are Rural Gang Members Similar to their Urban Counterparts? Implications for Rural Communities." *Youth & Society, 30,* 267-282. Available online.

Finn-Aage, Esbensen. 2000. "Preventing Adolescent Gang Involvement." OJJDP Juvenile Justice Bulletin, U.S. Department of Justice, Washington, D.C. Available online.

Finn-Aage, Esbensen and D. Wayne Odgood. 1999. "Gang Resistance Education and Training (GREAT): Results from the National Evaluation," *Journal of Research in Crime and Delinquency, 36,* 194-225. Available online.

Fritsch, Eric J., Tory J. Caeti, and Robert W. Taylor. 1999. "Gang Suppression through Saturation Patrol, Aggressive Curfew, and Truancy Enforcement: A Quasi-Experimental Test of the Dallas Anti-Gang Initiative." *Crime & Delinquency, 45,* 122-139. Available online.

Galindo, Letticia D. 1993. "The Language of Gangs, Drugs, and Prison Life Among Chicanas." *Latino Studies Journal*, 4, 23.

Gang 2000: A Call to Action: the Attorney General's Report on the Impact of Criminal Street Gangs on Crime and Prevention by the Year 2000. California Department of Justice Division of Law Enforcement, Bureau of Investigation, March 1993.

Hasan H. A. 1998. "Understanding the Gang Culture and how it relates to Society and School." In Park Hyun-Sook and Meyer Luanna, et al., (Ed), *Making friends: The influences of culture and development*, 263-283. Baltimore, MD: Paul H. Brookes.

Henderson, Eric; Kunitz, Stephen J. Levy, Jerrold E., 1999, "The Origins of Navajo Youth Gangs." *American Indian Culture and Research Journal*, 23, 243-64. Available online.

Herbert, Steve. 1997. *Policing Space: Territoriality and the Los Angeles Police Department.* University of Minnesota Press.

Hutchinson, Ray. 1993. Blazon Nouveau: "Gang Graffiti in the Barrios of Los Angeles and Chicago." In *Gangs: The Origins and Impact of Contemporary Youth Gangs in the United States*, Eds. Scott Cummings & Daniel J. Monti, 137-171. Thousand Oaks, CA: Sage.

Jackson, George. 1970. *Soledad Brother: The Prison Letter of George Jackson.* New York: Bantam.

Jackson, Robert K., and Wesley D. McBride. 1986. *Understanding Street Gangs.* Custom Publishing.

Klein, Malcolm W. 1992. "Attempting Gang Control by Suppression: The Misuse of Deterrence Principles," *Studies on Crime and Crime Prevention, 2*, 88-111, October.

Klein, Malcolm, Cheryl Maxson, and Jody Miller. 1995. *The Modern Gang Reader.*

Klein, Malcolm. 1995. *The American Street Gang: Its Prevalence, Nature and Control.* Oxford.

Klein, Malcolm W., and Lois Y. Crawford. 1967. *Groups, Gangs, and Cohesiveness,* Los Angeles: University of Southern California, Youth Studies Center.

Lane, Jodi, and James W. Meeker. 2000. "Subculture Diversity and the Fear of Crime and Gangs." *Crime & Delinquency, 46,* 497-521. Available online.

Lasley, James. 1998. "'Designing Out' Gang Homicides and Street Assaults." *National Institute of Justice Research in Brief.* U.S. Department of Justice, Washington D.C. Available online.

Levitt, Steven D., and Sudhir A. Venkatesh. 2000. "An Economic Analysis of a Drug-Selling Gang's Finance." *The Quarterly Journal of Economics,* August, 755-789. Available online.

Ley, David. 1974. *The Black Inner City as a Frontier Outpost.* Annals of the Association of American Geographers.

Ley David. 1974. "The Street Gang and in its Milieu." In *The Social Economy of Cities,* 247-273. Prentice-Hall: Englewood Cliffs, N.J.

Ley, David, and Roman Cybriwsky. 1975. "Urban Graffiti as Territorial Markers." *Annals of the Association of American Geographers, 64*(4), 491-505.

Maxson, Cheryl. 1995. "Street Gangs and Drug Sales in Two Suburban Cities Series." *NIJ Research in Brief.* Available online.

Maxson, Cheryl, and Malcolm Klein. 1996. "Street Gang Migration: How Big the Threat?" *NIJ Journal, 230,* 26-31.

Meehan, Patrick, MD, and Patrick WO 'Carroll, MD. 1992. "Gangs, Drugs, and Homicide in Los Angeles." *American Journal of Diseases of Children, 146*(6), 683.

Miller, Jody. 1998. "Gender and Victimization Risk Among Young Women in Gangs." *Journal of Research in Crime and Delinquency, 35,* 429-453. Available online.

Moore, Joan. 1991. *Going Down to the Barrio: Homeboys and Homegirls in Change.* Philadelphia, PA: Temple University Press.

Moore, Joan. 1994. "The Chola Life Course: Chicana Heroin Users and the Barrio Gang." *The International Journal of the Addictions,* 29(9), 1115-1126.

Moore, Joan B. 1978. *Homeboys: Gangs, Drugs and Prisons in the Barrios of Los Angeles Temple.*

Office of Justice and Delinquency Prevention. 2000. "Youth Gangs, Programs and Strategies." U.S. Department of Justice, Washington D.C. Available online.

Office of Justice and Delinquency Prevention. 1994. "Gang Suppression and Intervention: Problem and Response." U.S. Department of Justice, Washington D.C. Available online.

Office of Justice and Delinquency Prevention. 1994. "Gang Suppression and Intervention: Community Models." U.S. Department of Justice, Washington D.C. Available online.

Patton, Peter L. 1998, "The Gangsters in Our Midst." *Urban Review, 30*(1), 49-76.

Puntenney, D.L. 1997. "The Impact of Gang Violence on the Decisions of Everyday Life: Disjunctions between Policy Assumptions and Community Conditions." *Journal of Urban Affairs,* 19(2), 143-161.

Rodriguez, Luis. 1994. *Always Running: La Vida Loca: Gang Days in L.A.* New York, NY: Simon & Schuster.

Romotsky, Sally, and Jerry Romotsky. 1975. "Plaqueaso on the Wall." *Human Behavior, 4,* 65-69.

Rosenthal, Lawrence. 2000. "Gang Loitering and Race." *The Journal of Criminal Law & Criminology, 91,* 91-100. Available online.

Schatzberg, Rufus. 1993. *Black Organized Crime in Harlem: 1920-1930.* New York: Garland.

Shakur, Sanyika. 1993. *Monster: The Autobiography of an L.A. Gang Member.* Penguin.

Sheley, J.F., et al. 1995. "Gang Organization, Gang Criminal Activity, and Individual Gang Members Criminal Behavior." *Social Science Quarterly,* 76(1), 52-68.

Sikes, Gini. 1997. *Eight Ball Chicks.*

Sipchen, Bob. 1993. *Baby Insane and the Buddha: How a Crip and a Cop Joined Forces to Shut Down a Gang.* Doubleday.

Spergel, Irving A., et al. 1994. *Gang Suppression and Intervention: Problem and Response.* Research Summary Washington, DC: U.S. Dept Of Justice Office of Justice Programs Office of Juvenile Justice and Delinquency Prevention.

Spergel, Irving A., et al. 1990. "Community and Institutional Responses to the Youth Gang Problem." *National Youth Gang Suppression and Intervention Program.* Washington D.C.: Office of Juvenile Justice and Delinquency Prevention. Available online.

Stenson, Kevin. 1997. "Crimes of Style: Urban Graffiti and the Politics of Criminality." *Sociological Review,* 45(3), 527-529.

Thrasher, Frederic. 1927. *The Gang.* A Study of 1,313 Gangs in Chicago. Chicago: University of Chicago Press.

Tyler, Bruce M. 1983. *Black Radicalism in Southern California: 1950-1982.* PhD dissertations, University of Southern California.

Venkatesh, Sudhir Alladi. 1997. "The Social Organization of Street Gang Activity in an Urban Ghetto." *American Journal of Sociology,* 103, 82-111

Venkatesh, Sudhir Alladi. 2001. *Community Justice and the Gang: A Life-Course Perspective.* Columbia University, New York: NY. Available online.

Vigil, James Diego. 1997. "Learning from Gangs: The Mexican American Experience." Washington D.C.: Office of Educational Research and Improvement, U.S. Department of Education. Available online.

Vigil, James Diego. 1996. "Street Baptism, Chicano Gang Initiation." *Human Organization*, 5(2), 149-153.

Vigil, James Diego, and Steve Yun. 1990. "Vietnamese Youth Gangs in Southern California." In Huff, C. Ronald (Ed.) *Gangs in America*. Newbury Park, CA: Sage Publications.

Werthman, Carl, and Irving Piliavin. 1967. "Gang Members and the Police." In David J. Bordua (Ed), the *Police: Six Sociological Essays*, 56-98. John Wiley & Sons: New York.

Whyte, W.F. 1943. Street Corner Society Chicago: University of Chicago Press.

Wilson, James, and Geogre Kelling. 1982. *Broken Windows, the Atlantic Monthly*, 29-33. Available online.

Yablonsky, Lewis. 1997. *Gangsters: Fifty Years of Madness, Drugs, and Death on the Streets of America*. New York: New York Press.

Recommended Publications

Final Report of the Select Committee to Study
Governmental Operations with Respect to Intelligence
Activities of the United States Senate, Ninety Fourth
Congress, First Session, U.S. Government Printing
Office, No. 94-755, April 14, 1976, Vol 1-6. (Church
Committee)

Hearings Before the Select Committee to Study
Governmental Operations with Respect to Intelligence
Activities of the United States Senate, Ninety Fourth
Congress, First Session, U.S. Government Printing
Office, Sept. 16 - Dec. 5, 1975, Vol 1-7. (Church
Committee)

The COINTELPRO Papers: *Documents From the FBI's
Secret Wars Against Dissent in the United States*, by
Ward Churchill & Jim Vander Wall, South End Press,
ISBN 0-89608-360-8

Agents of Repression: *The FBI's Secret Wars Against
the Black Panther Party and the American Indian
Movement* by Ward Churchill & Jim Vander Wall, South
End Press, ISBN0-89608-293-8.

The Age of Surveillance: *The Aims and Methods of
America's Political Intelligence System*, Frank J. Donner,
and New York: Knopf, 1980. *Protectors of Privilege: Red
Squads and Police Repression in Urban America*, Frank
J. Donner, University of California Press, Berkeley,
1990. *COINTELPRO: The FBI's Secret War on Political
Freedom* by Nelson Blackstock, Pathfinder, 1975,
ISBN0-937091-05-7

Ideological Warfare: *The FBI's Path Toward Power*, Frank
M. Sorrentino, Associated Faculty Press, Inc.1985. *FBI
Secrets: An Agent's Expose* by M. Wesley Swearingen,
South End Press ISBN0-89608-501-5.

War at Home: *Covert Action against U.S. Activists and
What We Can Do About It* by Brian Glick, South End
Press. *In the Spirit of Crazy Horse* by Peter Matthiessen,
1991, Viking Press (Out of print)

Racial Matters: *The FBI's Secret File on Black America, 1960-1972* by Kenneth O'Reilly, 1989, Free Press. *Liberation, Imagination and the Black Panther Party*, Cleaver and Katsiaficas ed., 2001, Routledge

Break-ins, Death Threats and the FBI: *The Covert War Against the Central America Movement* by Ross Gelbspan, 1991, South End Press

Are You Now or Have You Ever Been in the FBI FILES: *How to Secure and Interpret Your FBI Files* by Ann Mari Buitrago and Leon Andrew Immermann, 1981, Grove Press Inc.

Political Repression in Modern America, Robert J. Goldstein, Cambridge: Schenkman, 1978

A Season of Inquiry. *The Senate Intelligence Investigation*, Johnson, Loch, University of Kentucky Press, Lexington, 1985.

Congress Investigates U.S. Intelligence, A-L & M-Z

VIDEO: "All Power to the People! The Black Panther Party and Beyond" [Electronic News Group, Los Angeles]

Monster: The Autobiography of an L.A. Gang Member by Sanyika Shakur

8 Ball Chicks: A Year in the Violent World of Girl Gangs by Gini Sikes

Do or Die by Leon Bing

Crews by Maria Hinojosa

Deadly Consequences by Debo Prothrow Stith

Street Gang Awareness: *An Identification and Resource Manual for Families and Educators* by Steven L Sachs,

Kids Killing Kids: *Managing Violence and Gangs in Schools* by Thomas Capozzoli

Hearts and Hands: *Creating Community in Violent Times* by Luis Rodriguez

The Gang intervention Handbook by Arnold P Goldstein

Makes Me Wanna Holler by Nathan Mc Call: Vintage Press ~ More than a story about gangs or life on the streets, Nathan Mc Call talks about racism in America and how it condemns many black men to dead end jobs, prison and death.

What's going on? by Nathan Mc Call, Vintage Press

Fist, Stick, Knife, Gun by Geoffrey Canada: Beacon Press ~ An excellent book on child-violence from the President of the Rheedlen Centers for Children and Families in New York City.

Monster by Monster Cody ~ The life story of a member of one of America's most infamous street gangs.

Blood in, Blood Out by Art Blajos: Monarch Press ~ Now an evangelist with Victory Outreach, Art Blajos spent a total of seventeen years in prison with four spent on death row. This is his story.

APPENDIX

1965 Watts Riot Referenced in Chapter One

When the smoke cleared on August 17, 1965, thirty-four people were dead and roughly one thousand buildings had been damaged or looted (*Blumberg, 163*). Containing the uprising had required more security personnel than had American military involvement in the Dominican Republic earlier that same year (*Horne, 3*). The national guardsmen and police officers involved had ended up sealing off a Curfew Zone one and one-half times the island of Manhattan (*Blumberg, 163*). The total damage was figured to have amounted to somewhere in the neighborhood of $40,000,000 (*Governor's Commission on the Los Angeles Riots, 1*). With such frightening statistics in mind, the rest of America was left to wonder how a routine drunk-driving arrest could have escalated into six days of looting, rioting, sniping, and vandalism. Even more incongruous with the destruction of those one hundred forty-four hours was the fact that, in the eyes of many, the 1960s had seen great advancements on the behalf of blacks. A government commission was quickly assembled, chaired by and named for former CIA director John A. McCone. Even this official report seemed shocked that the denizens of Watts could find anything to riot over, concluding that neighborhood was neither a slum nor an urban gem (*Governors Commission, 83*). While the

McCone Commission Report was a bold departure from the standard government paper on social problems, it reflected the errors and misconceptions of much of middle-class America in its treatment of the realities of the Watts riots (*Rustin, 149*).

Destroyed Businesses in Watts

National Guard patrolling the streets

Angry Black Citizens celebrating in front of News crews

Safeway on fire

A heavily-armed group of police and national guardsmen stand ready at an open manhole after dropping a tear gas shell inside during riots in the Watts section of Los Angeles. Escaped shooting suspects were believed to be using an underground storm sewer system to move around and evade capture following a gun battle between the police and Black Muslims (below).

American army patrol in Watts, Los Angeles after Black riots virtually destroyed the city in 1965.

Movie quoted from Chapter One

"The Fugitive" (1963) TV series 1963-1967
    Creator: Roy Huggins
    Release Date: 17 September 1963 (USA)
    Genre: Crime / Drama / Thriller
    Runtime: 60 min (120 episodes)
    Color: Color (1966-1967) / Black and White
    (1963-1966)

Referenced in Chapter Four

"BLOOD RISIN": A NEW WORLD OF GANGS
Gianmaria Bergamaschini (Milan)

The end of the black "unrest" of the Sixties, which had developed in various directions and along varied lines – from Martin Luther King to Black Power and the Panther Party, passing through Malcolm X and the Muslims – was often the result of the arrest, or the physical elimination of the leaders who had launched and developed these organizations. Basic questions, which had been expressed but not resolved, continued to exist; silence did not – as it had not before the Sixties – sign an end, but a shift in the way in which realities made themselves felt.

In the course of the Sixties young Los Angeles blacks had slowly abandoned the intra-group hostility and violence which had pitted neighborhood bands like the East side Slausons and the West side Gladiators against each other in the Fifties[1], until there were no more "gang wars". The black revolt gave a decisive, though temporary, change of perspective. With the leadership of resolute and dedicated figures from within the black community, young black gang members acquired political consciousness and took on the fight for black power with all the energy they had previous put into intra-group conflict. There was an end to struggle to control the neighborhood, the few blocks of "our territory" (however miserable, "ours" all the same – and, indeed all that was "ours").

The entire black community was now seen as "ours" and the confrontation shifted to its borders. Black Power theorized the need for an organized force, rooted in the neighborhood, but coordinated throughout the community to city and then to state level. This force was to dedicate its energy to the building of independent economic, social and cultural centers and to the defense of the black community – the black Nation – in the overwhelmingly white context. It insisted upon the need to recover and elaborate an "African political identity" and affirm its traditions as a nation within the nation. It represented an attempt to displace the black American community from a program of reform within the existing white contexts to a program of "revolutionary" nationalism which aimed at modifying those contexts.

So intra-group conflict had virtually disappeared in Los Angeles in the mid-Sixties and the gangs' names had disappeared from the news. Social workers and police were dumb-founded at the sudden and unexpected end of hostilities among gangs. Indeed former enemies set aside old feuds to face the hated Los Angeles police department and its Chief, Parker[2], OR California' National Guard. The birth of the Black Panther Party for Self-Defense in Oakland in 1966 marked a crucial moment not only for the struggle of American black citizens – a majority of whom (as a Time magazine survey would later show) felt proud of the existence of the Panthers, even as they affirmed they would not vote for them - but for the more limited history of black metropolitan street gangs. In Los Angeles two prominent members of the Slausons, Alprentice "Bunchy" Carter and Jon Huggins became local organizers for the Panther Party. A third, Brother Crook (Ron Wilkins) founded the Community Alert Patrol to record police abuse in the black community. Many other former gang members joined the US Organization, set up by Ron "Maulana" Karenga.[3] To show that hostility between gangs had ended, a parking lot near the Jordan Downs housing project, long a meeting place and a battleground for Watts gangs, became the recruiting center for the "Sons of Watts", a sort of law-keeping patrol of the neighborhood whose key function, according to Alejandro Alonso's was to "police the police".[4]

President Johnson, who thought he had resolved everything began cajoling the 1964 Civil Rights Act out of Congress and bullying it the next year into a stronger second law. He reacted badly to the urban unrest and the apparent stirring of revolutionary proposals across the nation. The war in Vietnam had absorbed more and more money and troops and no end seemed to be in sight. At the same time, antiwar activity was increasingly vociferous even among the middle classes who were part of the world of business.

What he thought he saw was conspiracy and possible revolt. His reaction was both harsh and rapid. Cointelpro (Counter Intelligence Program)instituted in 1967 by the FBI (which had always identified black protest as anti-American and communist inspired) to combat the" black nationalist groups instigating hate" and all "radical" black organizations. It succeeded with often illegal means (including CIA infiltration, expressly forbidden by its statute within the United States) in suffocating the impetus of Black America.

Once it was all over and the more charismatic promoters were either dead or behind bars, black Urban youth found itself without any points of reference that might serve to channel their existential frustration and their anger into civic engagement. Poverty, unemployment, discrimination, and the indifference of authority continued as it had before the heady mid-Sixties years; indeed, sometimes worse. The long list of the dead and the violence that had marked police action during those years combined with the unsuccessful to increase rancor towards the police; and more generally all public authority.

The Nixon administration took up the banner of repression – law and order – and completed it with a change in federal policy towards Afro-Americans, in line with the views of the Republican party's prevalently white electorate, which now significantly, included for the first time sectors of the working class population (which the media called "lower middle class" identifying its social status by its mentality rather than its economic role). Funds for states and cities were now allocated according to a formula based on population, taxes and pro-capite income and no longer on the basis of need. The new criteria reduced welfare and educational aid drastically to damage the black community. At the same time; Nixon offered a demagogic solution to the request for "black power", interpreting this central slogan of the Sixties to mean "black capitalism". The public presence now became – with the cooperation of business associations and the personal encouragement of figures from the world of finance[5] – the promotion of Afro-American businesses and the creation of a new strata of black entrepreneurs. As Manning Marable wrote in 1980:

That black capitalism worked mostly as a useful myth is demonstrated both by the continual appearance of tiny black firms, and by the fact that within two years of opening, nine out of ten go out of business.[6]

Johnson's civil rights laws and Nixon's policy had, in any case, made it possible for a "new black bourgeoisie" to come into existence. This new group immediately moved out to the suburbs: Substantial change in the traditional models of white/black interaction had put an end to segregation (though some forms of resistance persisted, especially in real estate; it had opened the road to power and prestige for many blacks. At the same time it created an inferior class of blacks who lived in a hopeless state of economic stagnation, far below the rest of society.[7]

The rise of this new middle class was, as Nixon's advisors had hoped, one of the important reasons for the failure of black political movements to gather the consensus they had enjoyed in the Sixties:

Besides government action and the wide-spread presence of heavy drugs, the prospects and the way of life of middleclass nationalists were most responsible for the lack of real goals in the black liberation movement of the '70s and '80s. They dropped away because of their needs and interests as a burgeoning black bourgeoisie[8].

Many scholars suspected that the capillary circulation of drugs in Black neighborhoods, inherited from the latter part of the Sixties, was the result of one of the many illegal gambits authorities had used to suffocate militancy; and many "political" films affirmed it confidently, contributing to the rise of an urban myth whose validity is still uncertain.[9] Whatever the case, it is certainly true that the huge market in drugs was a bonanza for ambitious ghetto youth; a way to status without education and without having to leave familiar contexts.

No subsequent movement succeeded in bringing together what was left of the anger which had activated black big city neighborhoods' in the Sixties and given it political weight.

Young blacks were the first to pay the price of this political and cultural vacuum. We need to add one more specifically cultural factor to our picture and it is an aspect which I consider important to an understanding of the rebirth of urban street gangs in the early '70s. As political engagement waned and criminal organization linked to drug traffic, a new film genre captured the attention of young blacks.

This genre was part of the action-movie tradition, a white Hollywood staple; it now became the vehicle for what has been termed blacksploitation. That is the action-film whose protagonists and directors were black. They were immediately popular – for different reasons – with both black and white audiences, some going into series, like Shaft, which would have a lucrative television career as well. Blacksploitation films brimmed over with heroes and heroines who were really, really cool[11]: pimps and dealers, "stallions" and whores, gangsters and detectives, junkies and militants. A series of stereotypes–sometimes nearly caricatures, often brass-faced and arrogant to suggest attitudes, if not models. In a scene without cultural or institutional anchorage like the neighborhood, the effects of these films are negative and damaging for black youth. As Italian literary critic Franco Minganti observes[12]:

In their "psychotherapeutic" dimension these films–though superficially exciting - work as palliatives with narcotic effect on a young black audience, displacing attention from collective engagement and shifting it onto the individual attainment of things, money and maybe drugs as well. They do present the themes of consciousness, militancy and black revolt, but they reduce them to folklore and show, almost is a game, and certainly without real weight. In other words, they reaffirm society in its existing structural patterns – so much so that the leaders of the black community and black intellectuals denounce their benevolence towards drugs, criminality and some kinds of violence. It is this disapproval which grows as the genre turns to ever worse themes and stereotypes that decree the end of blacksploitation as a genre (and, as well, the change of Hollywood policy as it emerges from a recession).

So now the only attractive models offered uneducated black urban youth in the '70s were comic book heroes, aggressive, cynical and essentially no less egocentric than the "me" generation of the new middle classes. Whether or not it was part of a conscious policy, the atmosphere was, of course, not a major cause of gang rebirth. But, at the same time, in some deprived social contexts, the prevalence of negative models in the mass media and the "normalization" of violence in everyday life, were contributing factors, legitimating the warped values of contextual reality.

So Afro-American – black – gangs are reborn in Los Angeles in this complex climate, and become again the points of reference for a new generation of poor black youth. But this rebirth was a good deal more than a "revival" and carried no nostalgia with it at all. Urban black youth had no "sense of history" and no "fathers" to repeat any tradition. The culture of the new gangs is discontinuous and firmly linked to the contemporary context. And that is what produced an escalation of violence and death.

A few of the first new gangs of the "new era" did try somehow to take up the heritage of the Panthers or other nationalist groups. But – like the Crips – they very soon abandoned vague ideas of a social or political nature for criminal activity of various sorts, sometimes as ends in themselves (to show they could; for the "fun" and "kick" of it, etc.). Such activity was often once more connected to the territory, but the territory was also the marketplace for drug trade. The little neighborhood "wars" now factored out in dollars and cents. They were yuppies, too, in the Nixonian model of the '70s, out for bucks and status symbols and they rose in their "business" using the tools of the field: violence, coercion and, if necessary, death.

It was Raymond Washington, a fifteen year old student at Freemont High School, who, in 1969 – shortly after the elimination of the Black Panthers – founded the first street gang of the new era on 78th Street, near Crenshaw Boulevard, with seventeen year old Stanley "Tookie" Williams.[13]

Washington was too young to have had a real role in the political and social movements of the Sixties, but he did try to give his gang the rhetoric of neighborhood control in the neighborhood which had been the Panthers', though he did not understand (or adopt) the goals for which they had established that control. What he did understand was the Panther aesthetic, adopting the black leather jackets which had been the Panthers' distinctive sign of belonging. He called his gang Baby Avenues. He got the name, like the look, from the past: Avenues had been the name of a gang active in Los Angeles in the early Sixties.

Given the age of its members, Washington's gang soon became known as the Avenue Cribs and, finally as the Crips. The ambition to take up the mantle of the Panthers and become leader and protector of the neighborhood was soon set aside, too. The Cribs were so immature and so lacking in political consciousness and experience that they were wholly unable to organize any sort of community project.

The look was the only thing that came "naturally" (and this would be, from several points of view, a significant indication of future developments in the black urban world). Besides the jackets, the Cribs carried canes and wore a gold ear ring in their left lobe. They shifted to criminal activity rapidly and violently. Purse-snatching, robbery, and hold-ups became the rule (and often served as rites of initiation into the group) and, inevitably, the press and television became interested in them.

In 1971 the Cribs assaulted a young Japanese-American woman who described them as " young cripples carrying sticks"[14]. Local newspapers focused on this detail and called them the Crips. According to one of the original members of the Crips, Danifu, it was the papers who named them: The Cribs was the original name of the Crips, but the term Crips was substituted by the use of the word Crips through a newspaper article that highlighted specific individuals who were arrested for a murder. Because some of the early Cribs carried canes, the entire notion of Crip as an abbreviated pronunciation of crippled caught on. Crippin' meant robbing and stealing, and then it developed into a way of life.[15]

According to still another reconstruction, the name Crips is an acronym of Continuous Revolution in Progress and indicates the fluid, a-political nature of the group. In fact, with a few months the situation had changed radically and "acting" in the form of violence had become central. The Cribs had vaguely hoped to emulate the Panthers, the "crippin' way" soon transformed the gang into a criminal group. From 1972, as Nixon is re-elected and Watergate in the offing, no one mentions the Cribs; only the Crips are on the scene, though they keep the look alive for some time and newspaper accounts of the period mention episodes of violence where white youth are attacked and robbed of black leather jackets. Jerry Cohen, reporter of The Los Angeles Sentinel described the Crips this way:

A group of juveniles that committed extortion of merchandise, mugging the elderly, and ripping off weaker youths, particularly for leather jackets that have become a symbol of Crip identity.[16] It is a tragic irony that only a few days after this article presenting the Crips as a bunch of innocuous petty thieves appeared, the first gang homicide was committed. The victim, who was beaten to death, was a sixteen year old boy, son of a lawyer and living on Los Angeles' West side; he belonged to no gang. According to the Los Angeles police department report, the group attacking the boy wore leather jackets and they killed him because he resisted their attempt to take his jacket. A few days later nine youths – some well-known Crips – were arrested. A month later a white fifty-three year old man was killed in South Los Angeles. The death was again attributed to the new gang because of the way it was carried out, but a lack of proof made it impossible to arrest anyone.

The Crips' increasingly frequent and violent crimes, and the growing fascinated attention devoted to them by a press interested in selling and creating an audience was not loath to feeding conflict between groups. This made the Crips increasingly "famous". It looked to many black youths like a "winning choice" – probably the only "wining choice" in their destitute environment. It became, as the earlier gangs had been, a fundamental point of reference for ghetto youth; often the only point of reference. Many joined; others formed new gangs drawn by the attention police, local government and the media afforded.

Within a few months, the Crips had extended their area of influence from 68th Street to near-by Inglewood and Compton, and to part of the West side. The new gangs were unwilling to accept the arrogance and dominance of the Crips which their smaller numbers made them less able to resist. The police began to monitor the situation more closely: the gangs descended from the pre-Watts generation were becoming numerous and all were violent. By the end of 1972 there were 29 gang-related deaths, seventeen within Los Angeles itself and nine in Compton.

As these few figures show, the situation was much worse than it had been in the Fifties. What had started up again as a form of adolescent "pack" delinquency, had turned into a form of aggressive behavior in which killing was an accepted symbol of power. But what pushed the situation to the level of "epidemic" was that the attitude had become somehow "fashionable". The papers began to talk about "Crip-mania", casting the glamour of folklore over criminal events. The gangs took on the aura of myth for young urban blacks. Belonging to a gang was frightening, but at the same time reassuring – especially if the gang was the by now famous Crips. Belonging was the guarantee of a respected identity for many youths whom society seemed to have discarded before even testing their capacities. The Crips were indeed the poor blacks' yuppies. Being a gang member meant fame, nice clothes and prestige.

From 1973 to 1975 while the federal government got out of Vietnam as loser and Nixon resigned from the presidency leaving the confidence in the Executive – and the CIA - in tatters, intra group hostilities appeared again after more than a decade. In 1973 a member of the LA Brims, an independent West side gang was killed by a Crip after a brief argument. The episode opened a sharp rivalry with the Crips and set the stage for the formation of an anti-Crips front. In fact the Piru Street Boys in Compton had already shed blood against the Crips and they wanted to end Crip dominance.

At the end of 1973, the major non-Crips gangs met at Piru Street. Besides the Brims other groups in the same situation were present – the Denver Lanes, the Lueders Park Hustlers and the Bishops. The legendary Bloods were formed at this meeting and became the prime adversary of the Crips. Though it seems to have come from the colors of Centennial High School where many of the members of the various gangs were students, it certainly appealed because of its powerful semantic field, almost biological in nature, symbolizing violence, but also manhood and courage (as in the image so classic to English literature of "blood rising" indicates or, in American literature, "the red badge of courage"). The Bloods' choice of a color, obliged the Crips to leave the black which had identified them (losing its connotation of fate, death and nihilism); they chose blue, probably because Washington High School in South Central, a Crips stronghold, had that color (but its field was also strong, as in the colloquial, though dated, "true blue" to indicate loyalty and fortitude, which dates back to the days with which pagan British warriors painted their faces before battle).[17]

Through the '70s the two principle gangs in Los Angeles County continue to grow and absorb almost all the other groups in and around the city. They developed codes including gestures and speech patterns as well as vocabulary which still characterize them today. Alongside the basic chromatic signs of red and blue they adopted other distinctive characteristics. Each gang includes its initial in graffiti or in the tattoos which they probably got from California biker usage. They also structure their look to be more specific and recognizable at a glance.

In this way, with rituals, codes, languages – a sub-culture – the two gangs created a dichotomous "Parallel society", moving more and more to the margins of local and national white and assimilated reality and making of this exclusion a banner. Being outside the two gangs meant being "surrounded "by enemy territory and without defense. From 18 in 1972, the gangs active in Los Angeles became 60 by 1978: of these, 45 were affiliates of the Crips and 15 of the Bloods.

Conflict between the two sides often led to killings ~ as early as 1974 there were seventeen gang-related deaths.

Besides increasing in number and in membership, the gangs expanded beyond the city limits, into Los Angeles county; by the end of the decade they were rooted in Inglewood, Compton and Athens, bringing with them fear and death. They moved out to the towns with the migration of many black Los Angeles inner city families at the end of the decade. Within thirty years gang territories would cover more than sixty square miles of the county. It is important to note that the areas dominated by Crips and Bloods are not at all well-defined; there is no territorial continuity. Los Angeles was never a city divided in two red and blue blocks, and it is not so today either. Red and Blue areas interlock in a complex mosaic because the gangs developed on the basis of casual friendships or unplanned dislikes and feuds. This pattern has always favored gangbanging.

In 1979, Raymond Washington, the Crips founder was killed, but gang's terrorism flourished without him. The sub-culture he reintroduced had put down its own roots in a soil that seemed just right for it. The death of an OG (Original Gangster) was just an irrelevant detail. If the causes of Los Angeles gang reality are various and we cannot as-sign responsibility to anyone a factor, it is certainly the case that not only white authority, but the increasingly influential black middle classes are conspicuous absent from the scene. Several generations of black middle class professionals, though living out in the suburbs, have continued to come into the city to work .In this sense the generational aspect goes beyond the step from gang to Panthers to new gang (some of whose members also indicate shifts within a gen-eration) but reaches forward with sure relevance to those Afro-Americans whose experience is no longer that of pov-erty and exclusion. Very often black middle classes have not done even what little they might have tried to do, preferring to "forget it" once out of it. As Cornel West put it:

We have created rootless individuals, hanging over the abyss, almost entirely without ties to the networks – family, friends, school – that give sense and purpose to life...As a result...we have lives that resolve themselves into what we might call "casual moments" fleeting occasions and lucky incidents of getting over...

---

1   The growth in the number and size of gangs had begun to be a serious problem for city government in the late '50s and early '60s, though most gang fights were still hand to hand and weapons were generally chains or bats. The six gang-related deaths of 1960 – whose number, compared to the statistics of recent years, appears negligible – was viewed with alarm as a sign of the times by Los Angeles authorities and by the press, while local television channels publicized and, in a sense, encouraged the trend exactly because it was virtually the only attention given to the neighborhoods and the people involved. Battles were linked in the '50s to defense of a gang's "territory", clashes between fans of different football squads, or over the gang's exclusive access to those girls it chose to consider its own or, finally, and perhaps more frequently than other reasons to the perception of the antagonist's socio-economic status as "different". In Los Angeles in fact the persistent clashes between East and West side in the '50s and early '60s had insistently, almost desperately, clung to the subtle shadings of social class in what was considered by those "outside" (white politicians and sociologists) to be "the greatest area of urban decay in the whole country".

2   William H. Parker was Chief of police in Los Angeles from 1950 to his death in 1966. His methods were violent and his Anti-gang policy was based on repression rather than prevention; he devoted the notable funds at his disposal to arms and to the reinforcement of special squads in South Central where there was a high concentration of gangs. A detailed analysis of Parker may be found in Mike Davis' City of Quartz, Vintage Books, New York, 1993 or Brian Cross' it's Not About Salary... Rap, Race and Resistance in Los Angeles, Verso Books, New York, 19933

3   For an over-view of Karenga and the US Organization as well as the contrasts, - which reach their peak in 1969 – between this group and the Panther Party, see Scot Brown's study The US Organization, Maulana Karenga and the Conflict with the Black Panther Party: A Critique of Sectarian Influences on Historical Discourse, published on-line at j store web-site.

4   See www.streetgangs.com and www.gangorus.com, as well as www.nagia.com.

5   For example that most classic of organizations, the National Urban League, and the National Alliance of Businessmen Headed up by Henry Ford II.

6   Manning Marable, Black Nationalism in the '70s. Through the Prism of Race and Class, "Socialist Review", March-June, 1980, p.95.

7   Paolo Bertella Farneti, "Repression, the Dark Side", in Bruno Cartosio, ed., Senza illusioni, Shake, Milan, 1995, p. 93.

8   Cornel West IL paradosso Della ribellione afro Americana, saggio contenuto in Bruno Cartosio, Op. cit., p. 53.

9   in Martin Van Peebles' 1995 film Panther, which tells the story of the Black Panther Party, drugs are represented as the keystone of the movement's demise. According to Van Peebles (who revives in a sense Malcolm X's theory) Hoover, then head of the FBI, decided to introduce heroin into black neighborhoods' to undermine militancy.

10   See, for example, the searing New Jack City (1991), directed by Mario Van Peebles.

11   Along with private eye Shaft and Priest, female figures whose characteristics paralleled the men's – like Cleopatra Jones (Tamara Dobson) in 1973, Coffy and Foxy Brown (Pam Grier) in 1974. African American women found here models more than difficult to relate to or adopt in these "comic book" transpositions.

12   Franco Minganti, IL cinema afro Americana, in Encyclopedia Del cinema mondiale, Einaudi, Turin, 2001, p. 1367.

13   Tookie Williams, was arrested in 1981 for four armed robberies and homicide. After his "redemption" in 1993, he began writing books on gangs for children, where he denounced their brutality and urged his young readers to keep away from gangs. In 2001 Tookie Williams received a nomination for the Nobel Peace Prize.

14   See National Gangs History at web-site www.gripe4kids.org.

15   Interview with Danifu, Alejandro Alonso, African-American Street Gangs in Los Angeles, in the Web-site www.nagia.com.

16   Jerry Cohen, "Los Angeles Sentinel", Feb. 10, 1972.

17   I am indebted to discussions with Loretta Valtz Mannucci for these considerations.

Gang Grief: Violence Wounds Teens and Communities

Members of the Bloods gang engaging in turf battles with rival gang the Crips—that might sound like something out of a movie, but it was real life for Seattle teen Jon Amosa. The Bloods founded in Los Angeles is one the biggest gangs in the country. It considers the Crips, another L.A.-based gang, its enemy. Amosa joined a local chapter of the Bloods at the age of 14, enticed by cousins who were already members. Amosa was "jumped in"~ beaten by other gang members ~ as an initiation rite.

Then he went on to beat up members of rival gangs. "Whatever my 'big homey,' or the older guys, whatever they told me to do, I'd go do it, no questions asked," says Amosa. In addition to fighting, he sold and used drugs. While rap stars may brag about being a thug or a "gangsta," Amosa, now 18, says it was anything but cool. "I've lost a lot of friends to gang violence, a lot of family members too," he says. "Really, it's not worth it." Amosa left the gang after becoming more involved in his church.

A Growing Threat

Gang violence claimed the lives of six teens in the Seattle area in an eight-month period last year and left many others injured. Such violence can affect whole communities, not just people involved in gangs. Recent incidents across the country include the following:

• A curfew for teens was imposed in Hartford, Conn., after a bloody weekend in which 11 people were shot, including a 7-year-old boy. The shootings are believed to be gang-related.

• A Kansas City, Kansas, teen was sentenced to life in prison for a shooting that killed a 2-year-old girl. The teen, a gang member, was ordered to fire at the house where the girl was staying with her grandparents according to court testimony.

• A gang brawl in Nyack, N.Y., north of New York City New York City, was sparked when a high school student ripped a bandana with rival gang colors off the neck of a student.

The most serious gang activity is centered in larger cities such as Los Angeles, New York, and Chicago gangs are also present in suburbs and small towns, says James C. Howell, senior research associate at the National Youth Gang Center.

The center's 2006 National Youth Gang Survey shows there are about 26,500 youth gangs in the States with 785,000 members' total. Gang members are responsible for a large share of the violent crimes committed by teens in large urban areas, studies show. In Seattle, gang members were responsible for 85 percent of the robberies committed by teens in 1998.

One study found that 8 percent of 12- to 17-year-olds joined a gang at some point in their middle or high school years. Almost a quarter of students surveyed in 2005 said there were gangs in their schools, up from 17 percent in 1999, says Howell. Gangs aren't just a guy thing, either: Experts estimate that up to 33 percent of gang members are girls.

Referenced in Chapter Eight
Lyrics to "The Heat is On" by Glenn Frey

The heat is on, on the street
Inside your head, on every beat
And the beat's so loud, deep inside
The pressure's high, just to stay alive
'Cause the heat is on

[Chorus]
Oh-wo-ho, oh-wo-ho
Caught up in the action
I've been looking out for you
Oh-wo-ho, oh-wo-ho
Tell me can you feel it
Tell me can you feel it
Tell me can you feel it

The heat is on, the heat is on
The heat is on
Oh it's on the street
The heat is... on

The shadows are on the darker side
Behind those doors, it's a wilder ride
You can make a break, you can win or lose
That's a chance you take, when the heat's on you
When the heat is on

[Chorus]

Referenced in Chapter Nine
"Timothy McGhee Wanted Fugitive"

What: Los Angeles Police Department Press Conference Regarding Murder Suspect Timothy McGhee and United States Marshals 15 Most Wanted Fugitive List

When: Thursday, February 13, 2003, at 10:00 a.m.

Where: Northeast Area Police Station, 3353 San Fernando Road, and Los Angeles

Who: Los Angeles Police Chief William J. Bratton, United States Marshals Service Chief John Clark, Los Angeles City Councilman Eric Garcetti, LAPD Officials

Los Angeles: Timothy McGhee, a local Los Angeles gang member wanted by the Los Angeles Police Department in connection with as many as a dozen killings, has been named to the United States Marshals Service "15 Most Wanted Fugitive List."

Timothy McGhee, 29 years of age, has been charged by the United States Marshals Service with a federal offense of Unlawful Flight to Avoid Prosecution. The federal charges are based on McGhee's efforts to elude capture and prosecution in connection with an arrest warrant that was issued in June 2000, charging him with the murder of 16 year-old Ryan Gonzalez. McGhee allegedly killed Gonzalez simply because Gonzalez happened to share the same nickname that McGhee uses. McGhee is also a suspect in a string of brutal murders that have been committed since then, including the murder of a 17 year-old boy who was sketching a picture at the Los Angeles River near the gang's stronghold in Atwater Village. Additionally, he killed a young mother of two, apparently because of the type of vehicle she was driving.

Investigators believe that McGhee continues to influence the activities of his gang while on the run. He is still involved in their criminal enterprises, which include drug trafficking, firearms violations and other criminal offenses, including murder and threats of violence to dissuade rival gang members, potential witnesses and unsuspecting community members.

Give Rampart Investigators a Big Stick and Then Turn Them Loose

"Code of Silence Must Be Crushed"
By Erwin Chemerinsky and Constance L. Rice
Erwin Chemerinsky is a professor of law and political science at USC.
Constance L. Rice is a civil rights attorney.
March 3, 2003
The truth about the LAPD's Rampart corruption scandal never has been learned. How many officers engaged in illegal activity or facilitated it with their silence? How high up did the scandal extend within the Police Department? Did other anti-gang units also routinely plant evidence or lie in court? What happened to honest officers who early on blew the whistle on "gangster cops"? And why has there been no coherent account of what happened?

Now Police Chief William Bratton is proposing such an inquiry. We applaud him for recognizing that much remains unknown. But unless the investigatory commission has the powers and adequate budget needed to do the job, there is little chance of success. And after 3 1/2 years of delay, it is uncertain whether an investigation now can succeed.

Although several reports were issued concerning the scandal, none engaged in a thorough, factual investigation of what actually happened within the LAPD. The failures of prosecutors, judges, police commissioners and politicians have yet to be documented publicly. A great deal has not come to light.]

The Police Commission committee, chaired by lawyer Richard Drooyan, focused on making policy recommendations for reforming the LAPD, not on learning what happened. The LAPD had a board of inquiry look at Rampart, but it was very much the institution's version of the scandal and minimized the extent of the problem, blaming it on mediocrity and a few wayward officers.

There were several proposals for an independent commission to conduct a full investigation, but then-Mayor

Richard Riordan and then-Police Chief Bernard Parks succeeded in quashing them.

Now is the time for an independent commission with the tools and a clear mandate to get to the bottom of what happened. The commission must have subpoena power to ensure that needed witnesses testify and that necessary documents are provided. Most important, it must be able to give immunity to police officers. Many officers, some of whom have told each of us about unreported serious misconduct, have said that they can't testify because they fear they will lose their badges for failing to report misconduct when it occurred.

Worse, the many good officers who wanted to testify know that the LAPD's command staff and Internal Affairs ended the career of Armando Coronado because he blew the whistle on Rampart Division officers Rafael Perez and Nino Durden years before the Rampart scandal exploded publicly. The commission must have the ability to provide officers anonymity and protection from the LAPD's Pavlovian response of silencing and retaliating against officers who expose wrong doing.

If a real investigation is not going to be done, at the very least, an independent panel of experts might do a post-mortem of what went wrong in the Rampart investigation and provide a blueprint for future inquiries.

The Rampart scandal involved police officers planting evidence to frame innocent people and then lying in court to gain convictions. The officers' misconduct violated the very core of the rule of law. Not nearly enough was done to expose what happened and to ensure that it never happens again.

Referenced in Chapter Sixteen

Wednesday, January 3, 2001
Homicide Rate: Up 27.6% for Year in L.A.
Violence: Central and south areas are the hardest hit.
Many of the killers are thought to be gang members.
By: SARAH HALE, Times Staff Writer

Los Angeles saw an alarming 27.6% upturn in homicides last year, with more than 75% of them occurring in south and central communities, authorities said Tuesday. A total of 545 people were slain, according to the Los Angeles Police Department's year-end crime statistics. And violent crime in aggregate was up 10% citywide.

"These statistics should be a real cause for concern for the mayor, the City Council, the city attorney, everyone in the city," said Erwin Chemerinsky, a professor of Law at USC.

"But it is important that we resist the temptation to find a single cause; undoubtedly, this is a product of many factors," he said. "They may include an increase in gang warfare, demographic shifts causing a rise in the number of males of a certain age group, low police morale and less effective policing."

The year's homicide victims were almost exclusively black or Latino males between 17 and 32, and most of the killers--many of them believed to be gang members, were between 14 and 24.

Several LAPD officials cited drug sales, high-powered weapons, and a decline in the number of youth programs in poverty-stricken pockets of the city as additional possible explanations, as well as attrition within the department. There are now 9,200 sworn officers; about 800 fewer than there were three years ago.

The department has begun to analyze the year-end totals to develop strategies this year and to increase enforcement of existing laws, such as curfews.

"The department and the chief plan to do everything possible to curb this climb," said a spokesman, Officer Jason Lee.

The 77th Division, which had one of the highest murder rates in the city, is reassigning many of its 400 officers to street patrols.

Some of the division's narcotics officers have been redeployed, Sgt. Kiyong Ma said.

"The bike unit here was canceled 2-3 weeks ago," he said, "and those officers were put in cars."

The division is examining every patrol officer's arrest records, citations and court appearances in search of patterns that might reflect a less aggressive approach by some officers.

If an officer is found lacking in certain crucial areas, "we will approach each one individually to find out what's going on," Ma said. "Then, the problem will be addressed."

Citywide, rape increased 11.5%; aggravated assault 10% and robbery 8.8%, less serious crimes increased as well. Motor vehicle theft and burglary each increased 13%, Lee said.

But Sgt. John Pasquariello pointed out that crime gang-related homicides in particular remain significantly lower than they were in the early 1990s, when gang warfare fueled by turf killings and drugs escalated to unprecedented levels.

Between 1991 and 1993, there were more than 3,000 homicides, he said. After that, the homicide rate crept downward, until now.

Pasquariello suggested that the recent spikes in crimes across the board reflect a cyclical pattern of violence. The crime rate, he said, had decreased for so long that it was only a matter of time before it hit bottom and started to climb.

"What goes down, must go up; what goes up, must go up," he said. "But that's just one theory."

Referenced in Chapter 20

Texarkana, TX...On Monday, May 4th; Freeway Ricky Ross will finally be released from prison after serving 20 years for being a "drug kingpin." The real Ricky Ross oversaw a Los Angeles based multi-state drug operation in the early 1980's, which earned upwards of $2 million dollars per day at its height.

Former Drug Kingpin, Ricky Ross, Returns To Society a Better Man

Texarkana, TX...On Monday, May 4th; Freeway Ricky Ross will finally be released from prison after serving 20 years for being a "drug kingpin." The real Ricky Ross oversaw a Los Angeles based multi-state drug operation in the early 1980's, which earned upwards of $2 million dollars per day at its height. After L.A.P.D. set up a sting operation to bring him down (The Freeway Taskforce), Ricky finally turned himself in, weeks after a rogue police officer attempted to set him up and murder him in an alley. Ricky was sentenced to prison and released in 1996. After 6 months, his former cocaine distributor, who was working for the CIA (unbeknownst to Ricky), asked Ricky for a favor—it turned out to be a set up, and in 1996, Ricky Ross was sentenced to life in prison for orchestrating the purchase of over 100 kilos of cocaine from an undercover federal agent.

Ross' sentence was later reduced through appeals and after a series of explosive articles by the late Pulitzer Prize winning journalist Gary Webb. Webb wrote a series titled "Dark Alliance" for the San Jose Mercury News, which exposed the C.I.A.'s role in importing cocaine into black communities to fund Sandinistas in El Salvador, as part of the Iran-Contra scandal. That series turned into the best-selling book, "Dark Alliance," that blew the lid off of the alleged CIA complicity in the importation of cocaine into the US, creating the exceptionally profitable, and damaging, crack cocaine epidemic spread through many inner city neighborhoods. Congressional Hearings, in the late-90s, found the book's facts to be true.

As Ricky Ross' story reads like a page-turning novel or a blockbuster film, it has inspired rappers to name themselves after him, and even retell his stories as their own exploits, gaining international success. Although a pawn in a bigger scheme, Ricky realized that the damage done to inner city neighborhoods was unacceptable. He has devoted himself to making a difference in his community by teaching financial literacy to urban youth and teaching legal ways to financially empower themselves. When Ricky first went to prison, he was illiterate—the educational system in South Central L.A. had failed him, even though he went on to become a multi-millionaire savvy at numerous legitimate businesses, and tennis pro. Reading a book a week during his lengthy incarceration has since made Ricky wise beyond his years.

Ricky oversaw an empire that reached numerous states and that is rumored to have brought in millions of dollars a day at its height. His plan is to return to society and accomplish that again, but this time through legal means. Upon Ricky Ross' release, he is focusing on:

- A book and a film (currently seeking deals for both),
- a new record label in conjunction with industry legend Wendy Day,
- a Foundation to help inner-city youth at risk,
- a reality TV show,
- his social networking site, www.FreewayEnterprise.com that he built while incarcerated.

A film crew is following Ricky's release from prison and his trek across the country to a halfway house in California where he will interact with, and impact youth in juvenile detention centers along the way. Already the topic of one of the most successful episodes of BET's American Gangster series (1st Season), the real Ricky Ross is a cultural icon and hero in communities across the US. Now he is able to make positive moves with that status.

Ricky can be reached through his social networking site www.FreewayEnterprise.com.

Referenced in Chapter Twenty

INTELLIGENCE ACTIVITIES AND THE RIGHTS OF AMERICANS _____ BOOK II _____ FINAL REPORT OF THE SELECT COMMITTEE TO STUDY GOVERNMENTAL OPERATIONS WITH RESPECT TO INTELLIGENCE ACTIVITIES UNITED STATES SENATE TOGETHER WITH ADDITIONAL, SUPPLEMENTAL, AND SEPARATE VIEWS APRIL 26 (legislative day, April 14), 1976

D. USING COVERT ACTION TO DISRUPT AND DISCREDIT DOMESTIC GROUPS

MAJOR FINDING

The Committee finds that covert action programs have been used to disrupt the lawful political activities of individual Americans and groups and to discredit them, using dangerous and degrading tactics which are abhorrent in a free and decent society.

Subfinding

(a) Although the claimed purposes of these action programs were to protect the national security and to prevent violence, many of the victims were concededly nonviolent, were not controlled by a foreign power, and posed no threat to the national security.

(b) The acts taken interfered with the First Amendment rights of citizens. They were explicitly intended to deter citizens from joining groups, "neutralize" those who were already members, and prevent or inhibit the expression of ideas.

(c) The tactics used against Americans often risked and sometimes caused serious emotional, economic, or physical damage. Actions were taken which were designed to break up marriages, terminate funding or employment, and encourage gang warfare between violent rival groups. Due process of law forbids the use of such covert tactics, whether the victims are innocent law-abiding citizens or members of groups suspected of involvement in violence.

(d) The sustained use of such tactics by the FBI in an attempt to destroy Dr. Martin Luther King, Jr., violated the law and fundamental human decency.

Elaboration of the Findings

For fifteen years from 1956 until 1971, the FBI carried out a series of covert action programs directed against American citizens. 1 These 'counterintelligence programs' (shortened to the acronym COINTELPRO) resulted in part from frustration with Supreme Court rulings limiting the Government's power to proceed overtly against dissident groups.2

They ended formally in 1971 with the threat of public exposure.3 some of the findings discussed herein are related to the findings on lawlessness, over breadth, and intrusive techniques previously set forth. Some of the most offensive actions in the FBI's COINTELPRO programs (anonymous letters intended to break up marriages, or efforts to deprive people of their jobs, for example) were based upon the covert use of information obtained through overly broad investigations and intrusive techniques.4 Similarly, as noted above, COINTELPRO involved specific violations of law, and the law and the Constitution were "not [given] a thought" under the FBI's policies.5

But COINTELPRO was more than simply violating the law or the Constitution. In COINTELPRO the Bureau secretly6 took the law into its own hands, going beyond the collection of intelligence and beyond its law enforcement function to act outside the legal process altogether and to covertly disrupt, discredit and harass groups and individuals. A law enforcement agency must not secretly usurp the functions of judge and jury, even when the investigation reveals criminal activity. But in COINTELPRO, the Bureau imposed summary punishment, not only on the allegedly violent, but also on the nonviolent advocates of change. Such action is the hallmark of the vigilante and has no place in a democratic society.

Under COINTELPRO, certain techniques the Bureau had used against hostile foreign agents were adopted for use against perceived domestic threats to the established political and social order. 7

Some of the targets of COINTELPRO were law-abiding citizens merely advocating change in our society. Other targets were members of groups that had been involved in

violence, such as the Ku Klux Klan or the Black Panther
Party. Some victims did nothing more than associate with
targets. 8

The Committee does not condone acts of violence, but
the response of Government to allegations of illegal conduct
must comply with the due process of law demanded by the
Constitution. Lawlessness by citizens does not justify lawlessness by Government.

The tactics, which were employed by the Bureau, are
therefore unacceptable, even against the alleged criminal.
The imprecision of the targeting compounded the abuse.
Once the Government decided to take the law into its own
hands, those unacceptable tactics came almost inevitably to
be used not only against the "kid with the bomb" but also
against the "kid with the bumper sticker."

Subfinding (a)

Although the claimed purposes of these action programs
were to protect the "national security" and to prevent violence, many of the victims were concededly nonviolent,
were not controlled by a foreign power, and posed no threat
to the "national security."

The Bureau conducted five "counterintelligence programs" aimed against domestic groups: the "Communist
Party, USA" program (1956-71); the "Socialist Workers Party"
program (1961-69); the "White Hate" program (1964-1971);
the "Black Nationalist-Hate Group" program (1967-71); and
the "New Left" program (1968-71).

While the declared purposes of these programs were to
protect the "national security" or prevent violence, Bureau
witnesses admit that many of the targets were nonviolent
and most had no connections with a foreign power. Indeed,
nonviolent organizations and individuals were targeted because the Bureau believed they represented a "potential" for
violence -- and nonviolent citizens who were against the
war in Vietnam were targeted because they gave "aid and
comfort" to violent demonstrators by lending respectability
to their cause. 11

The imprecision of the targeting is demonstrated by the
inability of the Bureau to define the subjects of the programs.

The Black Nationalist program, according to its supervisor, included "a great number of organizations that you might not today characterize as Black Nationalist but which were in fact primarily black." 12 Thus, the nonviolent Southern Christian Leadership Conference was labeled as a Black Nationalist-"Hate Group."

Furthermore, the actual targets were chosen from a far broader group than the titles of the programs would imply. The CPUSA program targeted not only Communist Party members but also sponsors of the National Committee to Abolish the House Un-American Activities Committee 14 and civil rights leaders allegedly under Communist influence or not deemed to be "anti-Communist". 15 The Socialist Workers Party program included non-SWP sponsors of antiwar demonstrations, which were cosponsored by the SWP or the Young Socialist Alliance, its youth group. 16 The Black Nationalist program targeted a range of organizations from the Panthers to SNCC to the peaceful Southern Christian Leadership Conference, and included every Black Student Union and many other black student groups. 17 New Left targets ranged from the SDS 18 to the Interuniversity Committee for Debate on Foreign Policy, 19 from Antioch College ("vanguard of the New Left") 20 to the New Mexico Free University and other "alternate" schools, 21 and from underground newspapers 22 to students protesting university censorship of a student publication by carrying signs with four-letter words on them. 23

Subfinding (b)

The acts taken interfered with the First Amendment rights of citizens. They were explicitly intended to deter citizens from joining groups, "neutralize" those who were already members, and prevent or inhibit the expression of ideas.

In achieving its purported goals of protecting the national security and preventing violence, the Bureau attempted to deter membership in the target groups. As the supervisor of the "Black Nationalist" COINTELPRO stated, 'Obviously, you are going to prevent violence or a greater amount of violence if you have smaller groups.' 4 The chief of the COINTELPRO unit agreed: 'We also made an effort . . . to deter recruitment where we could. This was done with the view that if we could curb the organization, we could curb the action or the violence within the organization. 25 As noted above, many of the organizations "curbed" were not violent, and covert attacks on group membership contravened the First Amendment's guarantee of freedom to associate.

Nor was this the only First Amendment right violated by the Bureau. In addition to attempting to prevent people from joining or continuing to be members in target organizations, the Bureau tried to "deter or counteract" what it called "propaganda" 26 -- the expression of ideas which it considered dangerous. Thus, the originating document for the "Black Nationalist" COINTELPRO noted 'that consideration should be given to techniques to preclude' leaders of the target organizations 'from spreading their philosophy publicly or through various mass communication media.' 27

Instructions to "preclude" free speech were not limited to "black nationalists;" they occurred in every program. In the New Left program, for instance, approximately thirty-nine percent of all actions attempted to keep targets from speaking, teaching, writing, or publishing. 28

The cases included attempts (sometimes successful) to prompt the firing of university and high school teachers; 29 to prevent targets from speaking on campus; 30 to stop chapters of target groups from being formed; 31 to prevent the distribution of books, newspapers, or periodicals; 32 to disrupt or cancel news conferences; 33 to interfere with peaceful demonstrations, including the SCLC's Poor People's Campaign and Washington Spring Project and most of the large anti-war marches; 34 and to deny facilities for meetings or conferences. 35

As the above cases demonstrate, the FBI was not just "chilling" free speech, but also squarely attacking it.

The tactics used against Americans often risked and sometimes caused serious emotional, economic, or physical damage. Actions were taken which were designed to break up marriages, terminate funding or employment, and encourage gang warfare between violent rival groups. Due process of law forbids the use of such covert tactics whether the victims are innocent law-abiding citizens or members of groups suspected of involvement in violence. The former head of the Domestic Intelligence Division described counterintelligence as a "rough, tough, dirty, and dangerous" business. 36 His description was accurate. [Emphasis added.]

One technique used in COINTELPRO involved sending anonymous letters to spouses intended, in the words of one proposal, to 'produce ill-feeling and possibly a lasting distrust' between husband and wife, so that 'concern over what to do about it' would distract the target from 'time spent in the plots and plans' of the organization. 87 The image of an agent of the United States Government scrawling a poison-pen letter to someone's wife in language usually reserved for bathroom walls is not a happy one. Nevertheless, anonymous letters were sent to, among others, a Klansman's wife, informing her that her husband had 'taken the flesh of another unto himself,' the other person being a woman named Ruby, with her 'lust filled eyes and smart aleck figure;' 38 and to a "Black Nationalist's" wife saying that her husband 'been make it here' with other women in his organization 'and then he gives us this jive bout their better in bed then you.' 39 A husband who was concerned about his wife's activities in a biracial group received a letter which started, 'Look man I guess your old lady doesn't get enough at home or she wouldn't be shucking and jiving with our Black Men' in the group. 40 The Field Office reported as a 'tangible result' of this letter that the target and her husband separated. 41

The Bureau also contacted employers and funding organizations in order to cause the firing of the targets or the termination of their support. 42 For example, priests who allowed their churches to be used for the Black Panther breakfast programs were targeted, and anonymous letters were sent to their bishops; 43 a television commentator who expressed admiration for a Black Nationalist leader and criticized heavy defense spending was transferred after the Bureau contacted his employer; 44 and an employee of the Urban League was fired after the FBI approached a 'confidential source' in a foundation which funded the League. 45

The Bureau also encouraged "gang warfare" between violent groups. An FBI memorandum dated November 25, 1968 to certain Field Offices conducting investigations of the Black Panther Party ordered recipient offices to submit 'imaginative and hard-hitting counterintelligence measures aimed at crippling the BPP.' Proposals were to be received every two weeks. Particular attention was to be given to capitalizing upon differences between the Panthers and US, Inc. (another "Black Nationalist" group), which had reached such proportions that 'it is taking on the aura of gang warfare with attendant threats of murder and reprisals.' 45a On May 26, 1970, after U.S. organization members had killed four BPP members and members of each organization had been shot and beaten by members of the other, the Field Office reported:

'Information received from local sources indicates[s] that, in general, the membership of the Los Angeles BPP is physically afraid of US members and take premeditated precautions to avoid confrontations.

In view of their anxieties, it is not presently felt that the Los Angeles BPP can be prompted into what could result in an internecine struggle between the two organizations. The Los Angeles Division is aware of the mutually hostile feelings harbored between the organizations and the first opportunity to capitalize on the situation will be maximized. It is intended that US Inc. will be appropriately and discreetly advised of the time and location of BPP activities in order that the two organizations might be brought together and thus grant nature the opportunity to take 'er due course.' 46 [Emphasis added.]

A second Field Office noted:

'Shootings, beatings and a high degree of unrest continue to prevail in the ghetto area of Southeast San Diego. Although no specific counterintelligence action can be credited with contributing to this overall situation, it is felt that a substantial amount of the unrest is directly attributable to this program.' 47

In another case, an anonymous letter was sent to the leader of the Blackstone Rangers (a group, according to the

Field Offices' proposal, 'to whom violent-type activity, shooting, and the like are second nature') advising him that 'the brothers that run the Panthers blame you for blocking their thing and there's supposed to be a hit out for you.' The letter was intended to 'intensify the degree of animosity between the two groups' and cause 'retaliatory action which could disrupt the BPP or lead to reprisals against its leadership.' 48

Another technique, which risked serious harm to the target, was falsely labeling a target an informant. This technique was used in all five domestic COINTELPROs. When a member of a nonviolent group was successfully mislabeled as an informant, the result was alienation from the group. 49 When the target belonged to a group known to have killed suspected informants, the risk was substantially more serious. On several occasions, the Bureau used this technique against members of the Black Panther Party; it was used at least twice after FBI documents expressed concern over the possible consequences because two members of the BPP had been murdered as suspected informants. 50

The Bureau recognized that some techniques used in COINTELPRO were more likely than others to cause serious physical, emotional, or economic damage to the targets. 51 Any proposed use of such techniques ~ for example, encouraging enmity between violent rival groups, falsely labeling group members as informants, and mailing anonymous letters to targets' spouses accusing the target of infidelity ~ was scrutinized carefully by headquarters supervisory personnel, in an attempt to balance the "greater good" to be achieved by the proposal against the known or risked harm to the target. If the "good" was sufficient, the proposal was approved. For instance, in discussing anonymous letters to spouses, the agent who supervised the New Left COINTELPRO stated:

'[Before recommending approval] I would want to know what you want to get out of this, who is these people. If it's somebody, and say they did split up, what would accrue from it as far as disrupting the New Left is concerned? Say they broke up, what then... [The question would be] is it worth it?' 52

Similarly, with regard to causing false suspicions that an individual was an informant, the chief of the Racial Intelligence Section stated:

'You have to be able to make decisions and I am sure that labeling somebody as an informant, that you'd want to make certain that it served a good purpose before you did it and not do it haphazardly.... It is a serious thing ... As far as I am aware in the black extremist area, by using that technique, no one was killed. I am sure of that.' 52a

This official was asked whether the fact that no one was killed was the, result of "luck or planning." He answered: 'Oh, it just happened that way, I am sure.' 52b

It is intolerable in a free society that an agency of the Government should adopt such tactics, whether or not the targets are involved in criminal activity. The "greater good" of the country is in fact served by adherence to the rule of law mandated by the Constitution.

Subfinding (d)

The sustained use of such tactics by the FBI in an attempt to destroy Dr. Martin Luther King, Jr., violated the law and fundamental human decency.

The Committee devoted substantial attention to the FBI's covert action campaign against Dr. Martin Luther King because it demonstrates just how far the Government could go in a secret war against one citizen. In focusing upon Dr. King, however, it should not be forgotten that the Bureau carried out disruptive activities against hundreds of lesser-known American citizens. It should also be borne in mind that positive action on the part of high Government officials outside the FBI might have prevented what occurred in this case. 53

The FBI's claimed justification for targeting Dr. King ~ alleged Communist influence on him and the civil rights movement ~ is examined elsewhere in this report. 54

The FBI's campaign against Dr. Martin Luther King, Jr. began in December 1963, four months after the famous civil rights March on Washington, 55 when a nine-hour meeting was convened at FBI Headquarters to discuss various 'avenues of approach aimed at neutralizing King as an effective Negro leader.' 56 Following the meeting, agents in the field were instructed to 'continue to gather information concerning King's personal activities ... in order that we may consider using this information at an opportune time in a counterintelligence move to discredit him.' 57

About two weeks after that conference, FBI agents planted a microphone in Dr. King's bedroom at the Willard Hotel in Washington, D.C. 58 during the next two years; the FBI installed at least fourteen more "bugs" in Dr. King's hotel rooms across the country. 59 Physical and photographic surveillances accompanied some of the microphone coverage. 60

The FBI also scrutinized Dr. King's tax returns, monitored his financial affairs, and even tried to determine whether he had a secret foreign bank account. 61

In late 1964, a "sterilized" tape was prepared in a manner that would prevent attribution to the FBI and was "anonymously" mailed to Dr. King just before he received the Nobel Peace Prize. 62 Enclosed in the package with the tape was an unsigned letter which warned Dr. King, 'your end is approaching . . . you are finished.' The letter intimated that the tape might be publicly released, and closed with the following message:

'King, there is only one thing left for you to do. You know what it is. You have just 34 days in which to do (this exact number has been selected for a specific reason, it has definite practical significance). You are done. There is but one way out for you . . .' 63

Dr. King's associates have said he interpreted the message as an effort to induce him to commit suicide. 64

At about the same time that it mailed the "sanitized" tape, the FBI was also apparently offering tapes and transcripts to newsmen. 65 Later when civil rights leaders Roy Wilkins and James Farmer went to Washington to persuade Bureau officials to halt the FBI's discrediting efforts, 66 they were told that 'if King wants[s] war we [are] prepared to give it to him.' 67

Shortly thereafter, Dr. King went to Europe to receive the Nobel Peace Prize. The Bureau tried to undermine ambassadorial receptions in several of the countries he visited

68 and when he returned to the United States, took steps to diminish support for a banquet and a special "day" being planned in his honor. 69

The Bureau's actions against Dr. King included attempts to prevent him from meeting with world leaders, receiving honors or favorable publicity, and gaining financial support. When the Bureau learned of a possible meeting between Dr. King and the Pope in August 1964, the FBI asked Cardinal Spellman to try to arrange a cancellation of the audience. 70 Discovering that two schools (Springfield College and Marquette University) were going to honor Dr. King with special degrees in the spring of 1964, Bureau agents tried to convince officials at the schools to rescind their plans. 71 And when the Bureau learned in October 1966 that the Ford Foundation might grant three million dollars to Dr. King's Southern Christian Leadership Conference, they asked a former FBI agent who was a high official at the Ford Motor Company to try to block the award. 72

A magazine was asked not to publish favorable articles about him. 73 Religious leaders and institutions were contacted to undermine their support of him. 74 Press conference questions were prepared and distributed to "friendly" journalists. 75 And plans were even discussed for sabotaging his political campaign in the event he decided to run for national office. 76 An SCLC employee was "anonymously" informed that the SCLC was trying to get rid of her 'so that the Bureau [would be] in a position to capitalize on [her] bitterness.' 78 Bureau officials contacted members of Congress, 79 and special "off the record" testimony was prepared for the Director's use before the House Appropriations Committee. 80

The "neutralization" program continued until Dr. King's death. As late as March 1968, FBI agents were being instructed to neutralize Dr. King because he might become a "messiah" who could 'unify, and electrify, the militant black nationalist movement' if he were to 'abandon his supposed "obedience" to "white liberal doctrines" (nonviolence) and embrace black nationalism.' 81 Steps were taken to subvert the "Poor People's Campaign" which Dr. King was planning to lead in the spring of 1968. 82 Even after Dr. King's death, agents in the field were proposing methods for harassing his widow 83 and Bureau officials were trying to prevent his birthday from becoming a national holiday. 84

The actions taken against Dr. King are indefensible. They represent a sad episode in the dark history of covert actions directed against law-abiding citizens by a law enforcement agency.

Referenced in Chapter Twenty

Government plots
CIA Allegedly Linked to Crack Epidemic in Los Angeles;
CIA Director Orders Investigation; African-American Leaders
Outraged; DEA Agent Supports Charges; Charges Minimized
CIA/DRUG ALLEGATIONS
October 1996
A series of articles in the San Jose Mercury News on
August 18-20 alleges that the CIA was involved with
Nicaraguan Contra rebels who raised money for weapons
by selling cocaine to Los Angeles area street gangs (Gary
Webb, "America's 'crack' plague has roots in Nicaragua war,"
San Jose Mercury News, August 18, 1996, p. A1; Gary Webb,
"Shadowy Origins of 'crack' epidemic," San Jose Mercury
News, August 19, 1996, p. A1; Gary Webb, "War on drugs
has unequal impact on black Americans," San Jose Mercury
News, August 20 ,1996, p. A1; Tony Perry and Jesse Katz, "As
Drug Debate Rages, Dealer to Be Sentenced," Los Angeles
Times (Washington Edition), August 23, 1996, p. B1; Gary
Webb, "The Crack Masters," New Times (Los Angeles),
September 12-18, 1996, Vol. 1, Num. 4; The San Jose Mercury
News series and supporting documentation is available at
http://www.sjmercury.com).

Mercury News Allegations

According to the San Jose Mercury News, Nicaraguan
Contras, run by the CIA, delivered tons of cut-rate cocaine
to a young Los Angeles drug dealer named "Freeway" Rick
Ross. Ross, a street-wise drug dealer of mythic reputation,
turned the cocaine into crack and supplied the Crips and
Bloods street gangs, which saturated the market with crack
and used the profits to arm themselves with automatic weapons. The Crips and Bloods developed chapters throughout
the west. Ross later moved to Cincinnati and helped spread
the crack epidemic across the country. Cocaine was supplied
to Ross by Oscar Danilo Blandon Reyes, former leader of the
guerrilla army named the Fuerza Democratica Nicaraguense
(Nicaraguan Democratic Force) or FDN. Blandon used the
millions of dollars paid to him by Ross to buy weapons and

equipment for his anticommunist army that unsuccessfully tried to overthrow Nicaragua's Sandinista government in the 1980s. "It is one of the most bizarre alliances in modern history: the union of a U.S.-backed army attempting to overthrow a revolutionary socialist government and Uzi-toting 'gangstas' of Compton and South Central Los Angeles," the Mercury News reported.

The newspaper series said the covert drugs-for-arms trade was implemented because the U.S. Congress had not appropriated funds to help the Contras. But in 1986, after Congress authorized $100 million in military aid to the contras, the operation finally came under fire. On October 27, 1986, agents from the FBI, the IRS, local police and the Los Angeles County Sheriff raided Blandon's organization, but the raids produced no incriminating evidence. Some agents suspected that Blandon was tipped off to the raid. "The cops always believed that investigation had been compromised by the CIA," said Los Angeles federal public defender Barbara O'Connor. But Blandon and Ross eventually received prison sentences for drug offenses. While in prison, Ross testified in 1991 about police corruption in the LA police department.

In 1995 Blandon was given early release on unsupervised probation after serving 28 months of a life sentence. Since then, Blandon has been paid $166,000 by the DEA to provide evidence against Ross and others in the drug trade. Ross, recently paroled, was set up by Blandon and arrested on March 2, 1995 for allegedly buying 100 kilograms of cocaine. During Ross' trial in March 1996, Blandon testified as a witness for the U.S. Department of Justice. Ross' attorney, Alan Fenster sought to question Blandon about his ties with the CIA, but federal prosecutors obtained a court order blocking all questions involving the intelligence agency. Assistant U.S. Attorney L.J. O'Neale objected to the questions because "injecting a false issue would only inflame the truth-seeking process." Fenster said the government's opposition to letting Blandon answer CIA-related questions is damning proof of the agency's culpability. Ross is facing a mandatory life sentence without parole. Sentencing has been postponed because of the allegations in the series.

Webb reports that agents from the DEA, U.S. Customs, the Los Angeles County Sheriff's Department and the California Bureau of Narcotics Enforcement complained that early investigations of the drug ring were hampered by the CIA or unnamed "national security" interests. These investigations included Blandon's boss in the FDN's cocaine operation, Juan Norwin Meneses Cantarero. Meneses, who ran the drug ring from his San Francisco home, never spent a day in a U.S. prison, even though the government was aware of his cocaine dealing since 1974. He was implicated in 45 federal investigations and is listed in the DEA's database as a major international drug smuggler. Still, Meneses managed to live a high profile life in California, buying homes and businesses. "I even drove my own cars, registered in my name," Meneses said during a recent interview in Nicaragua.

News Stories Trigger Demands for Investigation

Los Angeles City Council members voted unanimously on August 23 to ask the U.S. Attorney General for an investigation. Councilman Nate Holden's motion requested the office to "immediately conduct a complete, thorough and independent investigation of . . . allegations as to the ongoing sale of illegal street drugs . . . with the apparent approval of the United States Government" (Associated Press, "L.A. Probes CIA-Cocaine Report," Washington Post (On-line), August 23, 1996).

In a letter to Senator Barbara Boxer (D-CA), dated September 4, CIA Director John Deutch said the CIA inspector general would probe the allegations. "I consider these to be extremely serious charges," Deutch wrote. "Although I believe there is no substance to the allegations in the Mercury News, I do wish to dispel any lingering public doubt on the subject." Deutch added that previous examinations of the issue by the CIA and congressional committees support "the conclusion that the agency neither participated in nor condoned drug trafficking by Contra forces." In particular, he denied that the agency ever had a relationship with Blandon or Meneses, and rejected the allegations that the agency blocked information in the trial of Rick Ross. Boxer had requested the investigation, which Deutch said would be completed within 60 days (Associated Press, "Deutch Orders CIA Drug Probe," Washington Post (On-line), September 5, 1996).

CBC Forum; NAACP Director Arrested at CIA Headquarters

On September 12, members of the Congressional Black Caucus (CBC) called for federal investigations into the allegations. Deutch and Attorney General Janet Reno responded with official denials in separate letters to Rep. Maxine Waters (D-CA), who have led calls for an inquiry. More than 2,500 people attended a discussion of the issue at the Congressional Black Caucus' annual legislative conference in Washington. On the same day, political activist Dick Gregory and national NAACP board member and radio talk show host Joe Madison were arrested outside CIA headquarters as they attempted to hand deliver a copy of the Mercury News series to Deutch. On September 19, Deutch addressed the CBC on Capitol Hill and promised an independent investigation. Though CBC members seemed to be satisfied with Deutch's sincerity, they said it was just a first step (Michael A. Fletcher, "Black Caucus Urges Probe Of CIA-Contra Drug Charge," Washington Post, September 13, 1996, p. A20; Vanessa Gallman, Knight-Ridder News Service, "Talk of CIA coke ring fuels anger," Denver Post, August 13, 1996, p. 1A; Michael A. Fletcher, "Deutch Assures Caucus on Drug Charge," Washington Post, September 20, 1996, p. A4).

According to the Associated Press, the director of national drug control policy, General Barry R. McCaffrey, called for a high-level investigation of the allegations. During an Operation PUSH news conference in Chicago on August 14, McCaffrey said, "Until the American public is fully satisfied; there must be a full and thorough investigation." The charges have become a major topic on black talk radio. "This deserves a serious investigation and debate," said Jesse L. Jackson, head of Operation PUSH (Michael A. Fletcher, "White House Aide Seeks Probe of CIA," Washington Post, September 16, 1996, p. A17; "Drug Director Urges Investigation of C.I.A.," New York Times, September 16, 1996, p. A13).

DEA Agent Supports Charge

On September 23, former DEA agent Celerino Castillo III said he sent reports about Contra drug flights into the United States to the DEA and even spoke to Embassy officials. Castillo, who retired from the DEA in 1992, said he sent cables to Washington with specific dates and flight numbers out of Ilopango, an air base in El Salvador and CIA logistical support center for the Contras. He claims that Americans hired by Contra leaders piloted many of the drug flights. Castillo accused Edwin G. Corr, then-U.S. ambassador to El Salvador of ignoring the flights. According to Castillo, Corr told him: "My hands are tied because these are Contra operations being run by the White House." Castillo said he first revealed what he knew in 1994 when Oliver North, former Reagan White House aide, was seeking election to the U.S. Senate from Virginia. He strongly opposed north because he believed that North had sanctioned the drug flights. North has denied these charges (Robert L. Jackson, "Ex-DEA Agent Ties Contras to U.S. Drug Flights," Los Angeles Times, September 24, 1996, p. A23).

Washington Post debunks Mercury News Account

A Washington Post investigation into the Mercury News allegations found that the evidence does not support the conclusion that the CIA or Nicaraguans played a major role in the emergence of crack cocaine use. The article found that drug trafficking by Blandon, Meneses and other contra sympathizers accounted for only a small portion of the nation's cocaine trade. Blandon moved an estimated five tons of cocaine during the entire 1980s, when more than 250 tons of cocaine was distributed every year. "We are talking about mid-level operators who were not causes of these events but rather participants in something that would have occurred without them," said Jonathan Caulkins, a professor of public policy at Carnegie Mellon University (Roberto Suro and Walter Pincus, "The CIA and Crack: Evidence Is Lacking Of Alleged Plot," Washington Post, October 4, 1996, p. A1).

Gary Webb and attorney Alan Fenster said that Webb gave Fenster the idea that the CIA was involved with Blandon's drug sales. During Fenster's cross-examination of Blandon,

U.S. Attorney L. J. O'Neale objected that Fenster's questions were suggestions that Webb had made to him during breaks in the trial, according to a transcript of the trial. O'Neale complained in a recent court filing that the Mercury News articles depend on the Ross case "as the primary source of information" and Ross "then waves the articles aloft as 'proof' that he was right." Mercury News Executive Editor Jerry Ceppos said on October 3 that he did not know that Webb provided questions to Fenster to be asked of Blandon during the trial.

Testifying during Ross' trial, Blandon said he met Ross after Blandon had broken off with Meneses and had stopped sending money to the contras. He also claimed Ross was already "a big coke dealer" and had other sources of supply by the time he met Ross. Blandon testified that he gave Ross low prices because Ross bought in large quantities. Ross supported that testimony under cross-examination when he admitted that he started selling crack in 1979, years before he met Blandon, and expanded sales by emphasizing volume sales and bargain prices. Ross also said in a 1994 interview with the Los Angeles Times that God "put me down to be the cocaine man," and did not mention Blandon or any other Nicaraguans. According to Blandon, Ross was his only African-American client, a claim that discredits the idea that Blandon based his marketing strategy on race.

Senator John F. Kerrey (D-MA), chairman of the Senate subcommittee on terrorism, narcotics and international operations in the 1980s, said recently, "There is no question in my mind that people affiliated with . . . the CIA were involved in drug trafficking while involved in support of the contras, but it is also important to note that we never found any evidence to suggest that these traffickers ever targeted any one geographic area or population group."

In 1994, former DEA agent Castillo and writer Dave Harmon privately published Powder burns: Cocaine, Contras and the Drug War. The first 100 pages of the book is Castillo's autobiography illustrated with photographs, including pictures posed with former President Jimmy Carter and former Vice Presidents George Bush and Dan Quail (sic). Beyond the Contra-cocaine story, Castillo tells of a DEA agent's helicopter joy ride leading to the crashing and destruction of a $500,000 helicopter next to a Guatemalan primary school. The book reports how DEA agents would "use" cocaine smugglers as informants -- but the informants were using the DEA to refuel their aircraft and bring their loads to airfields where they knew DEA agents were not waiting. (Celerino Castillo and Dave Harmon, Powder burns: Cocaine, Contras and the Drug War, Mosaic Press, 1994) -- EES

"THE FBI SECRET WEAPON: COINTELPRO"

"COINTELPRO is an acronym for the FBI's domestic "counterintelligence programs" to neutralize political dissidents. Although covert operations have been employed throughout FBI history, the formal COINTELPROs of 1956-1971 were broadly targeted against radical political organizations.

The origins of COINTELPRO were rooted in the Bureau's operations against hostile foreign intelligence services. Counterintelligence, of course, goes beyond investigation; it refers to actions taken to neutralize enemy agents.

'Counterintelligence' was a misnomer for the FBI programs, since the targets were American political dissidents, not foreign spies. In the atmosphere of the Cold War, the American Communist Party was seen as a serious threat to national security. Over the years, anti- Communist paranoia extended to civil rights, anti-war, and many other groups. As John Edgar Hoover, longtime Director of the F.B.I. put it:

'The forces, which are most anxious to weaken our internal security, are not always easy to identify. Communists have been trained in deceit and secretly work toward the day when they hope to replace our American way of life with a Communist dictatorship. They utilize cleverly camouflaged movements, such as peace groups and civil rights groups to achieve their sinister purposes. While they as individuals are difficult to identify, the Communist party line is clear. Its first concern is the advancement of Soviet Russia and the godless Communist cause. It is important to learn to know the enemies of the American way of life.'

Although today this may sound ridiculous, the implications were deadly serious for the thousands of people who became COINTELPRO targets. After many years of investigating and disrupting these groups, the Bureau could not find evidence that any of them were foreign-controlled. These programs were exposed to the public following an unsolved break-in into the FBI's Media, PA resident agency, separate lawsuits by NBC correspondent Carl Stern and the Socialist Workers' Party, and then a US Senate investigation led by Senator Frank Church. Although the FBI's COINTELPRO's officially ended in 1971, there have been many examples of counterintelligence-type operations against political dissidents since.

Glossary of Gang Slang

BG: baby gangster, usually a youth between 10-15 years of age

Blessed in: being taken into the gang on the word of a current member

CK and/or BK: initials for "Crip killer" or "Blood killer" used by members of those rival gangs

Crack: cocaine in a rock-like form

Crackheads: individuals who are addicted to crack cocaine

Do work: committing crimes, including robberies and drive-by shootings

G-Ride: stolen car

Greens: marijuana; (syn.) trees

Half a bird: 10 ounces of crack

Jumped in: being beaten up as an initiation to joining a gang; you can also leave a gang by being "jumped out"

OG: original gangster

One time/5-0/K-9 or bait: is one of the many words or terms gang affected youth use for police

Rock it up: make powder cocaine into crack cocaine using baking soda and boiling water

Shermheads: individuals addicted PCP

Shot caller: a gang member, usually an OG who gives orders to younger members

Snow white: cocaine

Spot: a house or apartment run by a gang member for selling drugs and stashing guns and money

TG: tiny gangster, a youth under 10 years of age

Original Founders of the Crips

Stanley "Tookie" Williams

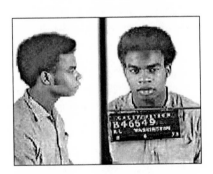

Raymond Washington

Compton Area Crips

Early big-shot members included Mack Thomas of the original Compton Crips, Michael "Shaft" Concepcion, Jimel "Godfather" Barnes, Greg "Batman" Davis and Stanley Tookie Williams.

A list of the original Leaders/ Founders of Crip Sets

The Compton Grandees Crips: Big Huncho, Big Mac Thomas, Too Sweet, Michael "Salty" Leblanc, Sugar Bear
   Avalon Garden Crips: Jimel Barnes, Godfather, Koonce, et al
   Neighborhood Crips: Gregory Davis, Batman, et al
   Mafia Crips: Karate Man, Mad Professor, Ba-Ba, et al
   Kitchen Crips: Skull, Cowboy, The Lees brothers, Red, et al
   Main Street Crips: James Compton, Squeaky, Moto, Little James, et al
   House Crips: Kenneth Jackson, Iron Man, Pee Wee, Crazy Black, et al
   BMCD: Foster Grigsby, Angelo "Barefoot Pookie" White, Deadly Blue, et al
   Boothill & Park Village: King Rat, Popcorn, Grasshopper, Cosmoe, Volcano, et al

Original Leaders of Pirus/Bloods

Compton Pirus street Pirus: Sylvester "Puddin" Scott, Tam, AC, et al
   Leuders Park Pirus: Marcus Nunn and family, Studderbox, China Dog, et al
   Bishops: Bobby Lavender, Ghost, Clay, Turp, Magoo, et al
   Athens Park Boys: Anthony & Michael White, Butch, Mooney, Cold Train, et al
   Bounty Hunters: Herman Coleman, Red, Ali, King Rat, McGowans, et al

Original Wardrobe of Los Angeles Crips

The Founder of Black P Stone Blood Gang

T Rogers

Blood Gang Graffiti

KEVIN LEWIS

The Original Wardrobe of
Los Angeles Pirus/ Bloods

Nonprofit Organizations to Help Prevent Gang Violence

To contribute support to inner city gang prevention groups, call CSDI at (323) 586-8793. Also call: (800) 722-TEENS for anti-gang support.

Mothers Against Gang Wars
42 North Sutter St. Suite 215
Stockton, Ca. 95202
(209) 464-6607

Amer-I-Can
Jim Brown
269 South Beverly Drive, #1048
Los Angeles, California 90212
Office Telephone (310) 652-7884
Office Fax (310) 652-9353

Barrios Unidos
1817 Soquel Avenue
Santa Cruz, CA 95062
(831) 457-8208
(831) 457-0389 Fax

Central Recovery & Development Project (CROP)
Agency Profile
5841 South San Pedro Street, Unit H
Los Angeles, CA 90003
(323) 231-5407

Clean Slate Inc.
Marianne Diaz, director & Founder
Gang Recovery & Tattoo Removal Program
(562) 770-0266

Community Coalition
Los Angeles, CA 90044
(323) 750-9087
(323) 750-9640 Fax

Community In Support of the Gang Truce
2822 S. Western Ave
Los Angeles, CA 90018
(323) 735-3637
(323) 733-2750 Fax

Family Service of Long Beach (FSLB)
Russell Brammer, Executive Director
1041 Pine Avenue
Long Beach, CA 90813
(562) 436-9893
(562) 435-4861 Fax

Gang Violence Bridging Project (GVBP) founded 1993
Pat Brown Institute, California State University at Los
Angeles
5151 State University Drive
Los Angeles, CA 90032-8261
(323) 343-3773
(323) 343-3774 Fax

Homeboy Industries:
Fr. Gregory Boyle
1916 E. First Street
Los Angeles, CA 90033
(800) 526-1254
(323) 526-1257 Fax

Homies Unidos Los Angeles (www.homiesunidos.org)
PO Box 642542
Los Angeles, California 90064
(213) 309-9724

Inglewood's Coalition
333 W. Florence Ave.
Inglewood, CA 90301
(310) 330-7999
(310) 672-6431 Fax

LA Bridges (City of Los Angeles)
215 W. 6th Street 7th Floor
Los Angeles, CA 90014
(213) 485-0016
(213) 847-2551 Fax

N.O.G.U.N.S.
Hector Marroquin
10910 Larch
Lennox, CA 90304
(310) 672-9348

Pico Youth and Family Center (PYFC)
Oscar De La Torre
828 Pico Blvd #9
Santa Monica, CA 90405
(310) 396-7101
(310) 393-7104 Fax

A Place Called Home (www.apch.org)
2830 S. Central Avenue
Los Angeles, CA
(323) 232-7653
(323) 232-0445 Fax

Project: No Gangs
Orange County Sheriff's Department
PO Box 28
Santa Ana, California 92702-0028
(714) 567-3900

Treasures out of Los Angeles (TOOLS)
13200 Crossroads Pkwy, Suite 135
City of Industry, CA 91746-3423
(800) 201-7320 ext. 1269
(562) 699-8856 Fax

United Community Action Network
www.ucan.av.org
44231 N. Division St
Lancaster, CA 93534
Telephone: (661) 948-3000
Help Line: (661) 266-HELP (4357)
Fax: (661) 948-4600

Unity One
Bo Taylor
4706 Lomita Street #5
Los Angeles, CA 90019
(323) 291-6623, (213) 963-5843, (213) 857-0959

Valley Unity Peace Treaty / Community in Schools
(since 10-31-93)
William "Blinky" Rodriguez
(818) 891-9399

Victory Outreach Inc.
www.victoryoutreach.org
Sonny Arguinzoni, Founder & President
250 West Arrow Highway
San Dimas , CA 91773
(909) 599-4437
(909) 599-6244 Fax

A World Fit for Kids
www.worldfitforkids.org
2550 W. Beverly Blvd., 2nd Floor
Los Angeles, CA 90057
(213) 387-7712
(213) 387-7507 Fax

Y.A.L.
Compton Youth Activities and Education Center Los
Angeles County Sheriff's Department Compton Division
Captain Cecil W. Rhambo, Sergeant Joseph H. Stephen, Jr.
700 North Alameda Compton CA 90220
(310) 637-2793

Gang Prevention Programs
We Help Kids off Streets & Gangs
www.clubkids414.org
(414) 380 3853

Portland Youth Redirection
1033 N Sumner St, Portland, OR 97217
(503) 281-2492

Office of Youth Violence Prevention
www.portlandonline.com/safeyouth
449 NE Emerson St.
Portland, OR 97211
(503) 823-3004 Fax

Portland House of Umoja
1626 NE Alberta St, Portland, OR 97211
(503) 282-3296

Credits

Alexander, Rod
Alonso, Alejandro A., Streetgangs.com
Bahr, Lorraine, Associate Artistic Director, Sowelu
Theater, Portland, Oregon
Bryant, Dr. Dexter Edward, Sociology, California State
University, Dominguez Hills
Carter, Ernest Yo-Yo, Fresno, California & Portland,
Oregon
Cat, Alley, Compton, California
Faust-Goudeau, Oletha, Kansas Senator 29th District
Gilkey, David, Wichita, Kansas
Henry, Ronald, Perris, California
Jackson, David, At Risk Youth Counselor, Portland,
Oregon
Larson, Kimberly, Academic Advisor, California State
University, Dominguez Hills
Leblanc, Michael "Salty" , Compton, California
Lewis, Cedric Henderson, Compton, California
Lewis, Chasity
Lewis, Dawn, Compton, California
Lewis, Jaqunta, Compton, California
Lewis, Jonathan, Compton, California
Lewis, Monique, San Francisco, California
Lewis, Roosevelt, Compton, California
Lewis, Rubye, Compton, California
Lewis, Sherree Henry, Perris, California
Lewis, Tamesha, Compton, California
Livingston, Kevin "Birdman"
Long, Glenna, Inglewood, California
Martin, Thomas, Compton
Miller, Brandon, Portland, Oregon
Molina, Jennifer, Hawaii/Seal Beach, California
Monroe, Shafia, Portland, Oregon
Quicker, Dr. John, Sociology, California State
University, Dominguez Hills
Richardson, Robert, Portland Youth Redirection, Youth
Outreach Counselor

Rowe, Sherri, Stockton, Kansas
Simovic, Sharon, Education Program Coordinator, Portland Community College
Sutton, Dr. Marylyn, English, California State University Dominguez Hills
Tyson, Michael, Wichita, Kansas
Wade, Steve, Portland, Oregon

CPSIA information can be obtained at www.ICGtesting.com
Printed in the USA
LVOW11s0819140816

500329LV00001B/3/P